8

BLACK DRAMA OF THE FEDERAL THEATRE ERA

Beyond the Formal Horizons

E. Quita Craig

Evelyn

THE UNIVERSITY OF MASSACHUSETTS PRESS   AMHERST, 1980

Grateful acknowledgment is made to the following for permission to reprint copyrighted material:

Atheneum Publishers, for selections from Alain Locke, *Negro Youth Speaks* and *The Legacy of the Ancestral Arts*, from Domingo, *Gifts of the Black Tropics*, and from Sterling Brown, *Negro Poetry and Drama*.

Alberta W. Browne (Mrs. Theodore), for selections from Theodore Browne, *Go Down Moses* and *Natural Man*.

Theodore Ward, for selections from his *Big White Fog*. Randolph Edmonds, for selections from his *Bad Man*. Elitea B. Allison (Mrs. Hughes), for selections from Hughes Allison, *The Trial of Dr. Beck, Panyared*, and *Foreword to Panyared*.

Abram Hill and Col. John D. Silvera, for selections from their *Liberty Deferred*.

Selections from the work of Owen Dodson are reprinted by permission of the author and of *Negro Digest* Magazine, copyright, 1968 by Johnson Publishing Company, Inc.

Selections from Langston Hughes, *Troubled Island*, are reprinted by permission of Harold Ober Associates Incorporated, copyright © 1963 by Langston Hughes, and from *Don't You Want to be Free?*, reprinted by permission of Harold Ober Associates Incorporated, copyright 1938 by Langston Hughes, copyright renewed.

Selections from Paul Green, *Hymn to the Rising Sun*, are reprinted by permission of the author and the publisher, Samuel French, Inc., 25 West 45th Street, New York, N.Y.

The calypso verse is reprinted from the *Black Scholar*, September 1975.

The Research Center for the Federal Theatre Project, George Mason University, for photographs of Federal Theatre plays on permanent loan from the Library of Congress, and for excerpts quoted from taped interviews with playwrights and personnel of the Federal Theatre.

FOR MY MOTHER AND "THE LION" WHO GAVE ME THE FUTURE.

FOR MY HUSBAND, WHO DIED FOR THE FUTURE.

FOR MY SONS, WHO ARE THE FUTURE.

CONTENTS

LIKE HALLEY'S COMET, once in a generation a book on a favorite topic appears and illuminates the previous work on the subject. A book of that scope gives one a vision of an entire landscape and requires a re-evaluation of history. Such a book is E. Quita Craig's *Black Drama of the Federal Theatre Era: Beyond the Formal Horizons*.

When in 1974 Professors Brown and O'Connor of George Mason University opened an old airplane hangar in Baltimore, Maryland, to uncover the "lost" archives of the Federal Theatre Project (FTP), they discovered more than manuscripts, photos, posters, scene designs, budgets, and all the other memorabilia of our nation's first and only national theater; they uncovered more than a treasury of the Negro Units of the Federal Theatre with their amazing playwrights. They unearthed a legacy that would contradict the weary platitudes about black drama which had been routinely shuffled along by white and black critics alike.

Among those who came early to examine the FTP archives, which had been moved from the hangar to George Mason University, was E. Quita Craig, a scholar of acuity. As she read the plays which she and so many others had only heard about, as she discovered scripts that no one had written about, Ms. Craig perceived that the black writers of FTP were not the isolated, culturally crippled amateurs she had been led to believe they were. Instead these playwrights stood out as shrewd, talented artists who had negotiated impossible dreams into possible productions. They had worked in a difficult time and place: faced with a segregated theater, and the racism of its audiences, they had cunningly worked into their dramas "dual messages"—one to be perceived by whites, the other by blacks.

Drawing on her knowledge of cultural anthropology, Ms. Craig was able to discern how these black writers used the European mode of viewing the world to speak through their plays to the Caucasian audience and, at the same time, how they were able to present the African aesthetic and philosophy to a second audience of Afro-Americans.

For many years there was a seldom questioned consensus among

students of black America that the horrors of mid-passage and of
slavery had destroyed nearly all remnants of African aesthetics and
philosophy in the American black population. Even after the publications of Herskovits and others in the 1930s and 40s, the concept of
"Africanisms" in Afro-American life was not popular, although some
gestures of acknowledgment were made toward residual influences in
the areas of farming and in the handcrafts. In 1976 I wrote an article in
Yale/Theatre's African theater issue suggesting that someone should
see if "Africanisms" could be found in the style and content of some
Afro-American plays. Ms. Craig is the only scholar, with the possible
exception of Paul Carter Harrison, who has developed that idea with
respect to the theater. Her chapter concerning the West Indian influence on American drama is a pioneering contribution.

Although the concept of the "dual message" is open to argument
and interpretation, Ms. Craig presents a very good case that white and
black audiences of the 1930s, attending the same production of a
play, often saw two different plays. Her analyses on that point of *Run
Little Chillun'* and *The Trial of Doctor Beck* are thought-provoking and
convincing.

From her analysis of these scripts, other important implications
tumble out. The black dramatists of the thirties were not the Uncle
Toms the revolutionary blacks of the sixties and seventies had labeled
them. Nor were these writers a group of pathetic naïve souls sustained
by the public dole, as white critics had implied. In light of the militant
black period with its emphasis on "all that is Black is beautiful,"
and its competition among scholars to be "blacker-than-thou," Ms.
Craig's attempt to find a balance between white and black racisms is
refreshing. Her argument that the FTP plays were not Uncle Tomish is
important, and her book opens a larger question: how did American
theater itself manage to assimilate black artistry without acknowledging its debt? This question did not occur to most theater historians,
and how could it? Our theater scholars were not equipped to pose the
question, let alone answer it. How many of the plays she discusses,
seen by thousands between 1935 and 1939, had been read by theater
students and teachers? At this writing, only two have been published
although Professor Lorraine Brown has promised that soon the others
will be available. It must follow that without publication of script or
summary, there could have been little critical discussion.

The next few years will certainly see several books and numerous
articles on the Negro Units of the FTP, but the quantity of material up

to now has been thin. Doris Abramson's *Negro Playwrights in the American Theatre, 1925–1959* devotes forty-four pages to "The Thirties." She gives five pages to *Run Little Chillun'* and four to a combined discussion of *The Trial of Doctor Beck, Turpentine,* and *Liberty Deferred.* Loften Mitchell's *Black Drama* gives twenty pages to the entire decade of the thirties. Jane Mathews in *The Federal Theatre, 1935–1939* gives nine scattered references to the Negro Units of the Federal Theatre Project. Hallie Flanagan's *Arena* contains surprisingly little history on the Negro Units of the Project she supervised. One recent book, *Free, Adult, Uncensored* by O'Connor and Brown, does provide an illustrated history drawn from information in the archives at George Mason University.

To put these observations into a larger context: recently I was leafing through H. G. Wells's *The Future of America* (1906). As an Englishman, an outsider, he could not contain his irritation with American ignorance of race issues. He wrote: "My globe-trotting impudence will seem no doubt to mount to its zenith when I declare that hardly any Americans at all seem to be in possession of the elementary facts in relation to this [race] question. These broad facts are not taught in school and what each man knows is picked up by accident." If one is to judge from the nationwide astonishment which followed the televising of *Roots,* one must conclude that after three-quarters of a century, Mr. Wells' comment is still valid.

Our nation's commitment to ignorance of race and racism, and its concomitant processes and products, still astounds the rational mind. Indeed, the basic issues of racism are so tied to our personal economy, to our sexual fantasies, to our self-image at home and abroad, and to our beliefs in ourselves and God, that we Americans, as a nation and as a culture, dare not seriously approach the issue at all; therefore, we devote almost no time in our schools, churches, government programs, and media to training our children, black and white, how to understand themselves, let alone how to live constructively with one another.

Into this general racial ignorance, Ms. Craig has thrown her light. Like all other sparks struck to illuminate an aspect of the human condition, hers will be seen by those who have committed themselves to the long march toward a national sanity. For the ultimate goodness of *Black Drama of the Federal Theatre Era* is that of one mind seizing upon one aspect of the American dilemma and bringing to that neglected and misrepresented subject the clear light of new facts, a careful analysis of the issues, and a balanced evaluation of truth. Although the subject of this book is the black playwrights of the Federal Theatre era, its greater subject is our nation's well-being.

James V. Hatch, Hatch-Billops Collection, August 1979

ONE

THE FEDERAL THEATRE LIVES AGAIN

T HE MYSTERY that has long shrouded an important period of black dramatic development was solved in the summer of 1974 when the missing treasure of America's first and only national theater was tracked down and once more brought to light. The recovery of this great mass of theatrical material—the fruit of an American dramatic era—was an event of considerable significance to American drama critics and historians, for it had been stored in great haste when the Federal Theatre was closed by Congress in 1939 and has remained in virtual oblivion for thirty-five years.

"But what was the Federal Theatre?" will, undoubtedly be some readers' first question, so before we can discuss the black drama of this period we must go back to the thirties—to the height of the Great Depression. It was a time when more than fifty percent of professional theater people in America were unemployed, and two-thirds of the legitimate theaters in the city of New York alone, were closed for the greater part of the year. It was a time when America's performing artists were in a sorry state. Economic relief was first attempted by theater organizations, on a basis of the greatest need, and by a few scattered communities which supported local theater groups with public funds.[1] Although such efforts were helpful, they were inadequate to meet the national needs, and the plight of theatrical workers grew steadily worse until the Roosevelt administration awoke to the fact that writers, artists, musicians, and actors, like the rest of America's army of unemployed, had to eat.

The President and Mrs. Roosevelt had long been interested in "the concept of a national theatrical project," and its affinity with their philosophy of social service was immediately apparent to the federal relief agencies.[2] Why, indeed, shouldn't the economic plight of American artists be relieved, and their talents used to enrich the American public? To the young administration, already deeply committed to the improvement of the depressed American economy, the additional incentive of reaping dual returns on a single investment was irresistible. In 1933 the president asked Harry Hopkins, his director of the Works Progress Administration, to look into the possibility

of establishing such a program, and the following year, when Mr.
Roosevelt repeated his request, Hopkins' assistant, Jacob Baker, was
put to work on the president's proposal.[3] In August 1935 the marriage
of art and politics was finally performed and the Federal Theatre was
officially launched as a branch of the Works Progress Administration.

The head of the new federal project, who was hand-picked by Harry
Hopkins and blessed by Mrs. Roosevelt, was a woman of exceptional
ability. Hallie Flanagan, a contemporary of Harry Hopkins at Grinnell
College, Iowa, was the first woman to be awarded a Guggenheim
Fellowship. She studied advanced techniques of theater production
in England, the Scandinavian countries, Germany, Italy, France,
Czechoslovakia, and Russia, and, at the time she was approached by
Baker and Hopkins to undertake the task of directing the new Federal
Theatre, she was the presiding drama genius of the Vassar Experimental Theater.[4] But there was also another reason why Hallie
Flanagan's selection as director of the project was a promising beginning for the new Federal Theatre; she was dedicated to artistic freedom and under no obligation to the commercial stage: of the twelve
men chosen as her regional directors, only Elmer Rice, the playwright,
had any connection with the Broadway stage.[5]

In his announcement of her appointment, Harry Hopkins also informed the theatrical world of his intention to preserve the creative
and artistic autonomy of the new Theatre:

> I am asked whether a theater subsidized by the government can
> be kept free of censorship, and I say yes, it is going to be free from
> censorship. What we want is a free, adult, uncensored theater,[6]

and with such assurance, Mrs. Flanagan began her new task of creating a national theater. She was soon to discover, however, that there
was no shortage of problems in such a union—they covered almost the
entire range of possibilities from the psychological to the political.

Two of the most immediate of these problems were fear and shame.
Some commercial producers feared that federal competition would
spell disaster for them at the box office, while some of the project's
participants began their federal careers with a sense of shame for
being on relief. Elmer Rice, Director of the New York Region of the
Federal Theatre Project, found it necessary to attempt to alleviate the
distress of his theater people by posting a notice which stated:

> . . . you are not being offered charity but WORK. The inter-
> viewers have been instructed to receive you with the same cour-

tesy and consideration that would be extended by any professional employment agency. . . .[7]

Nevertheless, some theater personnel refused even to fill out the
required relief forms, or to consider themselves on relief as long as
they gave the project a day's work for a day's pay; a few playwrights
also thought it necessary to hide their identities by writing for the
Theatre under pseudonyms.

Yet, in spite of these attitudes, the speed with which the Theatre
swung into action and achieved a leading role in the performing arts
was phenomenal. In a matter of months, its production units spanned
the length and breadth of the nation. Many of its productions were
highly innovative and of excellent quality, and commercial producers
began to look on the Federal Theatre as a source of inspiration and a
hunting ground for talent. They adopted many of the ideas and techniques it introduced, and even bid for a few of its more spectacular
productions, complete with casts. As the Theatre's successes multi-
plied, shame also diminished among its personnel, and participants
began to view their role in those successes with growing pride.

Although the commercial stage benefited from the project, the interests of the Federal Theatre were by no means confined to the tastes
of Broadway. Its professed aim was to be "National, Regional, and
American," and its scope included every phase of the performing arts.
During its short life it presented classical, modern, dance, religious,
radio, and children's drama, including puppet shows; it staged
pageants and spectacles, musicals, Americana, vaudeville, and circus;
it presented plays in several languages, including French, German,
Spanish, Italian, Chinese, and Yiddish; it encouraged community
theaters and sent touring troupes into small towns and rural areas; it
staged plays by unknown as well as famous playwrights; and, quite
predictably, it experimented with tremendous enthusiasm. By October 27, 1936, when It Can't Happen Here was performed under the
auspices of the Federal Theatre, the play opened simultaneously in
seventeen cities across the nation, in New York and Los Angeles in
both English and Yiddish, and in Tampa, in Spanish. Then, hot on the
heels of these successes, the same play opened in eight other cities in
what was a phenomenal display of vigor and efficiency for such a
youthful enterprise.[8]

The Federal Theatre Project undoubtedly ranks as one of the positive achievements of the Roosevelt administration, for, in addition to
attaining its primary relief goal, it stimulated creativity, brought first

rate productions to the economically depressed public at minimal cost, and introduced drama to a great many audiences in America who had never before been exposed to the performing arts. These were, indeed, multiple dividends on a single investment. Yet, in spite of the Theatre's remarkable achievements, the most persistent of its problems were not—perhaps could not be—solved.

One of the important initial aims of those who visualized the role of the federal project in American society was support and assistance for small theater groups, in their own local communities, and several of the regional directors expected that the major thrust of the national theater would be in that direction. But while Hallie Flanagan did support local theater groups, she chose, rather, to emphasize experimental theater, and, although her efforts in this area undoubtedly did much to revolutionize the performing arts in America, they also created political discomfort for many members of Congress. Experiments with advanced theatrical techniques, complex lighting, and other equipment necessitated professionalism and sophistication which, inevitably, resulted in the concentration of the Theatre's major effort in urban centers like New York, Chicago, and Los Angeles, rather than in decentralization.[9] Several states had no federal theater units at all, and their representatives in Congress felt that public funds should be more equitably divided.[10]

But the major problem that plagued the Federal Theatre's wedded bliss was the conflict between artistic freedom and political expediency, and the honeymoon came to a painful and abrupt end with the Theatre's preview performance of its first Living Newspaper, *Ethiopia.*

The Living Newspaper was Hallie Flanagan's personal brain-child. In an age when dramatic realism dominated the American stage, it was a radical experiment with some of the most modern dramatic techniques she had observed in Europe, and particularly with the techniques of the Russian revolutionary stage. The new form was a combination of journalistic and theatrical techniques that could present an astonishing amount of material in a short time, and the primary aim of this creation was to stimulate, through art, public awareness of vital current issues. After months of painstaking research and preparation on its first production, however, the staging of *Ethiopia* was prohibited because the administration feared that its highly effective dramatization of Mussolini's ongoing invasion of Haile Selasse's empire would antagonize the Italians, with whom America was then at peace.[11]

This was too much for some Federal Theatre directors—even those who had learned to live with, or to circumvent the boggling intricacies of bureaucratic red tape. Elmer Rice resigned, and when the furor over the imposition of such unexpected censorship subsided within the project the Living Newspaper transferred its attention, and its energies, from international politics to the domestic scene. In the domestic arena, however, there was also grave danger for the new project, and the smouldering conflict between artistic freedom and political expediency, although slower to erupt, was, ultimately, just as deadly.

Ironically, some of the Theatre's most effective artistic creations made its deadliest political enemies. Living Newspapers such as *One Third of a Nation*, which dramatized slum conditions in American cities, and plays like *Turpentine*, which revealed the economic plight of black laborers in Florida tapping camps, were artistically successful, and contributed to public awareness of the crying need for social and economic change, but their effectiveness also antagonized election-conscious members of the government. Perhaps it was too much to hope that the lawmakers could support, with real enthusiasm, a project that so forcefully dramatized their shortcomings, and some of them did not.

The Theatre's dedication to artistic freedom, and its efficiency, produced still another irritant for its political bridegroom. During the depression, economic hardship helped to promote widespread flirtations in America with left-wing political philosophies, and the fact that the federal project included among its creative artists a representative percentage of such radicals made some lawmakers very nervous. Political circles were stalked by fears of communist infiltration, and the efficiency displayed by the Federal Theatre in its simultaneous openings of *It Can't Happen Here* did much to heighten many lawmakers' nightmares of the possibilities of using such a nationwide organization for subversion, perhaps for a takeover. It is hardly surprising, therefore, that in June 1939, during a Congressional communist witch-hunt [12]—which achieved such proportions that Hallie Flanagan was even questioned about the political affiliations of Christopher Marlowe, sixteenth-century English playwright—the opponents of the Federal Theatre joined forces, and the marriage was terminated. [13] The Great Experiment was over.

Several attempts were made by concerned citizen organizations to protest the failure of Congress to vote funds for the continuation of the project, but they came too late to save the Theatre and, in view of the prevailing mood in the Congress, it is doubtful that they could have succeeded, even if they had come earlier.

Almost overnight the Federal Theatre was dead and its interment began. Masses of records and other theatrical material—property of the United States government—were packed in great haste, and they poured into Washington from all over the nation. Some of the records found a home in the National Archives, but most of the material, overwhelming in its sheer bulk, was stored in its original containers and slid into oblivion. Emmet Lavery, Director of the National Service Bureau of the Federal Theatre, recalled in 1970:

> Remember, when the project was closed out, there was about two million [dollars] of theater equipment, apart from all those records, that was just put somewhere in a warehouse,[14]

and as a result future generations of drama critics and scholars were left to wonder, to guess, and often to misinterpret the value of this unprecedented experiment. Thus, shrouded in mystery, the treasures of the Federal Theatre slept until 1974 when Lorraine Brown and John O'Connor, two tenacious English professors from George Mason University, resolved to make a concerted effort to find them. With the able assistance of John Cole, Reference Librarian of the Library of Congress, the search began; it led, ultimately, to an abandoned airplane hangar in Baltimore.

The discovery that climaxed this painstaking treasure hunt was itself dramatic. As the great warehouse doors were thrown open, nesting pigeons were startled into flight, and mice, whose sanctuary was being rudely invaded, scurried for cover. Streaks of light penetrated the accumulated gloom of a third of a century to etch the great pile of packing crates and metal filing cabinets within. Some of the original containers in which the materials had been hurriedly packed were intact, while others lay half open, their contents covered with dust.[15] Newspaper clippings from performances of *Power* and the "swing" *Mikado*, photographs of T. S. Eliot's first New York production of *Murder in the Cathedral*, original set designs for the spectacular "voodoo" version of Shakespeare's *Macbeth*, court scenes from Hughes Allison's *The Trial of Dr. Beck*, costume sketches from Hall Johnson's *Run Little Chillun'*, and the muted voices of countless radio drama scripts, all seemed to stir expectantly under their blanket of dust. Awed and excited, the explorers gazed on the great pile, eloquent in its silence. They brushed off a few manuscripts, and leafed through the ageing pages.

It was magic in the making! The youthful genius of Orson Welles and John Houseman, of Abe Fedder and Sam Leve, of Arthur Miller and Langston Hughes, of Eubie Blake and thousands of actors and actresses, the young and the old, the dead and the living, the famous and the long-forgotten, could now rise from the fluttering pages of production notebooks, playscripts, musical scores, posters, costume designs, research folders, to live again.

As the New Deal reaped multiple dividends on its investment, multiple now, too, are the rewards that this resurrection brings, for this massive collection, the essence of an American dramatic era, has been placed on permanent loan from the Library of Congress to George Mason University, and once more challenges the dramatic world to explore its turbulent, romantic history, and its achievements. Already, excerpts from the Living Newspapers and other plays are being re-staged on college campuses; in the nation's capital, the New Federal Theatre, with the assistance of a grant, has staged material from the Federal Collection in the Coolidge Auditorium at the Library of Congress; at the Research Center, which has been established at George Mason University, ethnic theater groups pore over the treasures of their dramatic past; historians and critics, who, for the last thirty-five years, have had to touch Federal Theatre productions very lightly—often to rely, for their evaluations, on synopses and reviews that were published in newspapers and periodicals at the time the plays were produced—now seek in this wealth of material the live vitality that has eluded them.

It will take time to explore the history and achievements of the Federal Theatre and the impact that the project actually had on American dramatic development: if the mystery of its lost wealth has been solved, the adventure of rediscovery has only just begun.

Although this recovery is exciting for drama historians and critics in general, it is doubly so for students of black drama, for the Federal Theatre had a tremendous impact on black dramatic development and the Collection includes published and unpublished, produced and unproduced works by the black playwrights who submitted their plays to the Federal Theatre. Some of these young black playwrights received much of their technical training and experience on the project, and wrote specifically for its black units. Indeed, the black drama treasure chest is one of the richest in the Federal Theatre Collection.

TWO

THE DUAL DILEMMA OF THE BLACK FEDERAL DRAMATISTS

BLACK DRAMA did not start with the Federal Theatre. In fact, it has been around the American continent as long as there have been blacks to practice the African arts and rituals in religion, in storytelling, in song, and in oratory. In the beginning, it was the spontaneous, living drama of a people whose physical actions directly reflected their spiritual and emotional being, or as Alain Locke phrased it, of a race that was "inherently dramatic" in its mode of expression. The actor and the dramatist were one, and every performance was an opening night since playscripts did not exist. It was not drama, therefore, but written drama that was forced to await the coming of Western education to the African dramatic arts in America.

The earliest surviving plays known to have been written by black Americans did not appear until the middle of the nineteenth century; by that time, the stereotyping of blacks as buffoons in white plays and in minstrel shows had already been accomplished. Black playwrights and performers were locked into this derogatory public image, and those who aspired to create serious black drama were forced to leave America for the more hospitable atmosphere of Europe.[1]

There were serious plays about the black experience in America written by black playwrights in the early years of the twentieth century, some of which are still coming to light. However, before the New Deal's Great Experiment was launched in 1935, few of those plays ever reached the footlights. Commercial producers had little or no interest in producing them since white audiences expected to see black actors only in comic or subservient roles, and there were not many blacks who could afford to pay the price of commercial theater tickets. Certainly, no black American could hope to support himself and his family by writing plays about the black experience, so the art could be practiced only as a hobby, and would-be dramatists were forced to engage in other occupations to make a living.

"It was the Federal Theatre," said black Federal playwright Theodore Ward, "that proved the open Sesame, providing at once a laboratory and the wherewithal for creative enterprise."[2] In fact, in no area of its endeavors did the Federal Theatre's efforts and influence reap more dividends than in that of black drama. For many young black dramatists, this was their first opportunity to concentrate on their creative efforts, free from the devastating effects of economic pressure, and to participate in stage procedures and production techniques on such a broad scale. The results of such participation, including the feedback they received from having their plays produced, were extremely valuable to these young playwrights, and were instrumental in their development.

"The Federal Theatre," wrote black dramatist Loften Mitchell, "dominated the Harlem area."[3] It also dominated other black communities where black Federal Theatre units were established, since it provided unprecedented opportunities, not only for black artists, but also for black audiences. The nominal prices charged by the Theatre for tickets made it possible for members of those communities to attend performances, and the increased degree of artistic freedom practiced by the Theatre made it possible for black playwrights to project a new and recognizable image for those audiences.

In the Manifesto of The American Negro Theater, which was formed in Harlem at the close of the Project, its founders also acknowledged their debt to the Federal Theatre, for the project had not only organized workshops for writers, and produced plays by unknown black playwrights, but it had also trained directors, technicians, and actors in the most modern and sophisticated stagecraft. Sterling Brown also stated that "the opportunity to direct plays, denied to Negroes except in musical comedy or amateur drama, was one of the finest things afforded by the Federal Theatre."[4] Thus, it seems clear that the Federal Theatre was considered by both black artists and intellectuals to represent a watershed in Afro-American dramatic development.

Nevertheless, the unprecedented opportunities that the Great Experiment offered its black playwrights did not automatically solve all their problems. Indeed, the Federal Theatre's opening of this door to the world of serious drama was a mixed blessing akin to the opening of Pandora's box: along with the advantages, out came the problems that had to be wrestled with. And the most awesome of these difficulties was white racism.

The theater of the thirties that was inherited by the federal project was a product of white racism. It was a segregated affair that varied considerably in degree from city to city, and even from theater to theater. By that time the majority of commercial theaters did include segregated sections for black audiences, but some of them still refused to admit blacks at all.[5] Even that rare phenomenon, the successful black playwright, could find himself denied access to a staging of his own creation.[6] In contrast, white theater-goers felt free to attend Harlem productions. As early as the preceding century there had been several attempts to establish and maintain black community theaters, but white rabble-rousers had wrecked the African Grove Theater, which was formed in the nineteenth century in lower Manhattan by Mr. Brown, James Hewlett, the black West Indian tragedian, and other black actors.[7] By the 1930s, the manners of some whites who attended black performances had hardly improved.

Then, too, segregation in the thirties was not confined to theater audiences; it usually extended also to casts. No black could play a leading role on the white stage, and any physical contact between a black man and a white woman was strictly tabu. Many white actors refused even to occupy the same stage with blacks, and theater unions, generally, excluded black performers from their membership.

The organization of the Federal Theatre reflected the prevailing practices by maintaining separate black units,[8] but segregation in the Federal Theatre was far less rigid than it had ever been before. In Boston, for example, the black unit occupied the same building as white, Yiddish, and other ethnic drama groups, and mixed casts, which hitherto had been almost nonexistent, were common. While only a few of the black federal units were headed by black directors, this could not always be credited to white racism. When the New York unit—by all estimates the most active and spectacular of all the Federal Theatre groups—was given a choice, the veteran black actress, Rose McClendon, "felt that since Negroes had always been performers and had had no previous means of learning direction and design, they would prefer to start under more experienced direction."[9] Thus, by choice, the unit acquired John Houseman and the flamboyant young Orson Welles as its directors. While Welles' association with the black unit was not always harmonious, it was spectacularly productive and instructive and amply justified Rose McClendon's judgment.

But segregation in the theater of the thirties was an effect, not a cause, and in the mood that prevailed throughout America, discrimination on the project was inevitable. The conditioning of the white American public, which included the vast majority of theater audiences and theater personnel, did not incline it towards either understanding or appreciating black American culture. Almost all of the plays about black life that had been produced had been written by white dramatists[10] who had little or no first hand knowledge of their subject, and who projected white interpretations of what black life was—or ought to be—in a dominant white culture. With this straight-jacket of expectancy already established, the young black playwrights on the federal project were faced with the task of trying to fulfill the needs of their black patrons for recognizable black images on the stage without antagonizing their white patrons.

The attitude of the white public extended also to white play readers, producers, and directors; thus, while the project did open the door for blacks, many of their plays, quite predictably, never reached the footlights. At no time was there a black representative on the National Play Bureau or the Play Policy Board, which were responsible for the selection of the plays produced by the black units,[11] and many of those selected distorted the black image, and had no appeal for the black communities.

The most immediate problem of racist expectancy, inherited by the black playwrights of the thirties, was the derogatory black stereotypes which had been established by the white stage of the nineteenth and early twentieth centuries. Even today, almost everyone is still familiar with these stereotypes: the "brute Negro," whose sole aim it was to drink, gamble, slash, rape, and otherwise attack white America; the "young Negro," whose ambitious mother pushed him relentlessly, and unsuccessfully, into the white domain of higher education; the servile "step'n'fetchit," who delighted in serving white folks; the vicious, vengeful, untrustworthy "black seductress," on whose shoulders the white man could unburden his responsibility for his promiscuity, and his miscegenation;[12] the ignorant, artless "ingenue"; the "black mammy," whose self-denying devotion to the white master's family brought her greatest joy and satisfaction in life; the "Negro minstrel," or singing, dancing fool, with nothing in his head, a perpetual grin on his face, and rhythm in his bones; and the "tragic mulatto," who had to die before the end of the play, because there existed no place at all for her within the framework of the white superiority myth.[13] Although the majority of these derogatory images have now been laid to rest, for the black dramatists of the thirties they represented an enormous and immediate problem that could not be ignored. Consequently, the black playwrights were immediately at war with the Broadway stereotypes.

Hand in hand with the expectations of the white public, that conformity to these stereotypes would be maintained, went the expectation that white aesthetic and ethical standards would also be reflected on the stage. To white audiences of the thirties, black was not beautiful, and black ethics were not even believed to exist. But even these

impositions were by no means the full extent of the attack on black
dignity by the white dramatic world. White critics, whose duty it was
to explain to audiences how they should interpret black characterizations, reinforced the black images projected by the white stage, and
extended their own stamp of inferiority to include both the black
dramatists' inability to achieve unassailable white standards, and the
mediocrity of their dramatic techniques and experiments. The circle
was a continuous, self-perpetuating one—from the expectations of
the white public to the producers, from the producers to the critics,
and back to the public.

The views of the white critics of the first two decades of the twentieth century have become so diffused and imbedded in the minds of
white audiences as to be generally familiar to most Americans.
Sterling Brown has noted the tone of condescension of some critics
toward black actors,[14] and Doris Abramson, in a daring article published some years after her evaluation of early black drama, has recorded and analyzed reviews of black plays in the twenties, and also
some of those produced in the thirties, and she shows that often,
under the umbrella of faint praise, the damage to black playwrights
was done by innuendo, and with derogatory tone and diction.[15]
Critics of such unassailable stature as Brooks Atkinson, of the New
York Times, described the images in the black plays as being caricatures of white caricatures. Alexander Woolcott of the New York World,
George Jean Nathan in Judge, Percy Hammond of the New York Herald
Tribune, Atkinson, and others, described plays and players with such
terms as "awkward," "naive," "childlike," or realistic "slices of
niggerdom." Even in the thirties some white critics continued to find
black characters, in black plays written by black playwrights, "less
real" than those black characters created by white dramatists in such
fantasies of black life as Porgy and Goat Alley.[16] By 1940 some critics
had become more direct in their assaults on black plays; John Mason
Brown stated in the New York Post, 24 October 1940, that Theodore
Ward's Big White Fog was "like an echo of every playwriting fault
committed in the worst of the scripts presented down at the erstwhile
Theater Union."[17]

Within the critical tradition of the thirties, also, was Carl Carmer, a
white reviewer for Opportunity. In fact, Carmer, and the rest of critical
America for that matter, failed to recognize the highly experimental
nature of Hall Johnson's Run Little Chillun', in which Johnson opposes
African and Western philosophies, and brings them to a spectacular
synthesis at his finale. At the time of its New York opening in 1933,

Carmer expressed regret that Hall Johnson had not been more "factual" with regard to Negro religion by opposing the Baptists to the Holy Rollers, rather than by opposing them to the pantheistic voodooism of the New Day Pilgrims he created for the play. Thus, in addition to the derogatory images and standards projected by white critics, black playwrights were also condemned both for realism and for nonrealism, and their achievements in experimental drama were either unrecognized or rejected. When *Run Little Chillun'* was produced in Los Angeles in March 1938 under the auspices of the Federal Theatre, its impact on the public was enormous, but its experimental nature, and its implications for the development of black drama, were still not widely understood.

Nor, unfortunately, have some of the black drama historians of the past been immune to the effects of the white superiority myth. In his doctoral dissertation, written at Yale University in 1945, Fannin Belcher did not include a single play by a black playwright in his choice of the six best plays that had been produced on black life. He chose, instead, plays by white playwrights such as *The Emperor Jones*, by Eugene O'Neill; *In Abraham's Bosom*, by Paul Green; *Porgy*, by Dubose and Dorothy Heyward; and *The Green Pastures*, by Marc Connelly.[18] Yet most of these white-authored plays alienated black audiences, who could find little or no relationship between them and black culture. Writing later about *The Green Pastures*, Loften Mitchell had this to say, "black blood flowed in those pastures as white knives ripped at the Negro image."[19] Belcher further bemoaned the lack of high quality plays by black playwrights, stating that to date not one was an artistic triumph.[20] In the same dissertation, however, in a brief discussion of *Troubled Island*, he contradicts this evaluation, in essence, by acknowledging that in this play Langston Hughes "becomes the poet playwright, wholly satisfying in language and portrayals,"[21] and states that "the writing is some of his best."[22]

Beyond the application of white critical standards, however, the few existing black critics did not go. The realm of derogatory tone and innuendo was the exclusive domain of the white critics, and the extent of misrepresentation on their part would, today, have all the earmarks of being both intentional and malevolent, were it not for the fact that their views were quite legitimately spawned by the racism inherent in the myths of white superiority that prevailed in the thirties.

The full extent of the effects of these myths can hardly be exaggerated. As Ralph Ellison showed with awesome clarity, they made of the black an invisible man.[23] They also made it virtually impossible

for white critics, and white audiences, to contemplate any other criteria of excellence than white criteria, since the myths, in fact even the
English language in which they were couched, defined all things
white as good, wholesome, and beautiful, and all things black as their
antithesis. The failure of critics to recognize black experimental drama
as such stemmed from the same source. The myths fostered the conviction that blacks were incapable of such creativity or such sophistication. They also fostered the belief that the black American's
African heritage had been completely obliterated during slavery and
replaced by Western cultural standards.[24]

But the twentieth century, which has gradually increased educational opportunities for black Americans—particularly in the years
since the Supreme Court's historic decision on desegregation—has
witnessed such a mushrooming of black intellectual achievements
that it is totally irrational for white America to cling to such myths. The
painstaking process of re-evaluation that has taken place in anthropology, sociology, and other related fields, has revealed, also, that the
African cultural heritage is still very much alive in black America,[25]
with the obvious implication that Euro-American standards are not
today, and were not in the thirties, the exclusive motivating force in
black culture. This fact has been in the past, and continues to be, one
of the most difficult for much of white America to accept since it
challenges, not only the cherished myths, but also the very foundation
of white judgment—the singularity of its criteria. Nevertheless, it is
precisely this reality, the existing plurality of standards, that has
characterized this nation of immigrants from almost all the world's
races and cultures.

The black dramatist of the thirties was a product of the African,
European, and other cultures that were scattered throughout slave-
owning America. He represented a synthesis that had been forged in
sorrow, compelled by the whip, and tempered by the continuous
flow, to black American communities, of black West Indians who had
experienced a somewhat greater degree of freedom to preserve their
African heritage.[26] Compression into urban ghettos, and the myths of
white superiority that defined and frustrated black expectations,
completed his education, and it would indeed have been remarkable
if such a synthesis had inspired in him exclusively Euro-American
standards. Nevertheless, it is little wonder that the conditions created
by these myths were more than enough to account for the cautious
ambiguity of the earliest plays by black dramatists. For those who
desired production, white-oriented plays were the only answer, and

such plays continued to be written by black playwrights even in the thirties, and beyond.[27] But by no means all of the black-authored plays of the thirties were white-oriented, and it is remarkable how many of the black dramatists of the Federal Theatre era chose to attack the white myths and stereotypes head on, in spite of the obvious threat to production that such heresy entailed.

To be sure, the inspiration for such a degree of dedication was not lacking. It came from a number of sources, of which the intellectual giant, W. E. B. Du Bois, and the charismatic leader, Marcus Garvey, are probably the best known. But the man who left his indelible stamp on black drama was Alain Locke. Locke, a Harvard graduate and Rhodes scholar, was for many years Chairman of the Philosophy Department at Howard University.[28] He was the father of black dramatic theory, and there is little subsequent black dramatic theory that has transcended the scope of his vision.

During the Harlem literary renaissance of the twenties, it was Locke who articulated the far-reaching significance of the black spiritual awakening,[29] and for Locke, this inevitably heralded a return to the ancestral arts, for

> there is in the mere knowledge of the skill and unique mastery of the arts of the ancestors the valuable and stimulating realization that the Negro is not a cultural foundling without his own inheritance.[30]

Locke was also passionately convinced of the potential of black American culture to parallel in drama its achievements in music, and to develop its own native dramatic mode, for "the supporters and exponents of Negro drama do not expect their folk temperament to prove the barren exception."[31]

His vision extended also to a future in which black drama would stimulate and invigorate all American drama, and apparently Max Reinhardt agreed with this view, for on one occasion, while they were observing black performers in action, Reinhardt remarked to Locke, "to me they reveal new possibilities of technique in drama, and if I should ever try to do anything typically American, I would build on these things."[32]

Even as far back as 1927, Alain Locke stated his visionary goals for the effective development of black drama:

> And while one of the main reactions of Negro drama must and will be the breaking down of those false stereotypes in terms of

which the world still sees us, it is more vital that drama should
stimulate the group life culturally and give it the spiritual quick-
ening of a native art.[33]

But he acknowledged that to recognize the "unemancipated resources
of the Negro actor" and to foresee "the extension of the freedom of the
American stage . . . and resources of the entire theater . . . one must of
course look over the formal horizons."[34] Locke's vision did, indeed,
penetrate the formal horizons, and several of the black dramatists of
the Federal Theatre who were inspired by it, and eager to seize the
unprecedented opportunities afforded them by the project, also set
their sights over the formal horizons.

But if the Euro-American criteria that were applied by the critics of
the thirties to their plays were inadequate for a just evaluation of
them, what criteria are adequate?

This, of course, is a complex question since critical criteria are also
cultural value statements, which vary considerably from culture to
culture, and even from era to era in the same culture. If Alain Locke,
for example, articulated the far-reaching significance of the black
spiritual awakening in the twenties, what was its significance to the
thirties, or to the seventies? One might state broadly that it was an
awakening to the validity of the existing black values and let it go at
that, but such an answer inevitably poses another question. What
were those existing black cultural values?

Certainly, in view of the varied, often conflicting orientations that
comprised the black heritage and the black experience in America,
they did not have a characteristic singularity such as those of the
Euro-American culture. On the contrary, they ran the gamut from the
entirely white orientation of those mulattoes who practiced the art of
"passing" to the wholly African orientation of the heirs of Marcus
Garvey. In addition, the white superiority myth had so penetrated
sections of black America—from academia to the sharecropper's
cottage—that a social hierarchy had even been established in many
black communities, based primarily on skin color, and several plays in
the Federal Theatre Collection acknowledge this. For some blacks,
then, spiritual awakening might accent a determination to achieve
equality through integration or even assimilation, while for others it
might entail a complete rejection of all white standards and a return to
their African heritage. For men of Locke's vision, however, it primarily signalled the end of enforced self-depreciation, and the beginning of a black self-awareness and self-appreciation that would lead to

an infinitely broader horizon; one beyond which the black dramatist could, with pride and without restraint, draw on his entire international and interracial heritage and experience. Locke's vision, therefore, went beyond self-awareness to complete self-assurance.

The spiritual awakening heralded by Locke was a significant step in that direction, but his ultimate goal for black drama still stretches into the future. This is another reason why the recovery of the Federal Theatre's black treasure is so important, for these plays represent a vital link in the chain of dramatic development, between theory and potential, that has too long been unrecognized.

In the late sixties and early seventies, zealous spokesmen for the Black Revolutionary Theater pronounced pre-revolutionary black plays too white-oriented and white dominated to meet their criteria for "valid" black drama. Plays from such a pre-revolutionary black "sensibility" were also considered of little value to the Black Revolutionary Theater's concerted effort to build black consciousness and a black nationalistic community,[35] and the dedicated black dramatists of the Federal Theatre era, who created an important link in the chain of black dramatic development, have been suspended in a DMZ—a no man's land—between the changing philosophical and sociological extremes that have spanned the last four decades. At one extreme, they experienced white rejection in their own time: black-authored plays were usually too foreign to the dominant white experience to be considered of much value beyond their titillating exoticism; in other words, they were "too black" either for white understanding or for white comfort. At the other extreme these dramatists have also experienced black rejection, or the contemporary downgrading of the value of their work. In 1971 Owen Dodson was asked about the unpublished sequel to his novel, *Boy at the Window* (1951), which was written by this novelist-playwright on a Guggenheim Fellowship, and he replied: "I was told that the novel was not "black enough.""[36] History has thus served the black playwrights of the Federal Theatre era with dual rejection an evaluation of "too black" as well as one of "not black enough," and in the DMZ which was made possible by the loss of the Federal Theatre records and playscripts, both evaluations have passed virtually unchallenged.

Now, however, the DMZ has been breached, the Federal Theatre material has been found, and both evaluations can be challenged through an objective analysis of the playscripts themselves. At the same time, it is obvious that the question of applicable critical standards is complicated. If Euro-American and Black Revolutionary

Theater criteria may both be inadequate for re-evaluation, then what criteria would be adequate?

There is no simple answer to this question, but the criteria will undoubtedly emerge as we relate the plays to the international and interracial cultural influences that produced them. We need, therefore, to examine the plays in their cultural context.

THREE

MYTHS, STEREOTYPES,

AND THE DUAL COMMUNICATION SYSTEM

BECAUSE of the power differential between blacks and whites in America up to now, and the calculated effort to eradicate ethnicity and force all minority groups into the same 'assimilationist' white Anglo-Saxon mold through the imposition of severe social penalties . . . blacks . . . have avoided the known risk of asserting their cultural norms in contexts governed by The Man.[1]

This statement by Thomas Kochman in his preface to *Rappin' and Stylin' Out* contains a veritable bouquet of reasons why black dramatists writing for biracial audiences were faced with problems far beyond those normally encountered by creative artists. In the thirties, they were forced to avoid the known penalties while attempting to create plays that were both acceptable to white patrons and meaningful to black patrons, because black drama occurred almost entirely in contexts governed by The Man.

Certainly, white America was in no way prepared to have its myths of white superiority disturbed and the system played both ends against the middle: on one hand, it demanded and whenever possible enforced conformity to its myths and stereotypes; on the other, its drama critics described the characterizations of black playwrights as "caricatures of caricatures" which accused them, in essence, of a lack of originality for accepting the stereotypes and presenting them in the settings of white superiority. The contradiction inherent in this mode of thought is inescapable, but it contains a far greater discrepancy, the presumption that the use made by the black playwrights of those myths and stereotypes inevitably resulted in white structures. Such a presumption is analogous to believing that because a cathedral in Paris, a suburban bungalow in Singapore, and a Chick Sales privy in a Southern sharecropper's backyard might all be constructed with bricks, they must all be identical structures. This is obviously a false assumption. The questions then are: what did the black playwrights actually build with the bricks they inherited? And if they did not build white structures, how did they avoid "the known risks of asserting their cultural norms in contexts governed by The Man"?

The answers to these questions lie deep in the Afro-American experience which, as early as the beginnings of slavery, forced blacks to develop a dual communication system as a means of self-preservation. From the very beginning, colonial slave owners in the Americas lived in constant fear of insurrection[2] and every effort was made to prevent communication between plantations. Initially, differing tribal languages were believed to be an adequate deterrent, but it was soon discovered that communication on a highly effective level was still possible; it was accomplished through the language of the African drums and dance, and in the British colonial systems, where the most stringent forms of control were practiced, both were forbidden when they were recognized as potential threats.[3] In spite of lofty talk by the Church of England, no real attempt was made at Christian instruction in the early days of slavery because the planters also feared the effects of Christian baptism. An admission on their part that slaves had souls might be considered equivalent to recognition of their humanity, and might result in demands for their freedom and equality as Christian brothers.[4]

In 1727 the Bishop of London, in a letter to the slave-owners of America, found it necessary to allay those fears, and while so doing he irrevocably placed the stamp of Christian approval on human enslavement:

> Christianity and the embracing of the Gospel does not make the least alteration in civil property, or in any of the duties which belong to civil relations. . . . The freedom which Christianity gives is a freedom from bondage of sin and Satan, and from the domination of men's lusts and passions and inordinate desires; but as to their outward condition, whatever that was before, whether bond or free, their being baptized and becoming Christians makes no manner of change in it.[5]

The bishop further pointed out to colonial slave-owners the advantages of slave conversions by stating, "It is certain that the Gospel everywhere enjoins not only diligence and fidelity, but also obedience for conscience sake."[6]

With white supremacy thus insured, and sanctioned by the Church of England, some efforts were made at religious instruction, for slave-owners were ready to cash in on the obvious advantages of having black leaders preach earthly submission and the delayed rewards of heaven to their slaves. But this brand of Christianity backfired with disturbing frequency. While religious gatherings were under constant surveillance, and attempts were made to enforce the cooperation of black preachers under a system of minimal reward and severe punishment, not all were meek and submissive; there were also courageous leaders among them who became thoroughly familiar with the white man's ways and experts in the art of dual communication.[7]

And the Bible stories spoke to these converts as they had not spoken to men since the days when Almighty God conversed with Moses in the mountain wilderness. Since God had delivered the Israelites out of Egyptian bondage, would he not deliver them also? And in this American wilderness of sorrow and suffering, the seeds of faith took root, and the waters of Christianity nurtured them into the great Negro spirituals and the hope of future freedom.

But the Biblical texts, the prayers, and the words of the spirituals seldom meant in the white man's language what they meant in the language of the slaves. The black converts used their inherent ambiguities to convey messages of hope, of the hatred of the slaves for their white oppressors, and often, of escape from bondage. A white overseer, pausing at the door of a shanty church to insure that the worship within did not include plans for insurrection, might have heard a soulful liturgical recitation of the deadly sins, such as avarice and gluttony—which no slave had the opportunity to commit—but instead of being an orthodox expression of repentance, it was just as likely to be an enumeration of all the reasons why no white man could enter the Kingdom of Heaven.[8] Such stories as Daniel's deliverance from the lion's den, Jonah's from the belly of the whale, and those of the Exodus—in fact, any mention of the name of Moses—were highly symbolic of freedom,[9] and lines from the spirituals, echoing across the field from plantation to plantation, were a potent means of signalling escape, or rebellion, or plans for either.[10]

As this system of dual communication developed, inversion of meaning became an important defense tool in black English. It was a method of pretending to adopt, but of not actually accepting, the white terminology that could, and often did, trap the black into self-depreciation and self-hatred.[11] No white man could understand how one slave could call another "nigger," a term which had such derogatory connotations in the white idiom, but because of inversion it became the term for "soul brother" and the mark of common suffering and united purpose.

A glance at the contemporary *Dictionary of Afro-American Slang* is most revealing with regard to inversion. Little Eva, that well-loved character from *Uncle Tom's Cabin*, is the term for a loud-mouthed white girl; "bad" means the very best, and a "bad nigger" is a black person who refuses to be meek, or who rejects the social limitations of poverty and oppression programmed for him within the structure of the white culture—in other words, a black hero. "Tough" and "terrible" mean really wonderful and great, "insane" is a positive, healthy state of mind; "lazy" is defined as calm and relaxed; and "ofay," which means foe in pig latin, is one of the common terms for a white man. The introduction to the *Dictionary of Afro-American Slang* also states that "this so-called private vocabulary of Black people serves the users as a powerful medium of self-defense," [12] and on the basis of these definitions alone, it is obviously no exaggeration to state that a black person and a white person can be engaged in a conversation which has diametrically opposed meanings for each.

In addition to inversion, inflation gradually became an accepted technique for pulling the sting of the white man's language and myths. [13] The whip-wielding slave-driver, or the supervisor of a black prison gang, became "cap'n"; captains were promoted to "colonels," and police patrolmen to "chiefs"; and any prosperous white male became "guv'nor," moreover, the meaning of these covert acts of ridicule never dawned on the ego-inflated white man—any more than did the later messages of the black dramatists which were intended to bypass white producers and audiences.

And, of course, every white Southerner is familiar with the black art of "shucking," or pretending innocence or repentance of real or imagined wrongs to avoid white penalties. [14] This ingredient of the dual communication system is a highly developed defense mechanism; it is learned and practiced from an early age not only in verbal but also in nonverbal communication.

In the medium of nonverbal communication, the black is an artist. He speaks with his facial expressions, his stance, the slant of his shoulder. In fact, he has an entire language of body movements which convey what he wishes to say without his uttering a single word, [15] and this language of the body is legitimately rooted in traditional African dance, which was an integral part of religious worship. Elkin T. Sithole, a native Zulu instructor of ethnomusicology and anthropology at Northeastern Illinois University, states that every African dance song "aims at controlling not only the movement of the feet but also the movement of the toes, knees, hips, stomach, neck, head, eyes, hands, and fingers. Each of these parts moves independently of others, yet simultaneously." [16] The potential of such controlled body movements, both in black culture and the black theatrical arts, is enormous, and its effectiveness in Afro-American communication is unquestionable. Since no technique in the art of self-preservation has been ignored by the Afro-American, this, too, has taken its place in the dual communication system. Its expert use in many contexts, including the art of "shucking," has cheated the whip, made the difference between freedom and imprisonment, or kept blacks from being lynched.

In "Stylin' Outta the Black Pulpit," Grace Sims Holt has recorded yet another reason for the continued development and proficiency of the dual communication system; it was in response to pressures within the black community. In later years the church had become the common meeting place of the black intelligentsia and the illiterate and destitute, and the black preacher was faced with the problem of reaching both segments of his congregation. He solved it by the skillful interweaving of two sermons. Grace Holt relates that he started with quiet, composed statements that were more rational and philosophical than religious, then he carried the congregation through the valley of the shadow—that common ground of slavery and broken promises that is the backbone of black unity—and burst forth into the religious realm of myth, superstition, and emotion, to transport listeners from both strata into an ecstasy of communion. [17]

As the product of such continuous development, the dual communication system has the broadest possible base. It spans and permeates the entire black experience from slave quarters to ghetto, and from pulpit to politics, and it is worth noting how many black political leaders have been trained in this art by the black pulpit: the Reverend Adam Clayton Powell, the Reverend Martin Luther King, the Reverend Jesse Jackson, and a myriad of others. As the products of black culture, it would be remarkable if the black dramatists of the thirties, who were struggling desperately for a toe-hold in the segregated world of the theater, were unaware of the enormous potential of such a system, or did not use it to communicate with their black audiences while avoiding white penalties. Like the early black preachers, they sent out their messages veiled in ambiguities so that interpretation of those messages depended on the medium of translation. On the one hand the messages were interpreted by the white experience, on the other they were decoded by the black experience, and the translations often differed; sometimes they were even totally opposite.

But let us look at some of the black plays and see what these playwrights built with the bricks they inherited.

The Trial of Dr. Beck was written by Hughes Allison, a young black playwright on the Federal Theatre Project. Allison, whose grandfather had been a judge during reconstruction, and whose mother was a concert pianist, had travelled extensively with her when he was young. He had attended Upsala College and majored in English and history before joining the Federal Theatre. His widow, Mrs. Elitea Allison, recalled that he believed man should live up to the best in himself, and that he was particularly impatient with those who betrayed their responsibility.[18] *The Trial of Dr. Beck* was produced by the Federal Theatre in 1937;[19] it opened in Newark, New Jersey, and was such a success that it was moved to New York for three weeks.[20]

In this play, Dr. Beck, a handsome and distinguished-looking mulatto, was accused of murdering his wealthy black wife, Amanda, and the drama unfolds through the evidence at his trial in New York City. Amanda Beck and her identical twin, Carrie, had grown up as cotton sharecroppers in Suffolk, Virginia, and had spent a great deal of time trying to find a concoction that could straighten their hair. Carrie recalled, "One time we got up a mixture we tried on Amanda first. Lawd! evah thing come out and off . . . but Amanda's ears" (II.4).[21] It was Carrie who had eventually discovered the right formula, and the business acumen of Amanda had then converted it into five million dollars and a fashionable New York City address.

In New York, Amanda employed John Beck, a struggling medical student, to promote their product because, as Carrie explained, "Th' customers and operators wuz all women. . . . It was Amanda's idea dat a man agent would help th' business more dan a woman agent" (II.6). Amanda then financed the last two years of Beck's education. A month before his graduation she went to his medical school and demanded that he be made to live up to his promise to marry her in return for her financial aid, and the school, concerned over the possible adverse publicity, withheld his diploma, although Beck had denied the commitment and stated that he had accepted her money as a loan. Under the prevailing system, however, Beck was trapped if he wanted to practice medicine, so he married Amanda. Beck then fell in love with Eleanor Hopkins, but Amanda continued to hold him captive by threatening to get his license revoked if he divorced her. According to Carrie, who lived with the Becks in New York, Amanda was hopelessly in love with John Beck: "She woulda done anything to git him. We had about two million den. So he wusn't hard to git!" (II.7) but,

"Amanda, as far as John Beck was concerned, was just as much a virgin the day she died as the day she first laid eyes on him" (II.9).

Dr. Beck claimed that on his return to his surgery, in their home, he had found Amanda murdered with one of his surgical knives and that he had immediately called Patrolman James from his beat and sent a telegram to his sister-in-law, Carrie, who was visiting a sick brother in Washington, D.C. He refused, however, to account for his absence from home most of the day. There was no concrete evidence of Beck's guilt: the surgical knife revealed no fingerprints, and there was no witness able to place him at the scene of the crime. However, it was District Attorney Madison's contention that the doctor had both the opportunity and the motive to kill his wife, and he built his case with a series of character witnesses whose prejudicial testimony ranged from alleged malpractice to the doctor's theory of eugenics.

It was soon apparent that Dr. Beck was, in fact, the prime suspect because of his theory of eugenics which was about to be published. His book strongly advocated that black leaders should marry the lighest-skinned women possible in order to dilute the race and make it more acceptable in America, and clearly his marriage to Amanda violated his theory. Over the objections of the defense counsel, District Attorney Madison also maneuvered the testimony out of Carrie that "John didn't love Amanda because she was black, because she was ugly, and because cullud men of his type ain't got no use for women of my—I mean her type." (II.10). And there, also present in court, was Beck's mistress, Eleanor, who was light-skinned and pretty, and who was intentionally pregnant with his child although they both knew that Amanda would not divorce him. All of this Eleanor was forced to reveal as a hostile witness for the prosecution, and even to respond, "Yes, I told him that I wished that the baby could have his name" (II.30), and the district attorney pointed out how convenient it would be for Dr. Beck if he was acquitted of his wife's murder since this would make him heir to Amanda's fortune, leave him free to marry Eleanor and practice his theory of eugenics, and, as he succeeded in commenting loudly to the Judge, "By this time it should be evident to the Court that John Beck was really advocating a mongrelization of the American race" (II.11), and "if this book is allowed to be published there is no telling . . ." (II.12).

But as Mr. Brooks, the novelist who had cooperated in the writing of "An American Spectrum," Beck's "sociological bombshell," testified: "Everybody knows that Negroes have always discriminated among themselves" (I.40). Beck's theory was an acknowledgement of a fact of the black experience that light-skinned mulattoes had the best chance for advancement under the white system that controlled black economic well-being. It also acknowledged the fact that many blacks had accepted the standards of white superiority and had created a social hierarchy based on education and shades of skin color—a hierarchy that placed Dr. Beck at the top of the social ladder in the black community.

The Trial of Dr. Beck was fast moving and humorous, tense with conflict, and highly dramatic. The highlights in court included an attempt by Carrie Jones to attack Dr. Beck with the murder weapon, and the marriage, by special license ordered by the Judge, of the doctor and his fainting, pregnant girlfriend, for Beck had been unable to get out of jail to obtain a license. The play was indeed almost too suspenseful, for with the appearance of an unexpected witness the defense counsel made it quite clear throughout the last act that he had discovered who the murderer was, and that it was not John Beck. Following this lead feverishly, he had a series of witnesses then identify a photograph of Amanda's murderer, without revealing who it was, and he teased the district attorney until Madison was driven to demand that the photograph be placed in evidence—a demand denied by the Judge who did, however, admonish the defense counsel for playing "now-you-see-it, now-you-don't . . ." (III.12).

There is certainly no doubt that Allison used the bricks of the white dramatic structures, but *The Trial of Dr. Beck* was much more than ordinary melodrama peopled with established stereotypes. Allison's direct confrontation of the myths of white superiority and their effects on the black community was daring, and he manipulated his stereotypes to condemn the whole system of white prejudice, and to show its effects on the black self-image.

White District Attorney Madison, like John Beck, was a distinguished looking man, a necessary characterization if the victory of Beck's colored lawyer, Collings, was to have any meaning, and his stereotypes included Assistant District Attorney Fields, who was a smug mulatto lawyer hired specifically for Beck's trial and whose manner reflected his Uncle Tomism; Carrie Jones was the untrustworthy black female stereotype, and an admitted physical replica of her twin, Amanda Beck; Eleanor Hopkins was the pretty mulatto in the usual tragic triangle, pregnant and unwed, and two of the State's other witnesses, George and Lulu Doolittle, were acknowledged to be ignorant and mentally deficient blacks who had produced about twenty children before Dr. Beck had sterilized Lulu during her last delivery, apparently without her knowledge. Dr. Beck, himself, was the young black stereotype who had been pushed into the white domain of higher education but whose parents had died before accomplishing their goal.

On the surface, too, this play appeared to commit no infringements of the philosophy of white superiority: on the contrary, District Attorney Madison's repeated proclamation that the doctor intended "to mongrelize the whole American race," (I.41, II.12) was guaranteed to strike responsive chords in a white audience. The efforts of the twins to straighten their hair, and Carrie's later attempts to persuade a Viennese doctor to use his newly-discovered bleaching cream on her also showed the extent to which white standards dominated black thought. The attitude of the district attorney and the State's entire parade of witnesses were aimed at convicting Dr. Beck by fanning the flames of white prejudice, and Hughes Allison even included in his stereotypes that of a white law enforcement officer dear to the hearts of white supremacists. Inspector O'Malley, who was born in Atlanta, admitted that he believed in Southern color standards. He could not tolerate the thought of a "nigger" doctor who numbered white women among his patients, he ordered the colored defense attorney to keep his voice down when speaking to him, and even commented sharply on his audacity in demonstrating such "smartness."

But what did Allison do with this array of stereotypes that was different from the established practice? Assistant District Attorney Fields was shown to be hopelessly prejudiced against the defendant, for John Beck had been forced to throw him out of his surgery when he had previously attempted to intimidate the doctor on behalf of a nurse whom Beck had fired for alcoholism and for seducing a fifteen-year-old boy in his surgery. The Doolittles did contribute a degree of pathetic humor, for immediately on entering the courtroom George began praying and shucking to the Judge: "Ah swear fo' God! Ah ain't done nothin', Mr. Jedge. Ah ain't done a thing!" (I.21), while Lulu thought she had about twenty children, but was not quite sure of the count. Yet with these humorous incidents Allison achieved a remarkable inversion of ethical values, for Lulu Doolittle, protesting vehemently that her children were all her husband's and that he didn't even allow her to talk to a white man, refused to speak to the white district attorney at all, and Madison had to call on his assistant to question her; she added to her refusal an emphatic "and yoh knows why!" (I.26) and her biting remark was an unmistakable denunciation of the black woman's rape by the white man.

Another of the prosecution's witnesses, the nurse who had been fired by Dr. Beck, was forced to admit, reluctantly, that he was the most capable and humane doctor she had worked for, while the white dean of Beck's alma mater stated, "John Beck was probably the most brilliant student ever to pass through our medical school" (II.36), and his sister-in-law confirmed his financial success in his profession. Although his earnings did not match Amanda's wealth, he had refused to be supported by her money after their marriage, and it was clear that Dr. Beck was a thoroughly successful intruder into the white domain of higher education and the medical profession. Allison also reversed the myth that the tragic stage mulatto had no place in society by triumphantly marrying the pregnant Eleanor to the doctor—who occupied the top rung of the social ladder in the black community. Finally, it is doubtful that anyone but the Carrie Jones stereotype, who eventually turned out to be her twin's murderess, could so effectively have delivered the agonized protest that closed the final curtain: "Goddam you God! Goddam you for making me so Black!" (III.17), for this desperate protest was not directed against the Almighty; it was a condensation highly reminiscent of the slave congregation's liturgical recitation of the white man's sins which, in her case, was the total subversion of her aesthetic values, and it was directed against the white myths' destruction of the black self-image.

As Carrie finally admitted, she herself had been in love with John Beck and had hated Amanda for having snared the handsome mulatto doctor, the fruit of her business acumen. Yet the final dramatic revelation of her guilt was not something that the defense counsel sprang unexpectedly on the Court. With the question, "Is it not so, Miss Jones, that your sister's will leaves you her part of the business?" (II.18) and Carrie's acknowledgement, he established that financially she stood to gain perhaps even more than John Beck. Her love-hate relationship to white aesthetic and ethical standards had also been carefully established, for she denounced the ethics that produced mulattoes: "Whenever you see a Negro dat's too light, yuh kin bet you last nickle dat some of his people get in th'bed wid white folks an' didn't have no marriage license to do it!" (I.17) whereupon the defense attorney asked, "and still you wanted your hair to look like white people's hair?" (II.17). Then, when it was revealed that Carrie had tried to get a Viennese doctor to use his bleaching cream on her, he commented, "I was thinking it rather inconsistent to hate Negroes with light skin and still be willing to pay a fabulous price to lighten your own skin" (II.19). She was also deeply in love with the handsome mulatto doctor, yet her capacity to commit murder as a result of her psychological disorientation was demonstrated in court by her attack on John Beck with the murder weapon.

The case presented by the district attorney was circumstantial and an outright appeal to prejudice: in the defense attorney's words, a case "which the State, like an old fashioned witch-doctor, has conjured up . . ." (II.33). In contrast, the defense counsel's case was based on fact. Mr. Collings produced a sidewalk radio interviewer and photographer who had photographed Carrie descending from a plane in Newark Airport the day of the murder and who humanely volunteered his testimony when he became aware of Beck's predicament. His testimony was followed by that of two airline employees who could identify Carrie on the flights from, and to, Washington, and the taxi-driver who had driven her from the airport to the Beck residence and back to the airport for the return flight to Washington in time to receive and sign for the cable from Beck, which had established her absence from New York at the time of the murder. Perhaps the accumulated evidence of Beck's innocence was a bit overwhelming, but Allison knew exactly what it would take to convince a white jury in the thirties, and in this play the audience was the jury. By opposing pure prejudice with unassailable fact, he also established that the black defense attorney was a man of higher moral and professional integrity than the white district attorney who was willing to convict a black man because his theories might "mongrelize the whole American race."

In addition, Allison's astute handling of this opposition succeeded in placing the entire white judicial system on trial along with Dr. Beck, the prevention of which was the acknowledged aim of the harassed presiding judge. After a particularly sharp exchange between the prosecuting and defense attorneys, the judge commented, in the course of a stern lecture,

> the Court is inclined to suggest that the prisoner, Dr. Beck, is not solely on trial, but is being tried in conjunction with tradition and dogma. Too much of this places the Court itself on trial. And this must not be so! (II.12–13)

Yet Allison's play did not antagonize his white audience, for it could point with satisfaction at the ultimate triumph of white justice, but it is difficult to imagine how he could have conveyed such diametrically opposed impressions without the ambiguities of the dual communication system, and perhaps Allison also succeeded in giving some

members of his white audience a deeper insight into black sociological problems than they had ever had before.

But the greatest achievement of Hughes Allison in this dual dramatization was the message he delivered to his black audience. By
confronting and exposing the white myths and the white standards
that had penetrated and become established within the black community, he showed how false and devastating they were and how
great was the need for a thorough re-evaluation and rehabilitation of
the black self-image.

FOUR

ALLISON DOES IT AGAIN

A FTER THE SUCCESSFUL production of *The Trial of Dr. Beck*, Hughes Allison was commissioned to write a trilogy for the Federal Theatre. Apparently it was not completed by the time the project was terminated, since only a foreword and the first play, *Panyared*, have been found in the Federal Collection, and no other plays have come to light.

The *Foreword to Panyared* is an interesting and valuable document which records the author's thoughts and theories on the function of black drama and the sociological role of the black dramatist. Apparently Allison intended the trilogy to span the entire period of Afro-American history, including its African "genesis." He was convinced that only a thorough knowledge of Afro-American genesis could destroy both white and black myths, and it was Allison's hope to promote better understanding between white and black Americans by dramatizing the truths of their historic relationship.

The title of the first play of the trilogy indicates the period of history which it dramatizes: *"panyared"*—kidnapped, or seized[1]—was a word in common use on the west coast of Africa during the slave trade, and the play dramatizes the seizure and transportation of Africans to American plantations, and the first year of their enslavement in the New World. This play predates Alex Haley's popular masterpiece, *Roots*, by thirty-five years, yet the similarity of some of Allison's incidents and many of the attitudes he dramatized, to those described by Haley, is striking. The role which was played by Haley's tribal elder on the middle passage, that of uniting men of many tribes and languages with the hope of achieving freedom, is played in *Panyared* by Allison's hero prince, who comes within a breath of successful mutiny. The mixture of compassion and fear with which newly-arrived slaves were received by blacks born to slavery in America is reflected by both authors, and similarly sets apart those born and raised in freedom from those who have known only the fear and degradation of slavery. The moral principles and practices of slavers, slave-owners, and those who voice the religious platitudes of their times, concern both writers; and both works reflect the effects of these

31

moral attitudes, not only on the enslaved, but also on the enslavers. The restraint of both writers in dramatizing white brutality makes the agony and the irony similarly effective, and there are also a striking number of similar motifs that appear in both stories.

Allison's concern with Afro-American roots, and his efforts to publicize them as far back as the thirties through drama, are particularly interesting since he wrote at a time when black playwrights were not recognized, by either whites or blacks, as having such a sense of responsibility and commitment to informing the black community. Even in the late sixties and early seventies, some theoreticians and spokesmen of the Black Revolutionary Theater categorized all black drama of this period as being hopelessly white-oriented. *Panyared* now corrects both misconceptions.

The first act of *Panyared* is set in Africa, where the English slave trader, Charles Chester, has the mission of opening a new slaving area by fermenting warfare between tribes, and making it profitable for the Africans to take and sell captives. He is attempting to make a quick fortune so that he can return to South Carolina and marry his love, Esther Wilson, daughter of a plantation owner. In Africa, Chester has tried to escape the psychological effects of his sordid profession by painting a portrait of Esther, using as a model his African mistress, Zema, who passionately hates the picture. Zema had not been allowed to see it until it was completed and was revolted to discover on the canvas the likeness of a yellow-haired white girl.

The play begins with the capture of Bombo, son of a native king's first wife, who is heir to his dying father. Bombo is a man of peace; he is humane, intelligent, and studious, and so far has been little concerned with the frivolities of courtship. He is betrayed to Chester by the king's second wife, Tavu, who is jealous of him and of his mother, Walu, and who intends, with the aid of the medicine man, to make her own warlike son, Promvo, the new king. While the drums furiously announce the old king's death, Tavu stabs Walu to death, and the prince and his personal slave, Kito, are panyared and chained by Chester. Chester notes that the betrayers of the prince are also magnificent physical specimens, but he dare not delay his retreat for he is already uneasy about possible repercussions from his having taken such an exalted captive. He immediately starts his return march to the coastal fort, pausing only to collect captives at arranged points along the way.

At the fort, meanwhile, white slavers taunt Zema into a frenzy of jealousy over the blond portrait, and when Chester finally returns she spits on it, and is whipped. Despite his belief in white superiority—a belief that is well supported, at the fort, by guns and chains—Chester is fearful that Bombo's leadership will stir the captives to revolt, so he orders Bombo to be chained separately to the auction block when the other captives are herded into the pens, and Zema, mad with jealous hatred, and impressed by the prince, sleeps with him.

The following morning, Zema flings her conquest in Chester's face, taunting him that she has chosen an African prince over a "nobody white man" (I.iv.9), and Chester's white pride is blistered by her preference for the black prince. He ships her out immediately on Captain Slade's slaver, the *Sally Mae*, as part of a cargo that includes Bombo, Kito, and Chester's portrait, on its way home to Esther Wilson. Also on board is Jefferson, a greenhorn white doctor who had only just arrived on the *Sally Mae*. Jefferson was horrified by his first glimpse of the slave trade and is fleeing from it immediately. By this time Zema's hatred for Chester is so deep that when she is dragged aboard she screams at him that if she has to leave her grave he will never touch the yellow-haired girl "with his lil' finger" (I.iv.14).

Act II, the middle passage on the *Sally Mae*, is a sharply dramatized nightmare. The slaves, lying shackled shoulder to shoulder in the uncleaned filth of three weeks, suffer horribly. The stench in the hold is unbearable enough even to drive out the sailors who must enter occasionally. With the exception of the experienced ship's captain, Slade, who banks on tribal rivalries and the five hundred different languages among his six hundred captives to prevent mutiny against the fifty whites aboard, fear of Bombo's leadership stalks the ship's crew. In the hold Zema has been shackled beside Bombo in the hope that she will keep him occupied, but the prince can think of little but how to free himself and his countrymen. A sailor who enters is torn to pieces by a male slave who has pulled his shackles loose from the rotten floor boards, and the slave frees Bombo. Soon, all the captives are released from their shackles and Bombo unites them, tribal rivalries and languages notwithstanding, and leads them in mutiny.

As Bombo emerges from the hold, followed by Zema and the African warriors, the doom of the slavers seems inevitable until the momentarily dumbfounded captain regains his wits and reminds Zema about the slave ship *Dolphin*. Zema, who does not want to die without her revenge, now frantically explains to Bombo that if they massacre the white men they will all die too: at the fort she had heard of such a massacre on the *Dolphin*, which brought death also to all the victorious Africans aboard since they could not sail the white man's ship. For a moment, the crew, frozen with fear, stares at the prince as he stands in front of the hatch, with Zema beside him and the warriors on the stairs behind him poised for his signal; then understanding contorts Bombo's face, and, to save his people, the prince, quivering with controlled anger, orders them back to the hold.

Allison's dramatization, in the thirties, of the events and horrors of the middle passage, is extraordinarily close to those described by Alex Haley in *Roots*: both writers record in tragic detail the inhumanity of the accepted system of transporting slaves, the suffering inflicted by it, and the frenzied efforts of the captives to regain their lost freedom. Both also demonstrate the capability of an intelligent and seasoned leader to overcome the barriers of tribal rivalries and differing languages, and to promote unity in the face of common disaster. As in *Roots*, there are those on the *Sally Mae* who choose death in the shark-invested waters rather than enslavement.

Act III of *Panyared* is staged on the Wilson plantation in South Carolina, to which Bombo, Zema, and Kito have been taken. Zema, who was familiar with the white man's customs, had succeeded in marrying Bombo before a preacher in Charleston, and at the plantation she is chosen to be the personal maid of her nemesis, Esther Wilson. A year later she gives birth to Bombo's son. Although Zema now loves Bombo dearly and idolizes their baby, she has not relinquished her obsession for revenge on Chester and on the eve of his return she locks Esther in her bedroom and sets fire to the house. Bombo is horrified by his wife's act and accepts responsibility for it: he enters the burning house and saves Esther's life; but Zema will not be thwarted, and when Chester arrives next morning she stabs him to death in the garden before he can "even touch her with his lil' finger" (III.iv.5).

In the last scene Mr. Wilson sits in judgment before his assembled slaves: he gives Bombo freedom for saving Esther's life, orders Zema sold down the river for murdering Chester, and refuses Bombo's plea for the freedom of their infant son and Kito. He leaves open the possibility of their future freedom, however, if Bombo can make the money to purchase it. Thus the prince is once more a free man, but there is no joy in Bombo's heart for his deliverance is accompanied by the destruction of his family. Mr. Wilson also makes it clear that Bombo must now leave the plantation and enter the alien white world, for as a free man he will be a disruptive influence among the slaves.

Chester has also brought back with him, as slaves, Tavu and Promvo, and on seeing their kinsman, Bombo, they throw themselves at his feet, pleading with him to forgive their treachery and to secure their freedom from the white man. Bombo replies sadly that he would if he could, but that he is unable even to secure the freedom of his wife and baby. With no other choice open to him, Bombo then places his son under the protection of the adoring Kito and leaves the plantation, but his last words hover ominously over the future: "Maybe dis will take a long, long time, Kito. But someday....we all be free. I only hope dat in gittin free....dey ain't much blood spilled!" (III.v.9).[2] Kito, twisted with the agony of despair, sinks slowly to the ground as the final curtain falls.

If Allison created suspenseful drama in *The Trial of Dr. Beck*, he certainly surpassed it with *Panyared*. The slavers' kidnapping of the African prince and their return march to the coast are not a cut-and-dried affair with a single possible outcome. A continuous news bulletin, broadcast by the talking drums from village to village along their route, make the possibility of the prince's rescue very real and, in fact, it almost occurs when one chief, with many warriors, is incensed that Chester appears to be no longer satisfied to seize the "branches" but would also attack the "roots." The slavers and their captives are also continuously stalked by hungry lions, and there is always the danger that the leadership capabilities of the prince might turn the slightest opportunity into a successful revolt. The male captives, despite their fear and suffering, are intensely alert for any signal from him. Throughout the middle passage the frantic efforts of the slaves to free themselves from their shackles, and the crew's recognition that this is a constant danger, also sustain a high degree of suspense, which reaches its peak when the prince comes within moments of achieving a successful mutiny. In the deceptively peaceful setting of the Wilson plantation, the suspense continues to be feverish as Zema attempts one murder, fires the plantation house, and achieves her revenge with another murder.

In addition to being suspenseful, *Panyared* is a spectacular play. The incidents Allison selected, with which to portray the genesis of black enslavement, were inherently dramatic, but he also exploited their full potential by dramatizing a series of stark, intimate details that flash through the range of human emotions from the poetic and noble to the purely bestial. At one end of the spectrum, the love scenes of Bombo and Zema are sheer poetry. When Bombo, at the auction block, begs her to take away his chains so he can go free, Zema replies: "Then.... Zema would feel as the earth would feel without the sun, the moon and the stars. But could she free Bombo....Zema would do it" (I.i.2). But Zema is not always poetic; the range of her emotions dramatized by Allison is tremendous: when Chester returns to the fort she flashes from love to jealous pain, followed almost instantly by intense hated for him. These emotions, mingled with admiration for Bombo, lead her to his seduction, and to new love. Within a few hours, however, Zema returns to a state of screaming hatred and fear as she is dragged off to the slave ship. On the middle passage, her suffering and terror alternate with tenderness for Bombo, hatred for Chester, and clear, cool-headed judgment. At the Wilson plantation, a year later, when Bombo shows jealousy over her preoccupation with her unabated hatred of Chester, she soothes him: "When I think of him....it wid my head, when I think of yuh....it wid my heart." Then she explains:

> First I see a prince; I say....sleep wid him and Chester eat dirt; like he make Zema eat dirt . . . Zema's lips....jest her lips....touch Bombo's lips. And Zema find her mate . . . . In my heart, Bombo. (III.ii.5–6)

Yet in a short while Zema will also attempt one murder, and achieve another.

Bombo's aristocratic dignity and self-control are a dramatic contrast to Zema's instantly flammable passions. Even when Bombo is in chains, the grace and eloquence of his salutation to the chief who meets the slavers on their march startles and disturbs Chester. Chester would prefer to recognize only the physical attributes of his captives. Peaceful by nature, Bombo is nevertheless a charismatic leader who needs no words to unite the slaves on the *Sally Mae*. He is a fearless warrior when the occasion demands, and clear-headed in extreme anger. When Zema explains that victory will bring death to all aboard, his concern is for her and for his warriors, not for himself, and he later jeopardizes his own life to save Esther Wilson. Even in slavery Bombo is still a prince and a hero.

At the other end of the spectrum, Allison dramatizes greed and bestiality. In Chester's absence from the fort, white slavers, who are impatiently awaiting his return with their cargoes of human misery, discuss with a Catholic priest their respective attitudes toward black enslavement, and their discussion is a highly effective piece of dual communication, filled with Biblical quotations and riddled with hypocrisy and irony. The priest expresses the generally accepted religious platitudes; some of the slavers admit that they dislike slaving, but are not about to let morality interfere with business; others hold that "all them that ain't white . . . is animals." But many of the slavers who are amassing material wealth are becoming drunkards in the process, and Chester's use of Esther's portrait as a fetish betrays the effects of his brutal profession on his stifled conscience. The white superiority myths hover like malevolent, corrupting clouds over the African continent, and even Zema's hatred for the portrait of a white girl she has never seem stems from the shameless way she has been exploited as an inferior being. The Africans, Tavu and Promvo, and the chief who could have freed Bombo had he not had captives of his own to sell to Chester, are also infected by greed.

But although Allison dramatizes spectacular incidents and emotions in spectacular settings, he is not concerned primarily with spectacle. It is his vehicle of truth, and his truth is stark tragedy. In 1946 W. E. B. Du Bois stated in his Appeal to the World:

> If, however, the effect of the color caste system on the North American Negro has been both good and bad its effect on white America has been disastrous. It has repeatedly led the greatest modern attempt at democratic government to deny its political ideals, to falsify its philanthropic assertions, and to make its religion to a great extent hypocritical,[3]

and it is precisely these facts that Allison's play reveals, for *Panyared* is a dual tragedy, the tragedy of both the enslaved and the enslavers, and Allison has tailored its structure to meet the complex demands of two interacting stories divided between two worlds. In acts I and II— Africa and the middle passage—all his characters, black and white, are individualized. In act III—the Wilson plantation in America—all his characters, black and white, with the exception of the newly arrived Africans, Bombo, Zema, and Kito, are stereotypes. This is an unusual switch in characterization, but one that achieved a high degree of unity since it dramatized the logical relationship between cause and effect by contrasting the thoughts and actions of psychologically free men with those of people who had been conditioned by a couple of hundred years of slavery. Continuity is also insured by the ever present myths of white superiority, by common tragedy, and by Allison's multiple motifs, Chaucerian in scope and complexity, which he manipulates so that incidents are repeated to achieve extreme irony in situations that reverse the roles of victims and victimizers.

This reversal of roles begins in the first act. As Chester nears the fort on his march, the greenhorn doctor, Jefferson, meets him and has his baptism of horror. Jefferson examines the captives for signs of disease and is expected to reject those who are unlikely to survive the middle passage. This examination is no act of mercy on the part of the slavers; it is a practical business safeguard. But Jefferson believes that those he eliminates will be allowed to return to their tribes and compassionately rejects as many as possible, only to find that they are taken aside and massacred. Among the rejected is a young woman whom he does succeed in saving from death, but he is horror struck when her baby is dashed to death by the slavers, before her eyes.

Allison now pulls a superbly subtle switch to drive home to his white audience the horrors of slaving. The slavers are met by an African chief who has captives to sell to Chester, and he offers to the highest bidder a young mulatto girl who is being followed by a white, Catholic missionary priest—an agonized-looking old man. The priest implores her release in the name of God, and Chester, recognizing instantly that she is his daughter, would release her provided the priest will acknowledge the relationship; lacking such an acknowledgement, the girl is extremely valuable property in his eyes. But the priest, who is sworn to celibacy, makes no such acknowledgement, and the chief has the girl stripped so that the slavers can admire the beautiful body of the girl "so like the women of your own world" (I.ii.22). A lascivious white trader bids for her instantly and attempts to approach her, but the terrified girl plunges a knife into her breast, and is left by the slavers with the priest kneeling over her dead body.

On the middle passage, Allison then repeats the self-destruction motif, this time in its familiar pattern. The grief-stricken black mother of the murdered baby is also on the slave ship and Jefferson has got her released to him from the hold. He follows her around the deck constantly, begging for her forgiveness, but at the first opportunity she hurls herself overboard into the water that never ends.

It is clear from Allison's dramatization that none of those involved in the slave trade, either victims or victimizers, are immune to its devastating effects. He presents both stories, sometimes with stark clarity, sometimes veiled in platitudes and the ambiguities of the dual communication system, and leaves the interpretation to his audience: the ultimate interpretation would depend on their convictions, their medium of translation, and their capacity for understanding and compassion.

After the mutiny on the *Sally Mae*, Jefferson delivers a prophetic warning to the ship's captain, and to posterity:

Chester kidnapped and wrangled from the jungle the best Negroes he could. I helped separate the unfit from the fit....

helped kill off the unfit. You put the best of the fit in the rotten
hold of your ship, Slade. Only the best among them will survive
the disease, the filthiness, the terror, the bloody muck in that
hold.

You're filling the States with super-fit Negroes, Slade. (II.iii.16)

Jefferson's warning is another jewel of ambiguity, for "best of the fit,"
and "super-fit" do not refer exclusively to the physical attributes of the
blacks, as the white idiom in the thirties would have interpreted. It
took a whole lot more than physical fitness to endure the horrors of the
middle passage, to remain sane, to think clearly, to achieve unity
across language barriers, and to renounce a victory that could only be
temporary, at best. Jefferson's prophecy continues:

We live....because they didn't know how to operate this ship,
because they didn't know our ways, (II.3.16)

And even while he speaks, Zema, shackled beside Bombo in the hold,
has begun to teach the prince the white man's ways.

In act III, on the Wilson plantation in America where the myths of
white superiority have been entrenched for over two hundred years,
there are both white and black stereotypes, and here, even more
comprehensively than in The Trial of Dr. Beck, Allison uses stereotypes to show the effects of the myths on both its black and its white
captives. Mr. Wilson, in the God-role, embodies all the traits of the
mythical, paternalistic slave-owner who dictates the terms of life and
morality, not only for his slaves, but also for his family. His own moral
standards are reflected in his relationship with June, one of his young
mulatto slaves; as Mr. Wilson's mistress she, too, is stereotypically
arrogant and tries to lord it over the other house slaves, even ordering
one of them to make her bed. Mr. Wilson's daughter, Esther, a stereo-
typical young white Southern belle, also reflects the effects of her
father's moral code and the contradictions inherent in the slave system: she rubs old Uncle Ben's rheumatic back for him in the morning
with kindly concern, then petulantly harasses the house slaves to tears
at night while she is impatiently awaiting Chester's return to marry
her; she accepts all the benefits, and exercises all the prerogatives of a
slave-owner's daughter, but she does not morally approve of the
system; she is aware of her father's relationship with June, but pre-
tends that it does not exist. The white overseer, too, conforms to the
myth of the compassionate slave-driver, and the Wilson slaves contrast his humanitarianism with the severe punishments inflicted on

slaves of neighboring plantations. Hannah, Esther's black mammy, is the privileged stereotype who rules over the Wilson household and keeps the other house slaves in their "places" as Mr. Wilson's code demands. All of these stereotypes constitute a very purposeful setting: the mythical, benevolent, and paternalistic Southern plantation. Certainly Allison could have chosen a more brutal setting, but nothing less than the mythical ideal could have produced such extreme irony.

The newly arrived Africans are the only individuals—black or white—in the American setting who are capable of thinking entirely independently of the system. When Zema remarks to Bombo that in little over a year they have learned to talk like the other "darkies," he replies: "But I don't think like 'em. Bombo still think of being a free man. . . . De Baby make me think mo' and mo' 'bout being free" (III.ii.4). Bombo's plight is highly reminiscent of the isolation felt by Haley's young Kunta Kinte in *Roots*, and in this act of *Panyared* Allison shows, as Haley will later do, that slavery, even at its mythical best, was a sordid and inglorious sytem that perverted the values of both masters and slaves, and inflicted infinite misery on its victims.

The final scene of *Panyared*, in which Mr. Wilson usurps the judgment throne and metes out justice, is a masterpiece of dual communication. There is no doubt that any white supremacist in Allison's audience of the thirties would have considered the slave owner's judgment just. It is also certian that no black would have considered any such form of punishment, inflicted by the forces of slavery, to be just; even Zema's murderous vengeance is the direct result of the injustices of the slave trade. The scene also dramatizes some classic ironies similar to those inherent in the liturgical enumeration of the white man's deadly sins in the early slave churches: Mr. Wilson's response to Bombo's plea for the freedom of his son and his slave, Kito, is that they are valuable property, but that perhaps in time Bombo may be able to buy their freedom: avarice is clearly this white God's God, and if he metes out white justice, at best, and in its own Christian terms, it is the justice of an unjust system that is devoid of mercy. Paradoxically, avarice even limits the value that Mr. Wilson places on the life of his own daughter; his reward to her savior, in essence, is a life for a life, although Mr. Wilson also believes fervently that a white life is superior to a black one, and he has no sense of guilt for dismembering Bombo's family.

In marked contrast to Mr. Wilson's code of ethics is the moral code of the prince—his faithfulness to Zema, in spite of her haunting hatred of Chester; his personal acceptance of responsibility for her vengeful act and his heroic rescue of Esther, at his own peril; his deep affection and concern for his own slave; and his compassionate forgiveness of the half-brother and step-mother who had betrayed him—mark Bombo as a prince among paupers.

As the final curtain falls, the agony of Kito also leaves no possible doubt that the whole happy, paternalistic, plantation setting is a mirage, as false as all the stereotypes that inhabit it.

Allison was not the only black federal playwright to use the inherited myths and stereotypes—the bricks—as the structural components of their own self-destruction, or to manipulate the dual communication system to bypass white producers and audiences and deliver meaningful images to his black audiences; but his plays probably reflect the most sophisticated use of them in serious black drama in the Federal Theatre era. Unfortunately, *Panyared* was not produced before the Federal Theatre folded, but its recent discovery in the Federal Collection leaves no doubt of its author's commitment to black history, or of the determination and daring with which he attacked the major black dramatic problems of his day.

FIVE

THE TRANSFORMATION OF THE STEREOTYPES

I N CONTEXTS governed by "The Man," the name of the game was subversion, and there were black playwrights, besides Hughes Allison, who excelled at it. The black dramatists rejected, subverted, and replaced the stereotypes that the white culture had established, and the white playwrights had accepted, with legitimate black images, and the dual communication system was an indispensable asset in this process of transformation. One of the most interesting examples of such a transformation by the black dramatists was that of the "brute negro." Although this stereotype was used by both white and black playwrights, a comparison of white-authored and black-authored plays reveals the entirely different images that resulted and the process by which change was achieved.

Paul Green and Eugene O'Neill were white playwrights of considerable stature and both were attracted by the dramatic possibilities of the black experience; they both also made positive efforts to dramatize the black as honestly as they could. Green's *Hymn to the Rising Sun* and O'Neill's *The Emperor Jones* were produced by the Federal Theatre in 1937[1] and they were hailed as breakthroughs in the development of black characterization.

Hymn to the Rising Sun is a hair-raising glimpse of a Southern chain gang, at daybreak on the fourth of July. During the assembly, Runt, a white prisoner who has kept the camp awake most of the night with his screams for help, dies in the sweatbox while the white camp boss is sadistically enjoying his own lecture to the men on the subject of freedom and good citizenship. His speech is an ironic exposé of conditions on the chain gang, including a reminder that they are strictly within the law, enacted in accordance with the democratic will of the people: the judge said hard labor, and that is exactly what he meant, and the Captain agrees that hard labor is what it will take to acculturate these prisoners.

The veteran and Hercules of the gang is a black, Pearly Gates, and it is clear that Pearly, unlike Runt, will survive. At first glance, it would seem that this will be so primarily because of Pearly's superior strength, but it soon becomes apparent that it is primarily because he is no stranger to the doctrine of white superiority and has learned the art of survival in the white world:

> Captain. I was just wondering, boys, whether I oughta make you that Fourth of July speech or not . . . What say, Pearly?
> Pearly Gates. Yessir, Cap'n, we'd sure like to hear you. (8)
> . . . .
> Captain. . . . A nigger is a nigger, ain't that so Pearly Gates?
> Pearly Gates. That's the gospel, Cap'n.
> Captain. Right. And you niggers that's in here didn't have sense enough to know that and so you went around trying to stir up trouble, thinking maybe you were just sunburnt white men and could do as you pleased. . . . (10)

Pearly may once have had heroic notions, but he now makes all the right answers. When he is called, after assembly, to hold a boy down for the Captain to lash, he feels great compassion for the victim, but the lids of the Captain's "eyes are snapped back and his dark brown pupils are filled with a fiery demoniac light" as he brings the whip down on the boy's back, and "with a cry Pearly Gates flings himself upon his plunging feet" (20). While the convicts are then eating, two guards who are "just celebrating a little" fire their guns, and several of the men, their nerves cracking, jump to their feet and drop their tin plates. Pearly's fatback falls in the dust, and Paul Green has him pick it up and eat it, "dirt and all" (9), without protest or hesitation. Certainly Pearly Gates is a sympathetic character, but in Paul Green's dramatization he is no hero.

In *The Emperor Jones* Eugene O'Neill deals with a physically superb black scoundrel, Brutus Jones, who bilks the natives of the island over which he has made himself emperor. It is also obvious that for him to have achieved such an exalted position he has that high degree of intelligence common to con artists. When he is threatened with revolt and revenge for his misdeeds, however, the Emperor takes refuge in the woods and here his intelligence is gradually conquered by superstitious fears.

Undoubtedly O'Neill dramatizes the power of superstition spectacularly. Jones' sins and superstitions join forces, are magnified by the subversive insistence of voodoo drums that mount steadily to a crescendo, and close in on him in the shadowy darkness. Jones is unable even to find the caches he had hidden, for just such an emergency, and is ultimately reduced to stark terror. But the effects of Jones' African religious heritage—which are precisely what O'Neill was attempting to dramatize—are all negative. Although this heritage is central to the dramatization it is completely shorn of its positive, all-powerful, life-giving force—the force vitale, and there is no sustaining strength whatever in it for the man who made himself emperor. Like Pearly Gates, Jones is robbed of all human dignity and crawls to his death, like a worm, writhing on his belly in the dust.

While the play was considered to be an artistic success, which it undoubtedly was, as black drama it was a failure. White audiences were quite satisfied to see the "brute negro" as the personification of degenerative fear, but there was no identifiable black image, either overt or covert, for O'Neill's black audience. Langston Hughes reported that the Harlem audience, at a complete loss as to what it should make of the emperor running naked through the forest hearing the Little Frightened Fears, howled with laughter, and shouted to him to leave the ghosts in the jungle and come back to Harlem.[2] Certainly, in O'Neill's dramatization, Brutus Jones is no more of a hero than Pearly Gates, and even less palatable to the black community.

Two of the elements that were central to O'Neill's dramatization in *The Emperor Jones* were also used by black playwrights Countee Cullen and Arna Bontemps in *Saint Louis Woman*, which was based on Arna Bontemps' novel of the same name.[3] These were the "brute negro" and superstition. Cullen and Bontemps do not transform the "brute" stereotype, but they shift him to a secondary role and glorify kindness and decency, while superstition is limited by the life-giving force.

In the gaudy world of race track betting, the cake walk, the jook, and prostitution, Lil' Angie, a successful and popular jockey, steals Della, who belongs to the saloon keeper, Biglow. Della is the toast of the district and she changes her men as their money runs out. But the mack, Biglow, is not broke, and although Lil' Angie is currently in the money, Della is also attracted to the jockey because he is kind and generous, whereas Biglow is cruel and beats his girls. Biglow is furious when he becomes a laughingstock for having lost his girl to the diminutive jockey, so he goes to Angie's house and beats up Della, just to prove his manhood. When Angie returns and sees her bruises, he heads for the saloon, gun in pocket, to confront Biglow, and thus armed the little man is a match for the brute. Biglow draws his gun, but, before Angie can fire, the mack is shot by an old girlfriend whose eye he had knocked out. Biglow believes, however, that the shot was fired by Angie and he dies putting a curse on the jockey's luck.

Throughout the community, superstition is rampant. All the men wear gold coins attached to their watch chains, and curses are not taken lightly. Lil' Angie is beside himself that he will now lose at the track, and his friends, too, are afraid to bet on him, but he covers his fears with bravado, and bets all he has on his next race. He loses it "by a wink." Economic reality now takes over; Angie can no longer support Della and she passes to the winner, Ragsdale, but she is not at all happy about the change and Angie, of course, is desolate. He is also convinced that he was jinxed by Biglow's curse. But in *Saint Louis Woman*, unlike *The Emperor Jones*, superstition is not the only motivating force. Angie is encouraged by his friend, Badfoot, to leave for the races in San Antonio, and Badfoot consoles him that "they's mo' fancy gals down there'n old Pharoah had in de lan' of Egypt. Old Biglow's ghost can't reach dat fur" (II.iii.6).

At Saratoga, Lil' Angie finds that Della, too, is there and is now accompanied by Jake, who has succeeded Rags. By this time, however, his confidence is restored and he wins three in a row and regains the delighted Della. Lil' Angie's superstitious fears did succeed in bringing his financial success, and his romance, to a temporary halt, but they did not drive him to despair and self-destruction: a man, after all, can escape the effects of superstition if he makes the effort.

In *Saint Louis Woman*, the "brute" stereotype has also been nudged out of the affections of the reigning prostitute, and cedes center stage to kindness, decency, and perseverance. By contrasting him with a hero who is his antithesis, Cullen and Bontemps also show that all blacks do not fit any single mold: the black community, like any other, consists of human beings, good, bad, and indifferent.

In far greater contrast to the portrayals of the "brute negro" by successful white playwrights, however, is the dramatization of the established stereotype by black playwright Randolph Edmonds. Edmonds did not write for the Federal Theatre; his play, *Bad Man*, was written in 1934,[4] and represents an important step in the total transformation of the "brute negro," a feat that was to be accomplished within the same decade.

In *Bad Man*, Maybelle, the ingenue sister of a sawmill worker, wheedles her way into the mill shanty to get a look at Thea Dugger, whose reputation as a bad man is guaranteed to attract any innocent. She meets Dugger and is properly awed as he expertly disarms a fellow worker who threatens him with a gun during a poker game. Dugger immediately prepares to shoot his attacker, for he knows that the only safe enemy is a dead enemy, but Maybelle pleads for the gunman's life. She naively believes Dugger is really a good man at heart who would not kill in cold blood, and Dugger is affected by her trust and spares his attacker. Not long after, a terrified black boy dashes into the shanty with the ominous news that white men with dogs are approaching; they have found a poor-white dead and they are automatically convinced he must have been murdered by a black.

The blacks in the shanty feel sure that the white men don't much care who they string up for the murder and that they are primarily out for a lynching, and their assessment of the situation is obviously valid since the white men threaten to burn down the shack unless the guilty black comes out and surrenders. None of these blacks are guilty, but it becomes a clear choice between one lynching or all being burned in the shack, including Maybelle, whereupon Dugger, emerging from the shackful of terrified blacks, struts toward the white mob and gives himself up with all the nobility of a Christ.

In this play Edmonds uses his stereotypes with great versatility. The ingenue's innocence is a powerful redemptive force for Dugger has admitted having killed several men in self-defense, and there is no doubt that he is all that the title of the play implies in the white idiom. He is an easy candidate for a lynching and not likely to be mourned. But the title of the play, *Bad Man*, is also a linguistic inversion; Dugger is also a black hero, with great respect for black womanhood. He is a doomed man, but in Edmonds' dramatization he does not crawl to his death like the Emperor Jones, or forfeit his human dignity like Pearly Gates. He does not flinch; he does not even groan when the white mob puts the fire to him.

While the crackle of fire, the howling of dogs, and the excited, barbaric voices of the white lynch mob invade the shack from offstage, the agony of those for whom Dugger dies is summed up by Maybelle's boyfriend, Ted:

> We ain't nothin' but sawmill hands. All we is s'posed tuh do is tuh cut logs, saw lumber, live in dingy shanties, cut, fight and kill each other. We ain't s'posed tuh pay no 'tention tuh a burnin' man . . . but ef de people wid larnin' can't do nothin' 'bout hit 'tain't nothin' we can do. 'Tain't nothin' we can do. [5]

Here at the finale Ted faithfully describes the "brute negro" stereotype, but it is in eloquent contrast to the actual dramatization of their savior who is being burned offstage by a white mob. Is Ted making a hopeless admission of white supremacy and assuring the white audience that the black will stay in his place? Is he making an agonized cry of disgust and protest against the savagery of a race that considers itself civilized and superior? Perhaps that depends on the translating experience, or from which side of the dual communication system one views the play. But one thing is surely clear: in either idiom, Dugger is neither Pearly Gates nor Brutus Jones; he dies like a hero.

Another young black playwright who was thoroughly conversant with the dual communication system was Theodore Browne, who wrote for the Federal Theatre. The story of John Henry, the legendary black steel-driver, had been dramatized by several playwrights, but Theodore Browne created a remarkable version in *Natural Man*. This play, which was first presented as a folk opera, was produced by the Federal Theatre in Seattle, in 1937;[6] it was revised for the American Negro Theater in Harlem in 1941,[7] and portrays the "brute negro" at his ultimate point of victimization and his highest point of dignity. Its setting, the contest between John Henry and a steel drill in the Big Ben Tunnel in West Virginia, provided enough ambiguity for the play to satisfy white audiences, and most critics interpreted it as the dramatization of the struggle between the natural man and the forces of mechanization. So it was, indeed, but Browne also completed the transformation of the "brute negro" into a black revolutionary hero.

The steel-driving contest around which the play is built is staged on a wager between John Henry's boss, Cap'n (by inflation?) Tommy Walters, and the steel drill salesman, and the Cap'n has no intention of losing, whatever the cost. Immediately before the contest begins, Walters informs John Henry that he has received his record from the Jasper County State Prison and that it is pretty bad. As John Henry then strides into the tunnel, the voices of the black spectators echo the meat of the Cap'n's warning to him:

> John Henry, if you don't win, well I won't be needing you around any more. You are an escaped convict. You killed a white man. You know what they do with a black man who kills a white man? They burn him alive. They string him up and burn him alive! (368)

and the steel-driver is left in no doubt: he has now got to win to stay free.

Cap'n Tommy further reveals his cold-blooded philosophy as he assures the drill salesman, who is watching the contest with him, that he would rather use cheap black labor any day than invest capital in a steam drill. He can employ the blacks when he needs them, push them around and pitch the fear of God into them, and lay them off without notice when business is slack. Browne thus makes it crystal clear that in his version of the legend, the Cap'n's exploitation, and not the rigor of the steel-driving competition, is ultimately responsible for John Henry's death.

The Creeper, a one man chorus with a guitar, joins John Henry and as the contest begins he reveals that John Henry's end is indeed near. The steel-driver is about to see his whole life pass before him during the contest, and the Creeper accompanies him through his "legend-in-the-making."

In a Beale Street dive in Memphis, John Henry gets drunk and has hot merchandise planted on him by a pickpocket who is being pursued by a policeman. He gets arrested and sent to jail, where he is taunted by white jailbirds with exalted opinions of their superiority. John Henry's replies to them express the whole black American attitude of disgust toward white oppression:

> White man's country. White man's world. Big Mister Great-I-Am. Change everything to suit himself. Black man got to bow and scrape to him, like he was God Almighty himself. . . . Even down when it comes to thinking. Black man got to go to him for that too. (373)

Yet, as with Hughes Allison's plays, in the Federal Theatre era these words could, and did strike different audience responses. Were they an acknowledgement of white superiority? Were they sarcasm? Or were they a cry of protest against the gross injustices that resulted from the superiority myths?

When the white jailbirds ask John Henry what it feels like to be a "nigger," his inverted interpretation of the term is clear, and the implied threat in his response is thinly veiled: "Like a giant in a straight jacket! . . . Like a great king without a throne to sit on!" (374). And the giant is becoming increasingly angry. All his life he has been pushed around by the system; he is peaceable and accommodating, but he has his limit: "I built that stone palace you live in. . . . You can have the swell palace and the golden throne, but don't mess up with my crown!" (374).

On the chain gang in a rock quarry, where John Henry is sent to expiate the sin he never committed, he states his simple philosophy as he works: "God . . . meant for every man to be a king" (375). It expresses the very essence of human dignity and equality, but taken in conjunction with his sermon to the white jailbirds—"When they shove dirt in his face [when he dies] his spirit's going rise up . . . and walk the earth for him . . . like a natural man . . ." (374)—John Henry is voicing the traditional African belief in the majesty of the eternal human spirit—the uncreated.[8] To John Henry, a man's eternal heritage is dignity, freedom, and justice, before, during and after incarnate life.

In the rock quarry, John Henry's growing need to take action in his own defense is expressed more urgently: "Cain't wait for God! . . . White folks git through with you, wouldn't be a black man left!" (375). John Henry is not Pearly Gates, and there is no servility in his attitude toward his white guard on the chain gang. Here, he also echoes the substance of Jefferson's warning to the Captain of the *Sally Mae*—"a handful of them holding us slaves!"—then he explodes, "I be blown to hell before I stays here the rest of my life . . ." (375).

It is extraordinary that the revolutionary doctrine voiced by John Henry, and the magnitude of his disgust with white oppression, were recognized only by the reviewer for *The Daily Worker*,[9] who would, no doubt, have preferred to find in John Henry's words a call for unified class action. Most white critics saw his contest as being with the "forces of mechanization," and decades would elapse before other critics, black or white, would recognize in Browne's version of the legend the creation of the first revolutionary hero in black drama. In an era when neither black nor white audiences thought in terms of "revolutionary" black drama, Browne's dramatization is quite remarkable; it is also a tribute to his ability to manipulate the ambiguities of the dual communication system.

With John Henry's emotions near the breaking point, it is little wonder that, when a boy on the chain gang drops dead, and the guard flogs his body to get up and work, John Henry is revolted by the indecency, and protests. The guard immediately reaches for his rifle and John Henry knows one of them will die. He seizes the rifle, kills the guard with its butt, and escapes.

After weeks of hiding out in swamps, John Henry stumbles into a black camp church meeting in search of help. He is hungry, filthy, and exhausted, but there too he is rejected. In this scene Browne, like Allison, dramatizes the devastating effects of the white superiority myths and of fear on black attitudes. He pours white religious platitudes and the doctrine of submission from the mouths of the black preacher and congregation, who dread reprisals if they help an escaped convict, and John Henry has no choice but to leave. He then encounters a group of hoboes who are bound for warmer climates and joins them.

But John Henry is no loafer; he is accustomed to hard work and the idleness of the hoboes soon drives him to distraction, so he decides to stop running and return to work. He sets out for the North and disappears into the Big Ben Tunnel, where, seething with anger at his shameless exploitation, he wins the steel-driving contest. But although it is now over, John Henry's rage is not yet spent and he keeps on driving steel, while his girl, Polly Ann, screams her fear and hate at Cap'n Tommy:

> You sick that steam drill on John Henry, done drove him clear out of his mind. You even down made him spite the Almighty. You turn him against the mountain . . . he hammer the rocks till he set them on fire, destroy himself and everything! (380)

And to the black spectators, everything is exactly what is in jeopardy, for, in the African cosmological heritage, the mountain is the abode of God, and God is in everything.[10] But John Henry is a builder, not a destroyer: he "gits still and quiet and very peaceful inside" (381) and, leaving the tunnel, he accepts death as freedom, confident that his spirit will rule the earth like a natural man, and a mighty king.

There is no doubt that in the white idiom John Henry, no less than Dugger, fits the "brute negro" stereotype; he is an escaped convict and has murdered a white man. But Browne's dramatization, like Edmonds', is also an inversion. He shows that there is nothing either paternal or benevolent about John Henry's white exploiters and that John Henry's philosophy of human dignity, justice, and freedom for all men, is superior to the hypocrisy and double standards of his oppressors. In Randolph Edmonds' *Bad Man*, the "brute negro" is transformed into a heroic savior while the protest against white brutality is made by his distraught friends. In *Natural Man*, Theodore Browne completes the transformation, for his hero and protester are united to make of John Henry a revolutionary hero: he fights back, and ultimately chooses death rather than submission to white exploitation.

Another fine example of such a transformation comes from the pen of Theodore Browne. His original version of *Go Down Moses* is also in the Federal Theatre Collection, but while a memorandum indicates that in December 1938 it was "being placed in rehearsal immediately as the next Negro production at the Lafayette Theater,"[11] *Arena* does not record that it was actually produced before the theater's demise. In *Go Down Moses*, Browne uses idealistic white themes—abolition and the Civil War are white patriotic notions not to be confused with fraternizing with blacks—as one element in his dual dramatization, the other being his exposure and inversion of the myths and stereotypes, accomplished through the glorification of a heroine of black history. The play is based on the life and exploits of Harriet Tubman, an escaped slave who ran an underground railroad up to the Civil War, and who then scouted for the Union army. Harriet had all the characteristics of the vicious, vengeful female stereotype; she hated her slave masters with a burning passion, she was considered dangerous enough to the slave system to merit an enormous price on her head, and, indeed, she was capable of any act of violence necessary to insure the safety of the slave passengers she led out of the South. But Harriet was also Moses, a giant among women and an architect of black freedom.

Go Down Moses makes full use of the religious symbolism of the spirituals, and the symbolism of the title is strictly observed throughout. In the last scene the symbolism is complete when, leading her people to the promised land, she falls to cradle the head of a dying black soldier who sees Canaan in the glowing sunset, while a procession of slaves, freed by the successful fighting, streams up the hill to Fort Wagner. Madonna and earth mother, giver of life and deliverer to freedom both in life and in death, a common field hand, Harriet is also a natural leader chosen, like Moses, by God.

As Browne presents his historic heroine, she has vision, determination, and the steel to do what must be done to free her people, even when it includes shooting the mulatto giant, Cumbo, who mutinies on the underground passage because he resents taking orders, and particularly taking them from a woman. Browne shows her under the most harrowing circumstances that demand the utmost courage and ingenuity; she repeatedly outwits the 'superior' white slave catchers, and later infiltrates Confederate lines to guide both slaves and soldiers. Her enormous vitality and purposefulness are reflected in Browne's instructions for the playing of the scene where Harriet, having just crashed the State House and talked the governor of Massachusetts into giving her a pass to the Union armies, leans dangerously out of the window and goes wild with excitement at seeing the newly inducted soldiers of the Fifty-Fourth Colored Regiment march by. Brown directs: "with an irresponsible abandon she plants a backward kick, catching the unsuspecting Jason [her brother] in his abdomen—throwing him backwards into the chair, exhausted— stunned" (II.ii.7).

But it is enough to read the prologue to recognize the speed with which Browne attacks both stereotypes and myths. It dramatizes the capture of Harriet's youngest Brother, Jason, aged seventeen, who had tried to escape to avoid that most feared of all disasters, being sold down the river. Harriet's mother, Reba, pleads with the overseer: "Massa Jim doan sell 'im. Do dis fo' yo' old mammy" (Prologue 7). But Massa Jim chastizes her sharply for interfering, and Jason is hauled off to suffer 125 lashes, to be administered by Massa Jim and his friends, who are all eager to try out his new whip. Reba is one of the thousands of old black mammies who nursed white children along with their own; she had nursed "Massa Jim," but the whole scene vigorously denies the myth of joy and contentment that was presumed to accompany that honor. It denies, also, the sincerity of paternalism, for not only is Massa Jim untouched by her plea, but Reba has been used as a breeder, and all of her other boys, one by one, have already been sold down the river. Harriet's burning hatred of the white man for brutalizing her mother, expressed as she prepares to escape to fulfill the call of God, also vigorously denies the happy slave myths.

At the slave mart in Richmond where the full range of slave types await their fate on the block, Theodore Browne draws a powerful picture of what has made these humans what they are, and his stereotypes burst their molds to emerge as flesh and blood. There is, like Harriet's mother, a breeder with a much-scarred back who confides, bitterly, that she has been forced to have children by six different men. A young girl and boy with "grins on their faces and rhythm in their bones" dance furiously, but it is no happy, carefree pastime; it is to cover the fear of being sold down the river that chokes the whole crowded room. A young boy hopes wistfully to be sold to the same owner as a girl to whom he is greatly attracted, but he abandons hope in the face of fear as he learns she has just been sold down the river. A young woman talks tremulously and meekly to a trader—dreading to be separated from her two children. Elderly house servants nurse their nervous dignity and acquired white standards by separating themselves from the field hands and dancers, as though proximity alone might endanger their hope for preferred status on the block. The powerful mulatto, Cumbo, reacts violently to an insult to his black mother, thrown out in the ritual fashion of the "dozens"[12] to try his frayed nerves. But the crowning irony of this scene occurs when Cumbo butts into instant insensibility a white trader who attempts to examine his teeth, and escapes to the underground railroad. To enable him to pass through the mart unnoticed, the mulatto dons the clothes of the unconscious white trader, and the slaves are awed that in the trader's clothes he looks so like a white man. The irony is very similar to that in Panyared when the priest's daughter, "so like the women of your own world," is offered for sale; but in Browne's play something more is exposed over the footlights. If the African sold his brothers into white captivity, the white man sold his sons, and through the use of breeders, often produced them specifically for that purpose.

At the mart, the desperate Cumbo had succeeded in gouging information out of a recaptured slave on the location of the collection point for the next underground passage North, and after his escape he makes it there, to Granny Sales' cabin. He is an uninvited, belligerent, and dangerous addition to the group since he is already being pursued by slave catchers, but Granny hides him in her storage bin nevertheless. Granny is also hiding Moses, and other contrabands, and the atmosphere is electric in the cabin as the overseer arrives, unexpectedly, to check for runaways. By this time the price on Moses' head has risen to thirty-five thousand dollars, dead or alive. The overseer senses that something is amiss, and Theodore Browne now demonstrates the enormous value of the art of shucking. At the critical moment, a chicken, encouraged by Harriet who is hiding above, flutters squawking out of the straw ceiling and switches the focus from contrabands to theft, and Granny instantly rises to the occasion:

> Granny. Mars Alan, Ah dunno heigh dat chicken get way up dar! Fust Ah knowed!
> Overseer. You didn't by any chance *steal* him?
> Granny. Me steal! Marse Alan! Dat chicken didn't hab no business up dar! (I.iii.11)

In the last act of *Go Down Moses* Theodore Browne also uses inversion with great effectiveness. Here Harriet, who is now scouting for the Union army, whips the tired and hungry black soldiers into a frenzy of activity immediately before the battle for Fort Wagner, in which so many of them died heroically for freedom and to prove their manhood (II.iii.3). Browne's instructions state: "The soldiers are grouped about Harriet clapping and beating time as she prances up and down, singing, wild with jubilation . . . ."

> Harriet. Massa gone, missy too.
> Soldiers. Cry nigguhs, cry!
> Harriet. Think ah'll see de blessed Noth, Fo' de day Ah die?
> Soldiers. Hi — hi.
> Harriet. Yankee shot 'im. Now Ah thinks de debbil's got 'im.
> Soldiers. Cry, nigguhs, cry! (II.iv.1)

Only in the context of inversion does such a scene of jubilation match the lyrics: in the white idiom the term "nigguhs" was far from uplifting; on the contrary, it would have been self-derogatory, but to the tired soldiers it is inspirational. Theodore Browne's instructions are also an invitation to his actors to subvert the white idiom with nonverbal communication and the scene could not but suggest, even to a white audience, that their standard interpretation was not quite what was intended. Thus, not only does Browne's dramatization of black legend in *Natural Man* transform the "brute negro" of the white stage into a revolutionary hero, but his dramatization of black history in *Go Down Moses* glorifies his female counterpart as one of the architects and heroines of revolution.

But there were also black playwrights in the thirties who did not use the dual communication system, and one of them was a woman, Georgia Douglas Johnson, the black poetess of Washington, D.C. There are several of Georgia Johnson's one act plays in the Federal Collection, among them *Frederick Douglass*, *Ellen and William Craft*, *A Sunday Morning in the South*, and *Blue Eyed Black Boy*, but in *Arena* Hallie Flanagan does not list any of them as having been produced by the Federal Theatre.

Georgia Johnson, whose home was for many years a meeting place for such black intellectuals as Alain Locke, Owen Dodson, and Langston Hughes, was passionately committed to promoting black pride and to publicizing the injustices of the white system, and her plays are written directly and unequivocally for a black audience. They are sociological commentaries, genre miniatures that dramatize, with the realism of a Vermeer, the condition of the black experience. In these settings, her plots have an uncomplicated, determinate, almost somnambulistic quality, and her protagonists either face their inevitable crises with heroic determination or become the symbols of black victimization.

In both *Frederick Douglass* and *Ellen and William Craft*, her slave-protagonists must choose between death-defying flight to freedom and being broken by the system. In both plays they achieve freedom through heroic determination and by keeping one jump ahead of their enslavers. In *A Sunday Morning in the South*, her protagonist has no choice; he is an innocent, hardworking, ambitious black youth and he is lynched by a bloodthirsty white mob after the local police have coerced a white girl into agreeing that "he looks something like" (1.5) her alleged attacker of the evening before. The efforts of the youth's aged grandmother to get the local judge to intervene in time to prevent this barbaric miscarriage of justice are fruitless. The judge is in church and resents being disturbed on this peaceful Sunday morning, and the lynching occurs while the music and song of worship pour blissfully forth from the white Christian church. The irony is enormous, the religious and sociological commentaries, profound.

In *Blue Eyed Black Boy*, the prospective lynch victim, Tom Waters, who is rumored to have "brushed against a white woman on the street" and whose sister is about to marry a local doctor, is also a hard working and ambitious young black. He is saved from the gathering mob by the timely arrival of state troops because the mother of the victim, knowing the inevitability of her son's fate unless he is rescued, succeeds in getting her plea for help to Governor Tinkham in time. Mrs. Waters' instructions to Dr. Grey are to tell the Governor: "They goin' to lynch her son born twenty one years ago" then "look in his eyes and you'll save him" (7). And the Governor's interest? Twenty-one years earlier he had fathered the blue-eyed black boy. Although in this play the victim is saved, Georgia Johnson's sociological commentary is every bit as ironic as in *A Sunday Morning in the South*; it is a forceful indictment of the double standards of the white system, and the blue-eyed black boy is a symbol of those standards.

The horrors and indignities of slavery, the barbarity of lynching, the injustices of the double standard, the blacks' thirst for education, and their courageous fight to achieve freedom and justice, all are simply, concisely, and clearly dramatized in Georgia Johnson's plays. They are quite as effective an exposé as some of the black plays of white flagellation that became popular in the late sixties and early seventies, but in the thirties, and particularly for a woman in the thirties, they were extremely daring. Yet the fact remains that none of these plays were produced by the Federal Theatre, and this poses the question whether Georgia Johnson's sharp blade of truth, untempered by the protective ambiguity and subversive qualities of the dual communication system, was not too radical for that era; a less direct approach might have achieved production and, inevitably, if a playwright wishes to contribute to changing an image, then he must have some form of access to the image makers.

Like Georgia Johnson, whose intellectual gatherings he frequented, the poet-playwright, Langston Hughes, also spoke directly and unambiguously to his audience. In 1937 he wrote *Don't You Want to be Free?* around a collection of his folk poems, specifically for the Harlem Suitcase Theater which had a seventy-five percent black audience,[13] and in it, his Young Man first exclaims exultantly: "I am a Negro/Black

as the night is black./Black like the depths of my Africa," then unequivocally denies the superiority of the white man's "circus of civilization";[14] Hughes also made the radical suggestion that workers
of both races unite to prevent the exploitation of the poor by the rich.
In several of his short plays Hughes also attacked the stereotypes of
the white stage with ridicule: *Em-Fuehrer Jones*, which was also produced by the Harlem Suitcase Theater, satirized the "brute negro"
image presented by O'Neill's play, and it was popular with his black
audience.

Nevertheless, Langston Hughes, like Georgia Johnson, was primarily a poet, and their unambiguous drama was unusual in the
thirties. Most of the young black playwrights of the Federal Theatre
era who were faced with the dual problem of destroying the derogatory black images while writing for biracial, or predominantly white,
audiences, used the dual communication system; with its subtleties
they achieved an originality that is probably unique in the history of
American drama.

SIX

AFRO-AMERICAN VERSATILITY

WITH EURO-AMERICAN TECHNIQUES

WRITING IN 1966 about white American playwrights, Brooks Atkinson recalled that they made the twenties "the most dynamic decade the American theater ever had."[1] In marked contrast to this superlative evaluation, the black playwrights of that period had been widely criticized for various and conflicting forms of ineptitude, including too much realism and non-realism. Doris Abramson, also writing in the sixties, recorded the prevailing opinion that they were not considered "ready artistically or intellectually" for experimentation; "they were hardly free of melodrama and the minstrel tradition,"[2] and of the Federal Theatre era she concluded from the available information that the Federal Theatre did not "live" long enough for its black playwrights to master the sophisticated techniques used by its Living Newspapers.[3]

But was this presumption, by white critics, of black ineptitude with the experimental techniques of the Euro-American stage, really justified? Were the efforts of the white American stage to master the latest European techniques really that much ahead of them?

Actually, in the first three decades of the twentieth century, realism, as a dramatic mode, dominated the American stage, and it continued to do so well beyond that time. Plays like *Processional* by John Howard Lawson, *The Adding Machine* by Elmer Rice, and *The Emperor Jones* by Eugene O'Neill were strictly in the minority, and white experimental drama was mostly confined to college drama units, such as the Vassar Experimental Theater over which Hallie Flanagan had presided.[4] Perhaps the most powerful deterrent to experimental drama was the fact that Broadway had its eye perpetually on the box office, and the eternally optimistic audiences in the land of hope and glory continued to demand euphemistically happy endings that did not disturb the American dream—at a time when most of Europe was already reflecting the sordid and disillusioning facts of life in dramatic modes created to cope with its changed vision. Not even the work of the great Bertolt Brecht, "who changed the face of European drama," succeeded on Broadway,[5] and black playwrights had much in common with Brecht's failure to scratch the surface of American complacency. They longed to dramatize all the sordid facts of the black experience—to tell it as it really was—but it was sufficiently difficult, sometimes even disastrous, for them to challenge the white American myths and stereotypes, without further indulging in overt efforts to disturb the American dream.

But the black dramatists had an additional handicap. Firsthand experience with European experimental modes and techniques was very difficult to come by except for those few blacks, such as Owen Dodson, who were exposed to it in college drama departments. Audience segregation made their opportunity to observe productions of their own plays, even in the prevailing mode, very uncertain; at best, they were seated too far from the stage for effective feedback. One such example was that of Wallace Thurman, whose *Harlem* was produced on Broadway in 1929; Thurman was denied orchestra seats for his own play and was ushered off into the rafters.[6]

Yet in spite of almost insurmountable handicaps, the same decade that produced *The Adding Machine*[7] and *The Emperor Jones*[8] also saw the creation of a veritable gem of expressionistic symbolism by a black woman; *The Purple Flower* was written by Marita Bonner and published in *Crisis* in 1928.[9] Marita Bonner was educated at Radcliffe College and wrote articles and short stories for *Crisis*,[10] and her play reveals that she was both artistically and intellectually capable of working effectively with European experimental modes. Its theme was unmistakably revolutionary, its technique was a complete departure from the dominant realism of the period, and it was written with the type of Brechtian distancing and symbolism that had been used by only a few white playwrights during the decade.

The purple flower that grows on top of the hill, Somewhere, is the flower of "life at its fullest" which is jealously guarded by the White Devils who live on the hill. The Uses, who are varied shades from white to black, live on the plane below, between Somewhere and Nowhere. They have worked hard to make the valley bloom, build the roads and even the houses of the White Devils, but are still Nowhere. The Uses would be Somewhere, too, if they could reach the fragrance shed by the purple flower, but so far they have not succeeded in getting to it, for the White Devils are ruthless and tricky. As the curtain rises, the White Devils are seen up on the hillside singing to the Uses to stay where they are, Nowhere. Some of the Uses, below, are having their siesta, with their faces, as always, turned toward

Somewhere, while others discuss their predicament: the hard work, so long advocated by their leaders, has got them Nowhere, for the White Devils have rewarded it only with a slap in the face; education has got them Nowhere, since the White Devils wrote the book and censored the instructions for success; religion has got them Nowhere, as they are usually so busy shouting at God that they fail to listen to Him; and the sacks of gold they have earned have got them Nowhere, for the White Devils have refused to sell them even a spoonful of the hill they labored to build. What the Uses need is leadership, and unified action.

As night falls, they are watched by a White Devil who hides in the bushes and amuses himself by pinching an Us who passes by; yet the Us must not defend himself, or even touch the White Devil, for that would surely bring death. Now, an old Us cries out for attention and relates a dream she had last night that she saw a White Devil dismembered, and the oldest Us recognizes that this is the signal for action. Into an iron pot he throws dust for all the generations of Uses who have died trying, followed by the books and the gold; the last ingredient he needs for revolution is blood, for "blood has to be let for births, to give life," and "the New Man must be born." [11] As with Abraham and Isaac of old, God has supplied the sacrifice, and Finest Blood is sent to perform the precarious task of enticing the White Devil out of the bushes; whichever of them is killed in the fight that will follow will supply the blood for the sacrifice. As Finest Blood pipes, and calls to the White Devil, all the valley from Nowhere to Somewhere listens; the final curtain falls, and Marita Bonner closes the play with the question: "Is it time?"

This short, compact play combines symbolism, song, rhythm, dance, and fantasy in a single act that ends in a crescendo of silent listening for the signal that awaits only the will of God and the coming of leaders to start the blood revolution; it is Messianic in scope. Technically, Marita Bonner's characters are depersonalized symbols of qualities: they are Young Man, Old Man, Cornerstone, Average, Finest Blood, White Devils, and so on, and her staging directions are a constructionist's delight. [12] The dynamics of social relationships, and of cause and effect, are projected through the skillful use of horizontal levels. On the hillside the White Devils, softly angelic in appearance, but with horns that glow red and tails decorated with bones—adroit, tricky—dance with acrobatic artfulness, sometimes erect and with dignity and sometimes writhing like snakes. On the plane below, the Uses, who may be any color from white to black, gaze longingly up the hillside and await the time for revolution. The stage is also horizontally divided by the Thin Skin of Civilization on which the main action takes place, and from time to time, when the White Devils and Uses become too loud or violent, the Thin Skin of Civilization breaks, and they tumble through, lying beneath in twisted, broken mounds. The lighting of the two levels also reflects their significance: the lower level is dim, but there is enough light to note that some actions that take place on the upper level are repeated on the lower, and in this shadow world lie the broken bodies of those who could not maintain their thin skin of civilization.

In addition to the dream symbol for action, drum beats supply immediate motivation to the sleepy Uses and they spring into dance to the rhythm that historically inspires black action. Symbolically, also, the drummer is a black Us. The multiple symbolism of the conjuring old Us is an abstraction of Brechtian scope, for not only does he mix the ingredients from which God will make the new man, but as he throws the dust of time and the fruits of effort into the iron pot, and awaits the blood of coming birth, he unites the past, the present, and the future into a Baal-like eternity. [13]

But Marita Bonner was not the first black dramatist to depart from the pure melodrama of realism. As far back as 1901 Joseph B. Cotter, Sr. had written *Caleb, The Degenerate*, which has been dismissed by critics as a "mere tract" peopled "with unbelievable characters spouting incredible lines," [14] and "chaotic in treatment." [15] In fact, the play is an impressionistic projection of black characters who are so vitally alive they virtually flash from the pages. James Hatch has already pointed out that at least one scene in the play—that between the Bishop, Olivia, and the Ministers, in act II, is as surrealistic as any in *Alice in Wonderland*, [16] and it is clear that Cotter was using the melody of dual communication to satisfy white readers while he created an accompanying bass for black recognition, for while the Bishop's white-oriented religious, patriotic, and work ethics ultimately prevail, Caleb's denunciation of the Christian ethics of the establishment are a powerful forerunner of black nationalism.

With the advent of the Federal Theatre in 1936, and with Hallie Flanagan's appointment as its Director, experimental drama was stressed far more than it had ever been before in American theater. Yet even then, the white stage was involved in a learning process. William McDonald reports that none of the three earliest Living Newspapers staged by the Federal Theatre, *Triple A Plowed Under, Highlights of 1935,* and *Injunction Granted* "achieved high standards of production," and that *One-third of a Nation*, the planning and production of which was personally undertaken by Hallie Flanagan, "was the first Living Newspaper to reach the full stature toward which the project had worked for two years." [17] While the white stage was learning, so were the black playwrights on the federal project. Edith Isaacs records that

> Negro playwrights, unwelcome in most theater audiences, had no opportunity to learn their trade by watching the work of experienced playwrights in performance. . . . The Federal Theater on the other hand welcomed its Negro audiences and gave its actors and technicians work and wages . . . . Moreover it encouraged initiative, invention, and experiment. [18]

Yet in spite of Federal Theatre policy at the highest echelon, the handicaps of segregation and discrimination persisted. A brief, prepared in 1939 by the Negro Arts Committee of the Federal Arts Council, specified a number of alleged acts of discrimination in employment practices, in producing adequate facilities for bringing black theater to the black population, and in the selection of plays by black dramatists for production; [19] and as one looks back with the hindsight of the seventies, one finds good cause for believing in the validity of its complaints about play selection. Several unproduced scripts in the Federal Collection, such as those of Georgia Johnson, contain strong racial protests, and there is no doubt that Federal Theatre audiences, who were predominantly white, were far from ready or willing to accept a doctrine of black equality and white guilt. It would have been remarkable, therefore, if those responsible for selecting and approving plays for production were willing to dare public disapproval too far, even if they accepted the doctrine themselves, and that some of them did not is evidenced by the necessity for a fight waged by Hallie Flanagan to get Theodore Ward's *Big White Fog* produced. Some of the characters in *Big White Fog* advocated a merger of black and white labor for their common good, and there were those in the Theatre who were revolted by the dramatization of such a doctrine and who were convinced that it would fan racial prejudice. [20] With Mrs. Flanagan's support, the play was produced in Chicago, without incident, but after a run of less than two months, it was transferred by local Federal Theatre authorities to a neighborhood school, allegedly to encourage greater black attendance, and there it withered on the vine in a matter of days.

There is also no reason to believe that white evaluators of black playscripts for Federal Theatre production were more capable of inter-

preting the black experience than the white playwrights who tried to
dramatize it, or were more capable of understanding the scope and
ingenuity of the dual communication system than the white critics
who did not recognize it. By and large, they were all products of the
same cultural indoctrination. In another three decades, Hoyt W.
Fuller, editor of *Negro Digest*, would demand informed black critics to
do justice to the work of black playwrights,[21] but in the Federal
Theatre era, that was still somewhere in the future.

Nevertheless, although production in the Federal Theatre era was
still sometimes elusive, young black Federal Theatre playwrights
achieved considerable experience under the guidance of such producers as John Houseman and Orson Welles, who directed the Negro
Unit of the New York Federal Theatre in such spectacular productions
as the "voodoo" *Macbeth*,[22] and they participated, also, in the most
coordinated experimental effort, and probably the most original contribution of the decade to the American stage, the Federal Theatre's
own creation, the Living Newspaper.

In an American era dominated by the American dream and by
realism, the Living Newspaper was an extraordinary phenomenon.
Like the Russian revolutionary stage, which influenced it greatly, it
was a theater of involvement with social and political issues. It combined the dramatic and journalistic arts in versatile and exciting new
forms to dramatize injustice with the hope of promoting change
through heightened public awareness. McDonald wrote:

> The Staff of the Living Newspaper, set up like a city daily with
> editor-in-chief, managing editor, city editor, reporters, and copy
> readers, began as Brooks Atkinson later remarked, 'to shake the
> living daylights out of a thousand books, reports, newspapers
> and magazine articles' in the attempt to create an authoritative
> dramatic treatment, at once historic and contemporary, of current
> problems,[23]

and the techniques used by the Living Newspaper were new to the
American stage. Its scope was panoramic, its presentation condensed,
its focus manipulated and concentrated to pinpoint essence rather
than event. Its most versatile liaison between eras, events, audience
and actors, was a Loudspeaker, vaguely reminiscent of Walter
Winchell-type newscasts but actually acting as a jack-of-all-purposes.
It announced datelines, named places, and introduced characters; it
provided factual information; it editorialized; it represented the Living
Newspaper, the Establishment, the underdog, the neutral observer;

and it played any other role as the need arose.[24] It could span days—even centuries—of history effectively, in seconds.

The Living Newspaper incorporated almost every desirable, sophisticated technical device Mrs. Flanagan observed during her extensive European tour, and although she was assisted in its planning by Elmer Rice, Arthur Arent, and others,[25] it was her personal brain-child. Yet in spite of the profusion of its foreign techniques, the final product was truly American in purpose and content, and there is no doubt that it left its indelible stamp on American drama and on the motion picture industry; indeed, the revolutionary influence of its telescoping techniques, which had the ability to drive points across to viewers in a minimum of time, are particularly apparent in the vast majority of contemporary television advertisements. So commonplace, in fact, have the basic techniques it introduced become that it is sometimes difficult to convince contemporary theater-goers, and even some contemporary critics, what is so revolutionary about their presence in Living Newspaper productions of the thirties. Certainly, American realism had previously found little need or inclination to introduce sophisticated techniques such as flash scene division, the bare stage, direct audience involvement, and Brechtian distancing; props such as portable trollies and symbolically used stage levels; or the simultaneous use of live drama, movie projection, journalistic commentary, and other varieties of communication to shepherd traditional drama toward happy endings. These and other European techniques were quite new and revolutionary when introduced to American drama through the Living Newspaper.

It is obvious that a form of such scope and versatility was ideal for the panoramic dramatization of case histories such as those presented by the Living Newspaper, and black federal dramatists who were exposed to it were quick to perceive that it was also ideal for the dramatization of three hundred years of enslavement, or for protesting the failure of the American democratic system to ensure freedom and equality for one tenth of its population.[26] Abram Hill and John Silvera who worked for the Federal Theatre Project, Hill as a play reader and Silvera in public relations and other capacities, used the Federal Theatre's own original art form to write *Liberty Deferred*, a veritable Afro-American history, which they researched and developed from factual cases. In 1977 Abram Hill stated that since the Federal Theatre "had introduced the experimental kind of a theater . . . it was a real challenge to break away from the basic format," also, that *Liberty Deferred* was an attempt to dramatize "Negro history in terms of the pattern followed by *One-third of a Nation."* He also pointed out that although the play was black history "it was really an integrated play," with both blacks and whites in the cast. Like Allison, Hill believed that plays must not only entertain but enrich, enlighten, and educate.[27]

Liberty Deferred was never produced by the Federal Theatre: it was rejected by Emmet Lavery, Director of the National Service Bureau, which was responsible for play selection, and this rejection was cited specifically as an incident of discrimination in the brief prepared by the Negro Arts Council. Mr. Lavery defended his rejection of it in March 1939 in reply to the Council, stating that in spite of the favorable publicity he had allowed on it "to encourage the authors" it "did not bear up the high hopes" he had for it.[28] The favorable publicity was recalled by Abram Hill in 1977: "John Anderson of the *Journal American* asked to read the script . . . and wrote a rather glowing report of the play, figuring that it would make an ideal piece for the theater." He also recalled that he had "several discussions with Emmet Lavery," and that "we got a tremendous amount of encouragement out of Mrs. Flanagan and one or two others in the higher echelons."[29]

In 1976, Mr. Lavery, however, had "only a vague recollection" of *Liberty Deferred*, and his interviewers, eager to learn more about the controversial decision to produce or not to produce this play, recalled that the files of Ben Russak in the National Archives mention the play, which seemed to be progressing well—"There would be a production conference and the word would be . . . it's getting very close to final form—and we'll have it in next spring's productions, or something like that"—before it suddenly dropped out. But Mr. Lavery could shed no more light on the matter; he replied that "oftentimes in a project like that the ultimate decision to produce or not to produce isn't necessarily a matter of discrimination."[30] It is interesting, however, that in a later interview Mr. Lavery commented on the Federal Theatre's black productions: "Now if there had been more Negro matter available in our particular sphere I have no doubt it would have been used . . . well I guess we did our share of what was available from Negro writers."[31] In any event, the script of this play does not appear to justify rejection.

The copy of the script of *Liberty Deferred* in the Federal Theatre Collection is rough—in several places the authors have indicated alternative staging suggestions, and scene numbering is so sketchy that it is difficult to tell if acts, or a series of episodes were intended for the structure of the final version. Nor does this appear to have been a final version—if indeed it was allowed to reach that point—for there are also among the Federal Theatre papers a separate first scene, which was reworked by the authors in response to a suggestion by Mr. McGee, Director of the Federal Theatre's Southern Region, and a memorandum which contains constructive suggestions for the play's development.[32] Yet even in this rough draft the dynamic nature and the potential of the Hill-Silvera play are apparent. It is also the most comprehensive example of the black dramatic skill with Euro-American experimental techniques among the unpublished Federal Theatre scripts, and it effectively uses the highly sophisticated Living Newspaper form throughout. In addition, it incorporates almost all of the ethnic problems contained in the other black federal plays: it presents black stereotypes for the express purpose of destroying them; it explodes the white myths; it dramatizes the injustices of racial discrimination; and it reflects the black's urgent need for the re-establishment of a valid self-image.

The central theme of *Liberty Deferred* is the historic fact of black enslavement and its inevitable effects on subsequent Afro-American history. The prologue starts with a rhapsodic review of black music which includes spirituals, blues, and jazz, and then swings into a night-club pantomime act in which two white supremacy representatives are in Harlem, seeking a thrill. This act is accompanied by all the sound effects of a Harlem night-club, and the black show-business stereotypes, as seen through their eyes, are presented in six elaborately colorful, satirical flashes—big apple dancers, a laden and subservient Red Cap, happy cotton-pickers in sateen overalls, players in a game of craps, the vaudeville act of The Black Crows, and Uncle Tom shuckin' to the judge; then the black protagonists, Linda and Ted, enter against this brilliant background of caricatures and for the rest of the play they lead the audience through the authentic black experience—a sharp contrast to the caricatures.

The Loudspeaker starts this contrast by completing the standard valedictory speech at Linda and Ted's graduation—opportunity, equality regardless of race, and so forth—but their diplomas do not purchase them equal employment opportunity and Ted, bitter and frustrated, moves quickly from the idea of the dancing stereotypes to the idea of dancing on the end of a rope, while an offstage chorus picks up the symbolic message of the spiritual, "Go Down Moses," in the line "Let my people go!" Blackout signals a new incident and the historic background of slavery begins.

While sound effects project emotional turmoil in the blackness, the

Loudspeaker and blue footlights announce the unemployed of London—it is economic crisis that motivates their emigration to America. The dialogue between the London merchants and the crowds is in sticomythia, depersonalized, condensed, kinetic, effective—blackout—and the Loudspeaker brings us to seventeenth- century America. A chart is projected on downstage scrim and a pinpoint whisks the travelers from the British Isles to Virginia. Sound effects re-create the difficulties of their journey and a storm at sea is topped by a piercing Indian war whoop when the pin point reaches Virginia.

At stage left, spots then pick up a scene between the Colonial planter, richly dressed and fed, and his indentured servant, whose term has just expired; the servant makes it clear that his labor will now become very costly. Brief blackout—and new lights flash behind the scrim on which England is projected. A dialogue follows between the English tobacconist and the planter in America: both are spotlighted, with action taking place both in front of and behind the scrim. The episode is fantastic in its literal portrayal because of its impossibility, but the essence of the situation is conveyed in seconds: the Englishman needs tobacco; the Bourbon needs cheap labor to produce it; and a Dutch sea captain materializes, conjured up by dramatic necessity like Madame Pace, in Pirandello's seminal *Six Characters in Search of an Author*—which was produced by the Federal Theatre in Los Angeles in 1936.[33]

Blackout now becomes pregnant with foreboding as African drums beat in the darkness and the sale of "black gold" in America begins, punctuated by clanking şhackles, the crack of the whip, and the herding of the Africans in great suffering. One black is struck and drops dead on the stage, and the new slave owners depart over the body of the dead black while the Dutchman tosses his whip to the planter as a bonus. When the lights flash off-on, the planter, on a high level represented by a huge bale of cotton, his face weirdly lighted by an overhead pin spot, is cracking the whip over the backs of his black slaves on the level below.

The above description is of only a small part of the play—accomplished with lightning speed—and yet the array of European experimental technical devices involved is incredible. The dramatists integrate pantomime, sound effects, offstage music, chorus, spirituals and drum rhythm for thematic symbolism, flashes of caricatured stereotypes, the Loudspeaker, separation of incidents by lighting effects, film projection, horizontal distancing levels in front of and behind scrim, literal symbolism, and character materialization by dramatic necessity. The authors now move to the apron and again display their technical virtuosity as they unfold a panorama which includes a slave auction, the stand for which is a portable truck that slides in from the wings; flashes of abolitionist activities; a performance of Shakespeare's *Othello*, done in pantomime and dramatic actuality by the great black tragedian, Ira Aldrich; slave revolts; a Supreme Court decision about blacks in tableaux and Loudspeaker combination; Christian religious hypocrisy; advocacy of Marxian socialism; and the Civil War, projected in the manner of movie montage with the legends intruding from a distant perspective— again in lightning succession.

The middle section of the play presents predominantly facts and figures—orators, politicians, and heroes who waged the war for freedom and equality. One scene in typically ballyhoo style shows a barker, Joe Lilly White, cracking his whip at a large map which is marked with the "black" and "white" states. On his call, heads pop out of the states and answer questions on black voting, school funding and other discriminatory practices, and pop back in. At this point the authors also break the bounds of the stage as a voice from the audience asks the definition of a Negro in America—that sticky question that has occupied many Americans in the past. Commenting in 1930 on attempts of Virginia legislators to establish legal "race purity," W. E. B. Du Bois stated: "But the Times-Dispatch gnashes its teeth and orders the legislature to pass a law defining a colored person as one having 'any ascertainable amount of Negro blood . . . .' Does the Times-Dispatch want its sister to marry a man who has an unascertainable amount of Negro blood? My God! What a loophole!"[34]

The focus now becomes more intimate as the play dramatizes the careers of four black ex-soldiers who fought for democracy in World War I. There are two doctors and a lawyer, who returned to be systematically deprived of their democratic rights and put back in their "places," and one soldier who remained in France because he did not trust the white American system. One scene from this post-war period ranks, in its ingenuity and its technical proficiency, with Elmer Rice's fantasy heaven in *The Adding Machine*—that interlude repair station between human reincarnations that dramatizes the hopeless plight of creatures, baited by hope and programmed to react automatically for all eternity. In *Liberty Deferred*, Lynchotopia is the fantasy heaven of lynch victims.

The Lynchotopia scene opens with the wild ringing of bells, horns, and other New Year's paraphernalia. It is 1 January 1937 and the

Keeper, seated at his desk, inspects new arrivals; compares yearly lynch figures; records what the various states did about those lynchings, which is always nothing; and stages the yearly contest between the old boys and the new for the best lynching experience. The winning story, dramatically presented and based on fact, is a hair-raising travesty of justice and decency. A mike then announces that a filibuster is in progress in the Senate, where the Wagner anti-lynch bill is being discussed, and the victims, in holiday mood, line up single file and march to Washington to the tune of Snow White's "Hi ho!"

In Washington, the filibuster, punctuated by the comments, boos, and popcorn-eating of the invisible victims, is even more ludicrous than usual, and this scene again unites a multitude of modes and techniques as Hill and Silvera move back and forth in time with psychological and physical agility: they flash from fantasy to fact, to demonstrate brutal tragedy, and then interweave illusion and reality, the dead and the living, to make a comedy of democratic government. Pirandello would have been right at home with such masking and unmasking, and one of the suggestions of a Federal Theatre editor for a revision of the play was that the finale should be set in the mythic Lynchotopia where the fact–fantasy potential could again be exploited.

A lapse of several years now ensues and the black soldier who had stayed in France has just returned to America, accompanied by his French buddy, Felix. From his chair in the audience, Felix interrupts a scene by insisting on a comprehensible explanation for discrimination, and the Loudspeaker is forced to invite him on stage, where, for the last third of the play, Jim Crow, the American race relations tzar, takes Felix on an indoctrination tour. This is done through flash scenes which include a segregated hospital, the athletic department of New York University, slum housing, the colored National Guard, and "the Harlem river"—"the old Swanee all over again." Hill and Silvera now put the flourish of supreme irony on their demonstration of the failure of democracy to include all Americans in its doctrine of equality. The black soldier emerges from the audience and joins his buddy, Felix, onstage, hand outstretched, but the Frenchman—the symbolic father of the Statue of Liberty—passes him by. In a remarkable reversal of the traditional pattern, the New Adam and the New Eden have become the corruptor of Europeans, for "that's what America has done to him!"[35]

The scope of *Liberty Deferred* is breathtaking, but Mr. McGee's suggestions for improvement of the draft are still valid. Some scenes, particularly in the middle section, are lengthy and could be cut, or condensed by the accelerating and telescoping techniques with which Hill and Silvera have demonstrated their facility. In addition, the finale is weak: it mushrooms unexpectedly into a newly introduced hodgepodge of social-political-philosophical themes, wedged willy-nilly into too parochial a container.

In this final scene, delegates from 585 organizations in twenty-eight states converge on the historic National Negro Congress where its President, A. Phillip Randolph, calls for black unity to meet the problems of black America, and, telescoped, this call for action could achieve an impressive finale by projecting into the future the purposeful stirrings of the black giant who will no longer be denied his rights. The scene, however, expands into spectacular agit-prop, with liberty as the battle cry; Randolph calls on all lovers of liberty and on the oppressed working masses, both black and white, to join in the fight for freedom,[36] and all of working America is now being addressed. This is a sound enough technique in agit-prop drama, but it is one which entails a finale that will emotionally engage and motivate an effective majority of its working audience; yet the song of national unity and liberty which accompanies marching scouts and the usual flag-waving hysteria is the Negro National Anthem. While no doubt appropriate to the real Congress, as a motivating dramatic technique in this scene it is entirely too parochial: it does not encompass all of working America and it is difficult to imagine a white audience of the thirties, even an audience bent, bruised, and shamed by the revelations of *Liberty Deferred*, going wild in the agit-prop sense over the Negro National Anthem.

I am well aware that many contemporary exponents of the black aesthetic have categorized "parochial" as a white aesthetic label which is too often applied by white critics to invalidate the universal implications of the black experience;[37] it is applied here, however, solely in terms of the play's own focus, the agit-prop technique applied, and the national audience it attempts to address. Even as synechdoche it fails, because it does not conjure up a vision of the whole, as the images, for instance, in the brilliant rhetoric of Malcolm X—by their very selective emphasis—do: his comment that "everything that came out of Europe, every blue-eyed thing is already an American"[38] is, in contrast, thoroughly effective. In the finale, too, the choice of such phrases as "unite for common attack upon the forces of reaction" subtly shifts black aspirations into the communist-democratic arena, and tends to equate liberty with the communist-socialist system, an orientation which, although perfectly acceptable in itself, was not suggested by the rest of the play.

In spite of these defects, the draft of *Liberty Deferred* is a potential knockout. Since the organization of the Living Newspaper was similar to that of a real newspaper, powerfully staffed with research workers, editors, and critics, and since other Living Newspapers that were produced were the joint efforts of editor and staff, and further, in view of Hallie Flanagan's all-out efforts within the project to find and train black dramatic talent, it remains a real mystery why this dynamic black play was rejected, instead of being re-directed. As McDonald pointed out, some of the Living Newspapers that were produced were not without faults of their own. Technically, the defects in *Liberty Deferred* were easily correctable, and certainly its potential was as great as that of anything which was produced by the Living Newspaper.

SEVEN

—AND THEIR AFRO-AMERICANIZATION

ALTHOUGH THE NEW vision and techniques of the European stage were digested en masse, and disseminated to nationwide audiences by the Federal Theatre's Living Newspaper, there had been prior attempts by a few of America's white playwrights to break the strangle hold of realism on the American stage. In *Processional*, which is considered to be a landmark in American drama,[1] John Howard Lawson sought to translate European dramatic techniques into an exclusively American idiom and he used them to express the mood of an American era. It is interesting to note that Lawson's chosen medium for the indigenization of the new techniques was the jazz idiom, which was the flower of black American culture. Apparently he, like Max Reinhardt, found the fruit of black culture most "typically American."

The indigenization of Euro-American techniques into black drama was accomplished by black Federal Theatre playwright Theodore Browne, although he was by no means the only black playwright to work successfully with the new modes. Browne, who was attached to the Seattle unit of the Federal Theatre, adapted classical drama for performance by its black units; he also wrote original plays, two of which, *Natural Man* and *Go Down Moses*, have already been discussed in connection with the black playwrights' transformation of the derogatory black stereotypes of the white stage. But Browne's hero, John Henry, was also an excellent candidate for technical transformation: he was no product of the euphemistic American dream; he was disillusioned and browbeaten by the racial inequities of the American system, and he virtually demanded new forms in which to express his reality. With the experience he gained on the federal project, Browne rewrote his folk opera, discarding the structure of the well-made play in favor of the episodes of Brechtian expressionism, and setting them to the tempo of Afro-American work songs and the blues, since the story dramatized life-as-it-was for black Americans. With these elements, he achieved a synthesis of form and content that perfectly expresses the mood, vision, and reality of the black experience.

Each of the episodes in *Natural Man* is an individual experience in the life of the steel-driver, but these episodes are not interchangeable since they represent the psychological progression of John Henry toward his participation in his own destruction. The flashback technique by which John Henry sees his whole life pass before him during the steel-driving contest in the Big Ben Tunnel has a dream-like quality since it all occurs within his mind. The Creeper, the garishly attired one-man chorus who accompanies him through his legend-in-the-making, unites the episodes, past and present, and projects them into the future, lending them also that quality of illusion that properly belongs to legend. The Creeper also symbolizes death, which usually precedes legendary fame, and John Henry instantly recognizes him as such and establishes his symbolic role by protecting him from the spectators who attempt to drive him away before the contest begins.

The setting for this play also pays no homage to realism; it is, in fact, reduced to symbolic essentials. The entrance to the tunnel is a stylized geometric design, a "frame-work of logs that form a crudely shaped rectangle that supports the earth above the dugout" (362). All of the episodes that emerge from John Henry's memory are dramatized outside this entrance, and as a reminder of the dream-like quality that knows neither time nor distance limitations, John Henry is silhouetted from time to time, wielding his hammer in the tunnel as the steel-driving contest progresses. Both lighting and sound are also stylized to enhance the atmosphere of illusion and the quality of conflict.

In the first two episodes the stage is dark, except for a dull, greyish light on the landing, into the shaft of which the steel-drivers emerge, one by one, from the blackness of the tunnel. In the second episode, Cap'n Tommy and the Salesman, who is nameless, wager on the coming contest, speaking "with rapid, staccato precision" like competing auctioneers, their hollow, metallic voices dominating the murmur of the crowd (367). The chanting of the spectators, who remind John Henry as he starts the contest that he is a victim of white oppression, also underscores the formal sociological cause of his psychological progression toward death.

The third episode, which occurs in a Beale Street dive in Memphis, continues the stylized lighting with a semi-darkened area between two lighted circles. In one circle there is a bar, and in the other John Henry is seated at a table with a gaudily dressed prostitute; black underworld characters are outlined in the surrounding shadows. All speech and action in this scene are performed in the slow, lethargic rhythm of the blues (369), which makes this expressionistic setting wholly Afro-American while at the same time it contributes to the dream-like atmosphere. But the reality dramatized is stark and immediate, for here John Henry is rolled and railroaded into jail for a theft he did not commit.

In the jail scene that follows, iron bars reveal the immediate predicament of the steel-driver, while soft blue light and the crouched, garish figure of the Creeper in the corner of John Henry's cell, continue to project a suspension of time. The disembodied voices of the white jailbirds, who taunt John Henry from offstage, support the suspension of time and expand the significance of the scene beyond the confines of the stage; yet the intensity of the dialogue between the caged "giant" and the jailbirds also projects the illusion of visible reality. The net effect is one of timeless significance packed into the immediacy of the present. John Henry's forceful denial of white superiority, his rejection of white oppression, and his warning that black complacence has its limits, also entirely express Afro-American disgust with the prevailing system and project the significance of the scene into the future.

In the fifth episode, the voice of the leader of the "hammer song" also penetrates the rock quarry scene from offstage and mingles with the responses of the convicts, who are seen "stripped to the waist," their bodies gleaming with perspiration in a "faint haze of light." Here, again, the combination of sound and light is multiply effective since it enhances the illusory quality of John Henry's memory while it expands beyond the confines of the stage the significance of the violent events being dramatized. John Henry is driven by the injustice and inhumanity of the chain gang to murder his guard, in self-defense, and the "weird prolonged blowing of a freight train whistle" (376) and a succession of rifle shots penetrate the total darkness that symbolically envelops the stage as he escapes.

The next episode, the black camp meeting, is spectacular. The "unrestrained religious fervor" as the congregation sings ". . . I want the light from the lighthouse . . ." and "I want Jesus to walk with me," swaying and clapping to the rhythm (376–77), is interrupted by the flashes of lightning and rolls of thunder that accompany the entrance of the ragged and mud-smeared John Henry and increase in intensity to the end of the scene. Here, as in the Big Ben Tunnel, natural instinct and an oppressive civilization clash. The preacher's main concern is that John Henry's very presence will place them all in jeopardy and he quotes to John Henry the famous Bible passage that recommends submission to earthly rulers; to which John Henry replies, "When Caesar git through with me, it be too late for God!" In this episode the spectacular natural forces and timid, fearful words contrast to create supreme irony. John Henry's plea for sanctuary and guidance is rejected because of the all-powerful influence of a system that perverts even the basic values of the Christian God, while lightning and thunder threaten—whom? Finally, John Henry, "laughing a loud, hollow, denigrating laugh," departs to hop the nearest freight train; his last act is to donate his only possession—the gun with which he killed his guard on the chain gang—to the flock of faithful who want to walk with Jesus. The victim moves one step nearer to his inevitable end.

In the seventh episode, John Henry is seen in a hobo camp near a railroad siding. Symbolically, the hoboes are "gathered around a dying fire" (379), and their commitment to endless motion is projected through sound effects as they expertly mimic the infinite variety of the train whistles that dominate their lives. John Henry contrasts their idle art with the constructive music of the steel-driver's hammer and it is more than his dignity can bear. He backs away from the hoboes toward the tunnel entrance and "the mouth of the tunnel begins to glow like an open furnace . . . as though the mountain were ablaze" (380). John Henry now struts into the tunnel, literally walking from the past into the present, and back into the contest which has been continuous throughout his mental trip into his past.

Certainly the dialectic in Browne's play is basically Brechtian. Like Brecht's protagonists, John Henry's conflict is with the oppressive and mechanized social system, and he is undoubtedly a victim who is more acted upon than acting. But the indigenization of the expressionist theory and techniques also produces something in Browne's hero that is wholly Afro-American; Browne does not entirely embrace Brechtian passivity but modifies it to express black reality, and his legendary hero has a limit beyond which he will not be pushed. He protests, he preaches a revolutionary doctrine, he kills in his own defense, and then, with the towering anger of outraged human dignity, he confronts and pre-empts the forces that drive him toward destruction—he chooses death as freedom rather than submit to the indignity and injustice of exploitation.

In the last episode, John Henry's death is symbolically, not realistically, portrayed. Having accepted death as freedom, he swings his hammer over his shoulder and struts majestically offstage, instructing the Creeper that "if any of the boys should ask for me, just tell them . . . he long gone from here to drive hell out of steel" (378). Symbolically, also, only the Creeper is left on stage at the finale to carry the legend—

and John Henry's revolutionary doctrine—into the future. It would be several decades before events would catch up with Browne's dramatization of John Henry's revolutionary doctrine, but his fusion of Afro-American content with Euro-American form resulted in a black play that was wholly American, perhaps more indigenous than Lawson's, which had borrowed, not only from Europe, but also from the black experience.

Another dramatic mode which had its roots in Europe, and which was developed by the American stage during the depression, was agit-prop. Its origin was, primarily, Russian revolutionary drama, and it had great appeal for the unemployed masses in America; but its revolutionary significance for the oppressed black minority was far greater than for the white majority. This mode, too, was used by black playwrights and modified to fit the needs of the black experience.

Agit-prop is a dramatic mode that is still disparaged by many critics and producers as being purely utilitarian in scope, devoid of artistic merit, and unworthy of production. But in *The Drama of Attack* Sam Smiley has made an impressive study of didactic drama of the Depression, and he points out that its utilitarian aspects do not preclude artistry. As Smiley shows, ideas are as much a part of the whole man as his physical and emotional characteristics, and since the dominant and unifying forces in this type of drama are ideas, the greatness of the play will be in direct proportion to the stature of the ideas and the artistry with which they are presented[2]—a fact to which much of the work of George Bernard Shaw, Clifford Odets, and other notable playwrights bears witness. John Howard Lawson, who also noted that great artists, such as Aristophanes, had historically utilized the significant ideas of their times to dramatize social injustice, also recorded his conviction that ideas were legitimate grist for the artistic mill in his *Theory and Technique of Playwriting*, and his theories had a great influence on all socially oriented drama of the Depression.[3]

The agit-prop that blossomed in this period properly belongs to the drama of ideas. It is a hybrid mode that basically utilizes realism to achieve immediate and unmistakable communication and audience response, but it is not confined to realism; it has also liberally borrowed its techniques for telescoping and dramatizing ideas from much the same experimental sources as the Living Newspaper.

As Sam Smiley has also pointed out, while agit-prop may use the same elements and structural progression as mimetic drama, it nevertheless differs significantly, since thought is not merely material to its characters but also performs organizational control, and all characterizations, action, plot progression, and spectacle are directed primarily toward this organizational purpose. The protagonist, who in literary realism, is generally expected to change or grow, has also made his ethical commitments before the agit-prop play begins, so change of this type should not be expected.[4] On the other hand, like the aims of the Living Newspaper, change in the villain—often the social system—is sought, and may well occur if the audience is forcefully enough impressed and engaged as participants in the drama.

Also like the Living Newspaper, agit-prop draws its material from immediate social injustices, and its greatest and most obvious disadvantages are first that it can easily become dated by achieving the social reforms it seeks to stimulate, and second that it may fatally antagonize political forces powerful enough to enforce censorship: this second disadvantage is similar to what occurred with the Living Newspaper's first intended production, *Ethiopia*. On the other hand it captures and records the essence of the era it dramatizes, together with the ideas and problems that were dominant at the time, and can thus reflect for the future, with intimate vitality, moments of history. Perhaps the best-known play in this mode is Clifford Odets' *Waiting for Lefty*, which sought to stimulate labor into unified action for the protection of exploited workers. It was an immediate success in both utilitarian and artistic senses, and is generally used as a popular comparative touchstone of excellence in the agit-prop mode.

Since Hallie Flanagan envisioned the federal project as "a theater which should reflect our country, its history, its present problems, its diverse religions and populations,"[5] it was inevitable that the Federal Theatre should include, among its productions, drama in this mode. Inevitable, too, was its appeal for black playwrights. Depression conditions, combined with discrimination, caused the highest unemployment rates and the greatest suffering in the ghettos: blacks were the last people hired and the first fired,[6] consequently theirs was the greatest need for reform, and several black dramatists advocated socialist solutions in their plays. In *Big White Fog* Theodore Ward suggested that integrated action by black and white labor for their mutual protection might be possible. The agit-prop solution in the finale of *Liberty Deferred* has also been noted. But neither of those plays was written entirely in the agit-prop mode, and the most successful Federal Theatre play in this mode was *Turpentine*, which was written by black dramatist J. Augustus Smith in collaboration with Peter Morell. It was produced by the Federal Theatre in 1936,[7] and was directed by its author, Gus Smith.[8]

The realistic setting for this play is a turpentine-tapping camp in Florida. The social necessity is that black laborers are paid 40¢ a barrel—the collection of which was a full day's work—for turpentine that eventually sold at $22.50 a barrel, while the resin sold for triple that price. Furthermore, all attempts on the part of the blacks to unionize, or strike for higher wages, have been suppressed for several years by the white population: the brutal white law enforcement officers, by their own admission, make up the law as they go along and indulge in lynching and other forms of violence. On the eve of the arrival of the absentee owner, Mr. Chase, the camp is in a ferment. Two young union organizers, Bud and Son, are attempting to persuade the men to join the surrounding camps that are already on strike, since solidarity is essential for success. The reforms desired by the strikers are a wage increase to 80¢ a barrel, free medical attention for injured workmen, better housing, and schools. The organizing idea is that the existing oppressive conditions can only be overcome by unified action.

Within the controlling framework there is a dialectic that presents the views of blacks and whites, both in logical terms and in action. On one side, Mr. Chase, the owner, wishes to prevent labor organization because it will increase production costs and cut profits; he is also negotiating a loan with a Northern bank which might fall through if labor unrest becomes too disruptive; the Sheriff wishes to control the "niggers" to the satisfaction of Mr. Chase and the white population because he has political ambitions to be the state's next governor; the camp boss, "Cap'n" Sap, needs to achieve a quick suppression of the unrest before the arrival of Mr. Chase; and the woodsrider, Hoss Crawford, fears that if the blacks successfully defy the establishment their next step will be to take his job, and perhaps even to vote. On the other side, the black laborers are starving on 40¢ a day, men wounded on the job die for lack of medical attention, the workers' shacks are almost uninhabitable, and their children are unschooled.

In this dialectic, Colonel Dutton, the commissary owner, is the mediator; he has motivations that tie him to both sides. On the one hand, he is a white man, and in addition, the underpaid blacks cannot pay for his merchandise; on the other hand, Colonel Dutton had a black mistress for many years, who bore him three children he could not acknowledge—under the existing customs he would have been tarred and feathered out of town if he had. But his sympathies are with the blacks, and he now regrets that he did not flout convention and acknowledge his children. He has written an endless stream of letters to the governor, protesting conditions in the camp—and this anti-white action would have made him a popular target for the crackers if he had not been the best shot in the county. The Colonel has two supporters for his mediate position, the poor-whites Stafford and Jenkins, who are beginning to believe that if the blacks succeed with their strike, the poor-whites, too, may benefit.

Since the central idea controls all aspects of the play, the costumes and settings are designed to support it. The clothes of the blacks are patched and torn; some blacks are without shoes, and wrap their feet in burlap to protect them from the resin; their shacks are dilapidated, but the clothes of the black stooge, Burrhead, and his pretty mulatto wife, Sissy, are neat and new, and their shack is in good repair. On the other side, the clothes of the whites consist of riding breeches, business suits, and leather boots; Mr. Chase wears white linen; and the clothing of the Northern banker, Forsyth, who accompanies Chase to the camp "to shoot turkeys," is expensive; the drawing room of the Chase home, too, is lavishly furnished. Again Colonel Dutton occupies the middle position, more from choice than necessity: his clothes are rumpled, his whiskers are tobacco-stained, and the seats in his commissary consist of cracker boxes. Stafford and Jenkins are only slightly better off than the blacks; they are neat, but barefoot.

In *Turpentine*, a major and a minor conflict are in progress, both stemming from the organizing idea: the major conflict is between the laborers and their white exploiters, and the major plot shows the progress of the young organizers in persuading the camp to join the strikers; the minor conflict is between the laborers and the black foreman, Burrhead, and the minor plot consists of the efforts of the men to prevent Burrhead from betraying them to the white bosses for his personal gain. These two plots are intricately interwoven and include the countermeasures of the establishment and its stooge.

To foil the efforts of the organizers, the sheriff and his deputies have crews out, with bloodhounds, to track Bud and Son, but the strike organizers outwit them by fouling the trail with pepper. The leaders of the camp laborers, Forty-Four and Shine, threaten Burrhead if he betrays them: they guard him and succeed in holding their meeting as soon as their lookouts bring news of Cap'n Sap's departure for town. Son and Bud persuade the laborers by logical argument to go out on strike, and the men elect Forty-Four, Shine, and Bud to present their demands directly to Mr. Chase—the news of whose impending arrival has been picked up by Bud and Son at the commissary, right under the noses of the sheriff and his deputies. The blacks wish to accomplish their ends peacefully, but are ready to fight if forced to defend themselves.

Their first encounter with Mr. Chase takes place in the commissary, with the sheriff and his deputies present. Before they can present their case, however, the trigger-happy sheriff shoots a young black, Turtly Eyes, and the enraged laborers break into the store to find that the whites have fled by the back door. Colonel Dutton then goes to Mr. Chase's house to mediate while the blacks hide out in the swamps, and Chase promises Dutton that he will listen to their demands if they will come out of the swamps and meet him at their evening church service. When Dutton leaves the Chase mansion, however, to carry the good news, the Northern banker advises Chase to give the sheriff a free hand to kill the strike, because banks are more interested in making loans in Southern areas that do not have labor problems.

The laborers trust Dutton, but not Chase, so they come to the church as requested but they are armed with shotguns, shovels, and other implements. Like Burrhead, the minister is servile to the white men, and before the blacks arrive the sheriff, his deputies, and Burrhead, reinforced by Ku Kluxers who are hidden in the bushes, enter the church, threaten the minister, and complete arrangements for their intended ambush. In the midst of the service, in which the minister preaches submission, as directed, the sheriff and his party enter. The sheriff shoots Colonel Dutton, the minister blows out the light, and general combat ensues.

But the tapping season is short—a month more and it will be too late to collect the turpentine—and Chase, realizing that this time brutality will not work and that he will lose a great deal of money, capitulates, and offers the blacks 80¢ a barrel, which they accept. They do not, however, achieve their other aims.

The plot of *Turpentine* is complex and action packed; its subplots are well integrated, and well balanced, and it achieves an effective agit-prop finale. In terms of the dialectic, the outcome of the conflict is a rational compromise that does not violate probability, but the closing words of both sides penetrate the future with foreboding. Mr. Chase indicates the temporary nature of the victory: "Give them 80¢ a barrel. It's only a month, then . . ." (III.iii.23). With his turpentine shipped, Chase will resume the fight; but this time, so will the blacks. As Colonel Dutton had stated in the first act: "Always will be trouble 'till they's treated like other human beings. . . . but mos' white folks are too blind to see it" (I.i.6), and at the final curtain Forty-Four's woman, Big Sue, tosses the laborers' determination challengingly at Cap'n

Sap—who is convinced they have all gone crazy: "An' Buckra, we's gettin crazier evah minute" (III.iii.23). Yet total capitulation by Mr. Chase would not have been believable in a white dominated Southern town, in the thirties; nor, for that matter, would such a fait accompli have been good agit-prop, for it would have given its audience no reason for concern or action on a very real and still existing problem.

In addition to set, costumes, and plot, the emotional appeal of Smith's characterizations and dialogue also supports the play's controlling idea. From the first scene in Colonel Dutton's store to the finale, the white bosses cannot understand what has gotten into these "niggers"; previous shootings, lynchings, and threats of violence have always brought them to heel. They are quick to notice, too, that Forty-Four and Shine, the leaders of the strike and the best tappers in the camp, are not cowed by their presence:

> Sheriff. That Forty-Four can't be trusted, he nevah dropped his eyes.
> Sap. He an' that dam' Shine nevah does.
> Sheriff. Any time a nigger looks a white man straight in the eyes, he ain't got the proper respect for him. (1.ii.26)

To the white men, Burrhead, bowing low and serving their aims for small favors, is the black as he should be. But even though he does their dirty work, he is not immune from their brutality. Sap's favors to Burrhead are partly motivated by his lecherous design on Burrhead's wife, Sissy, who is Colonel Dutton's unacknowledged daughter. She is pretty, good, and naive, and Sap, sending Burrhead on an errand, enters his shack and attacks her, tearing the front of her dress open. Burrhead enters unexpectedly during this attack and he informs the Cap'n that he'll do his dirt, but Sissy is *his* woman. In this instance he is quietly insistent; but he does not dare to use the rifle in his hands, and it is the women in the camp who, knowing Sap's capabilities, file into the shack and line the walls menacingly. Sap is armed, and he orders them out angrily, but Forty-Four's woman, Big Sue, answers him with quietly fermenting hate: "Better don't miss" (1.iii.35), and Sap is forced to retreat. Later when Burrhead fails to elude the laborers to warn Sap of their meeting, the Cap'n kicks him all over the woods, but Burrhead remains faithful and joins the ambush at the church. Sissy, on the other hand, joins the laborers.

Big Sue contributes powerful emotional support to the blacks' cause. Although Forty-Four had been shanghaied on to the chain gang for striking, two years previously, it is Sue who has the most cause to hate the white men: her sister had been raped by a white man, and when her father and brother learned about it, they shot him, and were both lynched; her sister had then also died of shock. Sue is a smouldering volcano, but her dignity is never shaken, and she, like Forty-Four, talks back. When the laborers fear to meet the organizers in the woods because the white men are watching—one is reminded of Marita Bonner's White Devil watching in the bushes—Sue precedes them as scout, and she encounters the woodsrider, Hoss, who wants to know where she is going:

Sue. (slowly) What is yuh, a white man, got ter do wid whar ah goes?

Hoss. Yuh black wench, yuh ain't foolin' me none.

Sue. How could ah fool yuh, white folks?

Hoss. Ah ax yuh again, what is yuh doin' in these woods?

Sue. Can't yuh see what ah'm doin'?

Hoss. Forty-Four sent yuh, didn't he?

Sue. If he did, ah wouldn't tell yuh.

Hoss. Well, yuh tell him, if he kno's what good foah him an' if he wants to keep his job, he'll leave strange niggers alone.

Sue. Forty-Four is man 'nuff ter pick his own company, which yer ain't Buckra. (I.iv.43)

To the white man, this kind of talk is sheer insolence, and when Hoss then propositions her with, "Ah lac' big black women, an ah could make things a whole lot easier foh yuh, if yuh is willin'," Sue further replies: "Why don't yuh make it easier foh one o' de big white women, Mr. Crawford" (I.iv.43–44), and laughs derisively at his anger, calling after his retreating figure: "De high an' mighty white man. De dirty, scrawny, red neck, Cracker. May God dam' his dirty soul!" (I.iv.44).

Sue is also kindhearted: she had borrowed meal and sow belly from Sissy when she and Forty-Four were starving, and repaid her debt by leading the women to save Sissy from Sap's intended rape. And she is quick-witted: it was she who showed Bud and Son the old slave pepper trick to confuse the bloodhounds that were hot on their trail. And she is scathing on the subject of traitors: when Son inquires how Burrhead found out about one of their meetings, she replies: "How does a buzzard know where dere's a dead carcas?" (I.iv.42). She is also the best revolutionary in the camp and spurs the men to action when Bud urges them to strike:

He's right, an' all mah life ah waited foh dis day ter come. De day dat we would grow tired of talkin' an' takin' what's lef' an have nuff guts to fight for de same rights others is got. Yuh can crawl an' beg all yuh want, but dey ain't no way ter git it but ter fight, no matter how many times we loses, fight. (II.i.64)

At the finale, the words that pierce the future ominously are also hers: "An Buckra, we's gittin' crazier evah minute" (III.iii.23).

But Sue is only one of the finely drawn characters in *Turpentine*, and similar cases can be made for the emotional and logical support contributed by other characters to the organizing idea.

The incidents in *Turpentine* touch a host of minor themes of violence, but this is precisely the essence of the black-white experience that its authors succeeded in capturing: the aesthetic texture of the realism is also enriched by symbolism, and the emotional appeal of the symbolism further supports the dominant idea. The work songs of the blacks echo through the woods, vibrant with their growing anger:

Mah belly's empty,
Ain't had no dinner terday
Lawd, lawd
Mah belly's empty,
Ain't had no dinner terday
Lawd, lawd
If they don't raise our wages, theres gonner be hell ter pay
Lawd, lawd. (I.ii.16)

Reflecting a vital function of the dual communication system, they also warn workers to fade into the woods at the approach of the enemy.

Git me away, good Lord
Git me away from dis weary land,
Git me away, good Lawd,   ·
I'm standin' on sinkin' sand. (I.ii.21)

In the tapping scene that follows Sissy's attack by Sap, the beat of the hoopers' hammers are African drum rhythms which become as savage as war drums when the baying of the hounds, which are tracking Bud and Son, floods the woods (I.iv.36–37), and the following evening, at the workers' quarters, the savage rhythm is again picked up. Sallymae, aged nineteen, asks the guitar player, Ben, to "beat it lac' it was befoh we was slaves in a stinkin' turpentine camp" (II.i.51), and the men beat out the African rhythm on porches and boxes while she dances herself into a faster, and ever faster, frenzy, in an eerie glow of moonlight that casts its spell over her poem of primitive, expressive motion. Later in the evening, when the blacks call Burrhead from his dinner to warn him of the consequences of betrayal, the dialogue, in the Southern black dialect, also repeats the angry staccato rhythm of the African drums:

> Shine. Sit down, yuh ain't goin' nowhere.
> Forty-Four. Yuh bet yuh life yuh ain't.
> Burrhead. My wife is waitin' fo me ter finish eatin mah supper.
> Turtly Eyes. Yuh tole her yuh was through.
> Shine. He is through.
> Burrhead. No ah ain't.
> Shine. Oh yes, yoh is. Sit down. (II.i.56)

And again:

> Forty-Four. Burrhead is yuh got any race pride?
> Burrhed. What yuh axt me dat foh?
> Shine. Tell him, is yuh or ain't yuh?
> Burrhead. Is y'all tryin' to start somethin'?
> Shine (Snapping). It's done started.
> Forty-Four. An' we givin' yuh a chance ter come in wid us.
> Shine. An if yuh don't its gonner be yo can.
> Forty-Four. An' we don't mean maybe. (II.i.57)

All of the dynamic interpersonal relationships, the symbolism, the dialogue, the musical and dance rhythms, the costumes, set, and plot form an organic and dynamic whole in *Turpentine* unified by the controlling idea, and they dramatize what Lawson described as "worthy goals." The goals for which the black characters in *Turpentine* were willing to fight, to kill, to die, were freedom and justice, and the techniques of agit-prop, in Gus Smith's hands, admirably reflected them.

But there is another important fact about *Turpentine* which makes it a play of great significance in the history of black drama. In the last decade, black critics, particularly those of Black Revolutionary Theater persuasion, have tended to dismiss early black-white collaboration on the grounds that it was dominated by "The Man" and was thus hopelessly compromised as black drama. While this was undoubtedly true in some instances, such an arbitrary dismissal of all plays that were the product of collaboration, and particularly of *Turpentine*, is

wholly unjustified. While some of the white elements which comprise
its dialectic may well have been contributed by Morell, the intimate
dramatization of the dynamic elements of the black heritage and
experience could have come only from the pen of Gus Smith. In spite
of the final dialectic compromise demanded by the agit-prop mode,
the play is wholly black-oriented, and it is the black elements that
dominate both the action and the atmosphere throughout. None of the
white characters, with the possible exception of the mediator, Colonel
Dutton, could be called either likeable, humanitarian, or just, by any
stretch of the imagination. On the other hand, the black characters
certainly are; indeed, so much so that in 1936 Federal Theatre performances of *Turpentine* greatly disturbed some white Southern industrialists and politicians who did not in the least appreciate the
attitudes it reflected.

At the American Theater Association Convention in Chicago in
August 1977 Dr. Margaret Wilkerson, who was reporting on activities
of black theater groups in California to the Black Drama Program,
stated that one group which was currently staging "integrated" drama
had actually succeeded in getting white actors to play oppressive
white roles. But this type of casting occurred with *Turpentine*, and it is
precisely this type of integrated dramatization of the black-white
experience that the collaborating authors of *Turpentine* achieved, forty
years ago. If the collaboration of actors in the staging of interracial
dramatic truth is considered valuable by some contemporary black
drama groups, then the fruitful collaboration of its creators must
be considered infinitely more so for the black-white experience in
America is precisely that—a dual experience. The script of *Turpentine*
stands as brilliant evidence that such black-white collaboration, however uneasy it may have been, was possible in the thirties, and was
successfully achieved in an experimental mode without the characterizations or the protests of its black author becoming compromised by
his white collaborator.

EIGHT

MESSAGE FROM ANOTHER CULTURE

ERETICAL AS IT may have sounded to American ears in the thirties, there were beyond realism, and even beyond the new experimental theories, dramatic modes and techniques which had not been immortalized by the European giants. The Noh drama of Japan,[1] the Chinese Wayang,[2] the Jatra[3] and Kutiyattam[4] of India, for instance, were dramatic gateways to other worlds. In view of the ethnic variety of America's population, certainly any definition of American experimental theater exclusively in terms of Euro-American modes and techniques was unjustified; it was also an unwarranted limitation on the very concept of experimentation.

There were those, however, who saw the potential of such ethnic diversity, and Alain Locke carried on a tireless campaign to make America aware of the artistic resources of its black culture:

> Here for the enrichment of American and modern art, among our contemporaries, in a people who still have the ancient key, are some of the things we thought culture had forever lost. Art can not disdain the gift of a natural irony, of a transfiguring imagination, of rhapsodic Biblical speech, of dynamic musical swing, of cosmic emotion such as only the gifted pagans knew, of a return to nature, not by way of the forced and worn formula of Romanticism, but through the closeness of an imagination that has never broken kinship with nature.[5]

For black American dramatists Locke specifically emphasized that one could "scarcely think of a complete development of Negro dramatic art without some significant re-expression of African life, and the tradition associated with it,"[6] for if

> the sophisticated race sense of the Negro should lead back over the track of the group tradition to an interest in things African, the natural affinities of the material and the art will complete the circuit and they will most electrically combine,[7]

and we now have, through the Federal Collection, new evidence that these affinities were recognized and exploited by black playwrights in the thirties. Their dramatizations of elements of their African heritage and their Afro-American experience were no less experimental than the efforts of American playwrights to emulate expressionism or the production techniques of the Russians: they were perhaps considerably more original since they aimed at new horizons which entailed the achievement of new syntheses. Pirandello shocked the West into recognizing that reality and illusion are interchangeable,[8] and we have only to recall that for three hundred years the white American dream has been the black American nightmare to realize that the recognition of experimental drama, as such, or even of realism, as such, depends on the cultural orientation and limitations of the interpreter.

The white beholder in the twenties and thirties—even much later than that—was ill-equipped to judge the merits of Afro-American experimental drama beyond its appealing vitality, since he little understood its African elements. While praising the vitality of the "voodoo" scene in Hall Johnson's *Run Little Chillun'*, the *California Eagle* for 28 July 1938 confessed, ". . . we are unable to fathom the mystery of this strange and weird form of religion."[9] White critics repeatedly referred to call–response church scenes, or voodoo, as "spectacular" but "perennial,"[10] but they might equally have referred to a myriad of such Western cultural conventions as *girl gets boy* or *justice will prevail* as perennial. African elements were used by black playwrights, and even by a few white playwrights but the question is not which spectacular or perennial African elements were used, but how they were used, and above all what they signified.

Consider, for example, the music of "perennial" voodoo, which has brought its enormous vitality to the entire Western culture. Ortiz M. Walton has pointed out the significant technical differences between Western and African music: in the Western world, and stemming from rational analysis by the Greeks, a system of musical notation developed in which melody was locked into a specific key, the notes progressing at regular and predictable intervals; no such regularity or predictability existed in African music, which had neither been rationalized nor systematized.[11] Elkin T. Sithole has traced the African prototypes of Afro-American music and he states that

There are as many scales in Africa as there are ways of improvisation. The nearest equivalent of this approach in contemporary art music is an arbitrary selection of notes in serial music,

and each group has its unique emphasis notes or focal points "round which the melody moves."[12] This characteristic is apparent in the work songs that have been transplanted to America and the Caribbean, while in most Negro spirituals the rest or emphasis notes are an invitation to improvisation in the African tradition.

As the product of a communally oriented culture, most African music was of the antiphonal, or call–response, type:

> the chorus could, because of antiphony, be unfamiliar with the melody, and yet be able to sing it. The soloist could vary his stanzas easily. . . . The more skilled the performer, the more adept he was in the art of improvisation.[13]

This call–response technique was basic to most African forms of artistic expression and applied also to instrumental music, with "the master drummer setting the beat and pattern followed by answer-like figures from the chorus of drummers."[14] These patterns might be infinitely varied, and could be extremely intricate, and Walton has further pointed out that

> the intricacy of African polyphony [the inter-weaving of many independent rhythmic patterns fitted into the overall pattern] is obscured by the masterful techniques and ease with which it is accomplished.[15]

It is these rhythms which, reflecting their communal base, characterize voodoo, and which have been transmitted to black church music, spirituals, blues, jazz, and all the popular dances, such as the rhumba and samba, that Africa has given to the United States, Latin America, the Caribbean—the world—and even if their origins and meanings are poorly understood, there is no mistaking the rhythms, since, unlike traditional European music that emphasizes the regular beat, African music emphasizes the offbeat.[16] There is also no mistaking the effect this music has had on white America, for as Rudolph Fisher observed, "it is almost as if a traveller from the North stood watching an African tribe dance, then suddenly found himself swept wildly into it, caught in its tidal rhythm."[17]

African rhythm formed the basis of many black musicals of the Federal Theatre era and its enormous vitality and potential were readily recognized by white playwrights and producers: Orson Welles' voodoo version of *Macbeth*, which was performed by the New York Negro unit of the Federal Theatre, was a tremendous hit; Eugene O'Neill attempted to interpret it dramatically in *The Emperor Jones*, capturing only its negative qualities; and other white playwrights translated whatever they felt they were able to understand. But the music of "perennial voodoo" had a great deal more to say than was translated by unindoctrinated Westerners; it spoke virtually the entire language of a different culture, and the potential of their medium was not lost on the black dramatists. They experimented with the words and rhythms of the spirituals, not only as messages and unifying symbols but in orchestrations and in choral call–response arrangements off- or onstage, or using both simultaneously; they experimented with them as voices speaking from level to level, in their entirety, or in fragments; they used African rhythms to raise or sustain emotional intensity, enhance nonverbal communication, dramatize significant elements of their cultural heritage—or just for their sheer beauty. Many of these elements were used by Theodore Browne in *Natural Man* and *Go Down Moses*, by Hill and Silvera in *Liberty Deferred*, by Marita Bonner in *The Purple Flower*, and by others, to create plays with an exclusively Afro-American quality; but in *Run Little Chillun'*, which was produced by the Federal Theatre in 1938,[18] Hall Johnson dramatized the very essence of the black musical heritage.

Hall Johnson was a musician and composer of great talent, and his famous Hall Johnson Choir was widely acclaimed for its performance in *The Green Pastures*.[19] *Run Little Chillun'* combined music and drama and proved that he was also an inspired playwright. He is said to have written the play to tell the story behind the spirituals;[20] but neither that story nor Hall Johnson's music had their inception in the West. Their genesis was in Africa, and if we are to evaluate the experimental value of *Run Little Chillun'* it is not enough simply to know the origin of its music and its rhythms. It is necessary for us to understand something of the cultural heritage they project. The report of Clarence Muse, who directed the Los Angeles production of this play, states that "research on African culture is very important before the spirit can be understood," and the original script submitted for copyright by the author, Hall Johnson, clearly specifies this need.[21]

The slaves of the Western hemisphere came predominantly from the bite of Africa—the west coast, stretching from Ghana down to Angola and extending into the Congo and the surrounding parts of central Africa—an enormous territory that encompassed many tribes and nations with diverse languages and cultures. But there were certain characteristics underlying almost all its cultures, and the most pervasive of these was the cosmological view. African metaphysics of the seventeenth century certainly were not systematized and written down; indeed, all philosophical, historical, and religious tradition was preserved by the highly developed oral method; but philosophy flourished, nevertheless, for the African lived his metaphysics.

To this seventeenth-century African, time was two-dimensional. It consisted of a present, a near future, and a rememberable past in one dimension, which was known as Sassa time, and a distant past in the other dimension, which was known as Zamani time. In this latter dimension the Creator and his associates lived, and to it dead heroes retired and the other dead gradually receded from living memory; thus, the future circled into the past. There was no real future dimension, as defined by Western philosophy, since time did not exist until it was created by man through experience: time was, therefore, a creative human act and was event rather than clock- or calendar-oriented. The activities of the day began with sunrise, not at a specific hour, and the planting season was heralded by the coming of the rains, not by a calendar. With this orientation, life was lived creatively in the present, and lived to the fullest possible extent.

The very basis of African music was cosmological. The African universe was a harmony of interacting rhythms, permeated and sustained by the continuous creative force of God—the force vitale. Each rhythm was a manifest quality of God, and the rhythms were personified by a hierarchy of spirits, the Orisha, who were God's associates in a manner reminiscent of the angels of Christian doctrine. In this rhythmic harmony, accident, illness, misfortune, and unusual natural phenomena were considered to be disruptions of the natural cosmic order, and the entire aim and efforts of the people were directed toward the restoration of cosmic harmony. There was not, and could not be, any separation of the visible and invisible (spirit) worlds since they were both integral parts of the universe and they interacted in the rhythmic harmony.

In the African analysis of the condition of being human, man was a combination of forces, and the metaphysics of the highest cultures, such as that of the Akan, named their sources. The okra—the spiritual, or true identity—derived from God and was eternal, having its existence before, during, and after incarnation (a fact of which Browne's John Henry was well aware). Several physical elements derived, one from the mother's blood, one from the father's, and so forth, but once all these elements were deterministically and harmoniously combined there was no further separation, or even thought of separation, during incarnate life. The African did not suffer from Descartes' ghost in the machine: man was not a warring physical–spiritual duality who recognized and reflected good and bad as abstract qualities which were separable from particularizing action; he was neither good nor bad except in the actual performance of good or bad, for the physical was a direct manifestation of the spiritual, in inseparable harmony. In such a metaphysical system, space too was defined by its content—the rhythms or potential rhythms it contained—and this definition is one which is still used by contemporary jazz musicians.

Adding further to the enormous significance of African musical rhythm, the rhythmic African universe was also a religious universe and the Creator was both transcendent and immanent. While God was greater than the universe, the universe was God's extension, manifesting his continuous creation, and thunder, lightning, and like phenomena were his vehicles and his voice. But the African had no religious creed for, like his philosophy, his creed was reflected in his daily life: his spiritual and physical worlds overlapped and harmonized since an incarnate, visible man today would occupy the spiritual, invisible world after his death tomorrow, and in the latter state he was revered and sustained—not worshipped—by the living. The sustaining act was mutual, for the living supplied food, honor, and extended life, through memory, to the dead, while the dead, whose access to knowledge and the force vitale had increased with their entry into the spirit world, and whose good will, except for specific causes such as murder, was presumed, acted as guides, guardians, protectors, and intermediaries for the living.

The social order of the African tribe also reflected its metaphysical and religious bases and every event, such as birth, puberty, marriage, procreation, and death, was of religious significance. Society, therefore was not oriented toward the individual but was organized to promote communal interaction, harmony, and welfare, which were an integral part of the universal, rhythmic harmony. The states were based on systems of duties rather than rights: justice was by retribution instead of punishment and polygamous marriage insured several welfare necessities—it took care of the surplus women who had lost their men to war, or the hunt, it provided communal training for children through multiple mothers, and it insured harmonious continuity for them in the event of a maternal death. Contributing also to this harmonious continuity, and minimizing the shock of bereavement, was the slow passing of the dead, who continued to be counted among the family for the span of living memory. No detail breached the philosophy of harmonious continuity and even the bodies of the dead were buried nude in preparation for their birth into the spiritual world.

Since the physical was but another manifestation of the spiritual, there were also no inhibitions about anything physical, including sex.

The West African forms of religious worship varied greatly from one tribe to another and even from one village to another—as indeed do the forms of the Christian religious sects that co-exist today—but all had their basis in the rhythmic harmony and there were many formal elements common to all. There was no such thing as salvation in any terms since man's spirit, being already eternal, had no need of it; consequently there was also no form of proselytizing. Man was born to his place in the physical, harmonized world and any attempt to subvert his acceptance of that place, or his beliefs, would have been unthinkable as it would have been an assault on the cosmic harmony of which he was an integral part.

Since prayers directed to God were often thought to denote presumptuousness on the part of man, the Orisha were usually addressed as intermediaries—also quite similarly to the custom of some Christian sects to pray to the Virgin and Saints—or as possible benefactors who had access to the source of the force vitale. Such rites usually took the form of placation or intercession, and in his relationship to the deity the African used every available means of communication and every mode of manifesting total man of which he was capable. The drums, the most basic manifestation of the universal rhythmic harmony, spoke a rich and diverse language and were central to the act of worship. The best known drummers in the world were the Ashanti, and their talking drums were capable of communicating anything relevant to African worship and culture. The dance, a physical manifestation of the spiritual and emotional, was another potent mode of communication, and every movement was pregnant with symbolic and psychological meaning. The word, the very utterance of which manifested metaphysical dimensions, combined concrete, kinetic, and poetic imagery with rhythmic sound, and it could cause the universe to burst into new life with its power. This power of vocal expression to generate, to transform, to create by very utterance was Nommo, and it embodied the act of creation described in the Christian Bible as "the word was made flesh." Speech, recitation, incantation, supplication, and exhortation were all potent manifestations of this power, and for the griots, too, the word and the song were the Nommo that "created rather than reflected the mood."[22]

All these major elements were combined in a variety of communal ritual forms, the ultimate religious aims being spirit possession—an aim also familiar to us in Christianity. But in many of the African religions, at this point in the ritual of worship man had some control over his interaction with the spirits, for the Orisha, too, had obligations to man. This convergence gave birth to the practice of magic, with which we are familiar in derivative Western forms such as voodoo. Since each Orisha had a specific rhythm peculiar to it, the expertise of the drummer could either call a spirit to the scene of worship or choose to lock it out of the ritual; thus spirit possession could be assured and controlled. The entire religious performance was a cosmic communion, at once the greatest act of psychological liberation and the greatest spectacle of living drama known to man.[23]

Also taking a prominent place in the communal cultures of Africa was the oral tradition, a masterpiece of artistic literary development that was highly functional. The primary purposes of the oral tradition were historical, nationalistic, and sacred,[24] but all of the themes and techniques learned and practiced for these purposes were also applied to the art of entertainment. The oral tradition comprised a continuous accretion spanning centuries and incorporating much experimentation and many refinements in techniques. Its practitioners were trained and indoctrinated, through apprenticeship, to exploit all the power and literary qualities of language such as association, repetition, suggestion, exaggeration, the subtly turned phrase, and the stylized or heroic image. These were enriched by the manipulation of sound qualities—alliterative, onomatopoeic, and so forth—in rhythmic and musical patterns, and were often accompanied by mime, dramatic gestures, or enactments. The raconteur's aim was to create a communal experience by promoting intellectual, emotional, and physical involvement, and the degree of his success depended on his virtuosity. Here was another manifestation of composite and communal artistic achievement with all the qualities of living drama.

The techniques of the raconteurs and the unifying characteristics of the oral tradition are particularly interesting to students of twentieth-century Afro-American culture because they live, much as they did in seventeenth-century Africa, in contemporary black American church services, in the best black preaching and political oratory, and through them in other black literary endeavors including black drama. The expert raconteur concentrated his efforts on remembering themes rather than characterizations, relying on his verbal skill to particularize and embellish his themes; the plots which conveyed these vital themes thus became infinitely varied throughout most of Africa. The most familiar of these stories to the Western world are the animal stories: Brer Rabbit, Anansi the spider, and many such others appeal to children and adults alike, but in spite of their apparent simplicity, they contain the crucial themes in highly effective forms and their great popularity bears witness to the timelessness of their wisdom.

In the art of entertainment, the dialogue was varied in accordance with the ability of the raconteur and depended on the composition of his audience, on topicality, on local usage, and on applicability. Character types, rather than individual, rounded characters, were used, and reflected the communal quality of the society. W. E. Abraham points out that in this regard European versions of African stories usually fall short because the rounded characters they invariably project violate the oral tradition.[25] The raconteur usually started his story with a riddle, a question, or a similar method of immediately launching the communal call–response technique. Song was frequently used for interpolation, and repetition was used to insure emphasis. There was always a dramatic pause at the crucial point in the story for deliberation, and this created or heightened suspense and also reflected the African's respect for thought and wisdom. There was a musical, rhythmic arrangement of language,[26] and the kinetic imagery, which resulted from a concrete, rather than abstract, linguistic representation of an action-oriented society, was vitally alive. Almost all of these elements have survived, and this imagery is still predominantly reflected in the language of black America;[27] it is, in fact, the primary source of the vitality of American slang, which is largely adopted from black English.

In this system of philosophy-in-action, traditional African art also reflected African cosmological beliefs and the African sense of harmony. It was a highly sophisticated, controlled, and stylized medium of expression that emphasized, with disciplined simplicity, qualities rather than physically accurate dimensions and perspectives. It was the living qualities of God, and his visible and invisible creation, that characterized the sculptures and the religious masks of Africa: the elongated breasts of the sculptured African mother, for example, denoted the sustaining quality of motherhood,[28] while the masks reflected a range of qualities from the divine to the demonic.

Like African music, African art has had a great influence on modern European artists, and in one of his many attempts to interest Afro-Americans in exploring its potential, Alain Locke pointed out its tremendous value as a "lesson of discipline, of style, of technical control pushed to the limits of technical mastery."[29] He also cited Roger Fry's enthusiastic recognition of the three-dimensionality and plastic freedom of the traditional African artist, who "manages to give his forms their disconcerting vitality, the suggestion that they make of being not mere echoes of actual figures, but of possessing an inner life of their own,"[30] and this observation of Fry's is generally true of all forms of African literary and artistic expression.

Certainly the stylized art of Africa had far greater significance for the Afro-American dramatists of the thirties than has been recognized, for it reflected a mode of vision that succinctly apprehended essential qualities and these dramatists were obviously not in unknown territory when they were introduced to the symbolic and stylized sets of European experimental drama. Yet European drama did have significantly different philosophical bases for its stylization, and the black dramatists found in these differences both a broad, fertile field for experimentation and many problems of synthesis which had to be solved.

Our glimpse of the African universe has revealed some of the major differences between the philosophies that governed African forms of artistic expression and those of the West. Indeed the two systems embodied beliefs that directly contradicted each other and the following tables summarize those which had the greatest significance for the Afro-American creative process in the thirties, particularly for those black playwrights who attempted to create an Afro-American dramatic idiom.

The Western philosophic beliefs need no elaboration as they are familiar to all Americans; the Western dramatic canons to which they gave birth were, in the thirties, still basically Aristotelian,[31] with an overlay of Christianity, and where listed they reflect this orientation. The African dramatic canons are based primarily on the drama inherent in the techniques and performance of the African raconteurs, but the ritualistic drama of worship was equally part of the African dramatic heritage.

Certainly, the differences shown in the tables can hardly be exaggerated, nor can the problems of synthesis with which Afro-American playwrights have had to wrestle. But above all, this glimpse of the African universe brings us a message from another culture that there are systems other than that of the West for creating and evaluating the dramatic art. Hall Johnson also brought us this message as far back as the thirties. As Alain Locke predicted, he completed the circuit. He opposed African and Western philosophies and achieved a most electric synthesis in *Run Little Chillun'*.

As we now explore Johnson's play I shall identify for the reader, in brackets, the African elements which he used and which we have just discussed.

The Philosophies

Western	African
Time: three-dimensional, chronologically measured by clock and calendar; a saleable commodity.	Time: two-dimensional, defined by experience, event-oriented—a creative act.
Space: defined by rational, abstract laws, harmonized.	Space: defined by interacting rhythmic content or potential, harmonized.
Energy: a physical potential with action its function and form of expression.	Energy: divine. Creative force vitale that permeates and sustains entire universe.

The following are separated:

Western		African
abstract ⎱ universal ⎰	concrete ⎱ particular ⎰	No separation of any of these possible. The abstract has meaning only as expressed in the concrete. The universal is expressed in particulars.
spiritual ⎱ ethical ⎬ physical aesthetic ⎰		The physical is a manifestation of the spiritual. Man's ethics and aesthetics have meaning only in performance.
(e.g., idea of good, evil, justice, etc.)	(e.g., their actual expression by man)	
art man made art	life natural art (e.g., drift-wood)	The universe is an interacting harmony. Art is a dimension of life, and the universal rhythmic harmony.

Western	African
Individuality based on rights. Effects: subjective vision, self-consciousness, egocentricity.	Communality based on duties. Effects: communality of vision, unself-consciousness, altruism.
Individual salvation based on performance, self-denial, spiritual revelation and grace. Gratification delayable, delayed, rewarded in heaven or hell. Effects: fragmentation, guilt, inhibitions in constant need of harmonization.	No salvation necessary; man spiritually eternal, partaker of divinity. Physically and spiritually harmonized. Effects: incarnate man is whole, uninhibited, joyful—gratification in incarnate life except where it threatens cosmic harmony, duties.

The Artistic Process (Dramatic)

Western	African
Art is not life; it is an imitation of life, based on probability.	Art is a dimensional manifestation of life. Actuality, not probability, manifests life.
Art pursued for its own sake is contemplative, formative, pleasure-giving.	Art is functional, a direct manifestation of experience; enlarging, confirmatory, supportive, solidifying, pleasure-giving.
Art requires imitators.	Art requires manifestors.
Subjective, imaginative vision of artist performs extraction, abstraction, universalization in accordance with laws of probability, and translates into particular action.	Traditional thematic base dominant; clothed in relevant, contemporary experience; projected imaginatively, directly; technical virtuosity of raconteur involves audience in creative process.
Apprended by viewer through emotions and intellect and retranslated contemplatively, subjectively, into relevant experience.	Basic themes generally familiar. Immediate apprehension by whole man who enters dramatic experience and contributes to it.
Through externalization of emotions performs katharsis, enlarges, forms, and gives pleasure.	A communal creative effort which is confirmatory, supportive, solidifying, pleasure giving through participation.

The traditional dramatic arts primarily stressed:

Western	African
Individual creation	Traditional accretion
Spectator audience	Creator audience
Formal unity	Thematic unity
Rationalistic	Ritualistic
Contemplative	Apprehensive
Mimesis	Spontaneity
Form over content	Content over form

NINE

THE WORD WAS MADE FLESH

R UN LITTLE CHILLUN' is the spectacular story of the synthesis of the African and Western philosophic elements that comprise the Afro-American culture. No black American in the audience could fail to recognize in the play the elements of his African heritage, yet members of the white audience who were unaware of the significance of those elements could still appreciate the play's acknowledged dramatic excellence and the beauty and vitality of Hall Johnson's music. *Run Little Chillun'* was highly successful and widely acclaimed when it was produced by the Federal Theatre in Los Angeles, and the *Hollywood Citizen News*, perhaps the most discerning of its enthusiastic critics, commented on 15 August 1938:

> If this had been done by the Moscow Art Theater or any group of foreign actors and actresses, it would be hailed nationally for its dramatic intensity and integrity, its brilliant direction and staging.[1]

Yet even this recognition of its dramatic quality says little about the experimental genius of its dramatist, and it is the experimental element that now interests us.

The story of *Run Little Chillun'* is set in a deep Southern black community where the Hope Baptist Church is strenuously engaged in a month-long revival. Church attendance has dropped, however, and the members are alarmed for they are convinced that this defection is caused by the recently arrived New Day Pilgrims, whose pantheistic worship is being held in the woods in a manner considered mysterious and pagan by the devout Baptists. The minister's son, Jim, who is also a preacher, is married to a good woman, Ella, but for the past year he has been having an affair with Sulamai, who comes from the tacky side of town known as Toomer's Bottom. Current gossip has it that Sulamai has bragged she will take Jim over to the Pilgrims, and the excited Baptist Council visits Reverend Jones, who has been unaware of his son's philandering, and calls on him to do something to rid the Christian community of the heathen Pilgrim menace. On learning of the latest gossip, Reverend Jones is horrified, particularly at the pros-

97

pect of Jim's deserting his religious training and his God and losing his soul to the devil because of his infatuation.

When the members of the council leave to attend revival, the Reverend Jones soon follows, and Ella, who is the soul of Christian understanding, confronts Jim with his father's distress. Jim reveals, however, that it isn't just Sulamai who has caused his alienation; he has religious doubts and is curious to see if the Pilgrims can supply him with some of the answers he seeks: for instance, why can't he follow his normal biological urge to live with Sulamai without affronting God and scandalizing the congregation? Jim does not feel sinful in his extramarital relationship with Sulamai.

After Ella too leaves sorrowfully for the revival meeting, Sulamai enters and Jim informs her of the result of her bragging. Sulamai explains to him that she had not really intended to brag; she had hot-headedly retaliated when she was snubbed by one of the good Christians and had "switched off," and Jim concedes that switching off is one of the things she does best. Jim is disturbed that his father is so stricken and Sulamai is distressed because she has hurt Miss Ella, who has shown her true Christian charity, but their feelings of remorse are forgotten when Sulamai arouses Jim's jealousy by her obvious admiration for the Pilgrims' preacher, Brother Moses. Moses is the "finest looking dark man"[2] she has ever seen; he speaks better than the white Episcopal minister—having been educated at Oxford—and he makes religion so clear and so beautiful. Sin, says Sulamai quoting Moses, is what human rules have arbitrarily decreed it to be, and Jim's urge to reform evaporates. Prompted by jealousy and curiosity, he accompanies her to the Pilgrim worship in the woods where he finds that Brother Moses is indeed easy on the eye and a "silver tongued orator."

The Pilgrims' meeting is a celebration of the full moon and it is very well attended. When Moses enters to begin the ceremony he is flanked by the African founder of the sect, Elder Tongola, who is a mysterious and stoic-looking ancient, and by Tongola's daughter, Kanda, who is a typical conjure woman. Elder Tongola has not spoken for seven years and his thoughts are spoken by his dedicated representative, Moses, and by Kanda. Kanda's daughter, Reba, who has been promised to Moses since childhood and who looks rather like a sleep-walker, also enters and sits dutifully at her mother's feet. The chattering of the congregation subsides and the worship begins.

Moses preaches a doctrine of joy in the Oneness of God and Nature, invites converts to join the Pilgrims' work, and informs his flock that

Tongola's job on earth is now done and that he will soon leave, in a storm, for higher planes. As the moon rises, the worship progresses to a pinnacle of frenzied expression with song, drum rhythms, music, and dance, and Sulamai, enchanted by the hypnotic power of the rhythm, sheds her garment and "self-expresses" among the dancers. The total abandon of her performance stirs Brother Moses' long-controlled passions, and on observing this unexpected development Jim seizes her and carries her off bodily.

After this experience Jim has had about enough of the Pilgrims, and particularly of Brother Moses' startling reactions, so he resolves to reform. Three days later he dutifully sets out for church services with Ella but he wavers at the crossroads and, leaving Ella with a muttered promise to rejoin her, he detours to Toomer's Bottom. Here he gives Sulamai a note, delivered to him by Kanda, requesting that she not return to the Pilgrims' meetings. This rejection again hurts Sulamai so when Jim taunts her about Moses and then insists on keeping his promise to join Ella, she retaliates by revealing that she is expecting his baby. Immediately contrite, Jim offers to leave town with her on the two o'clock train, but she refuses angrily. Sulamai now decides she will stay in Toomer's Bottom and flaunt Jim's baby in the faces of the good Christians. Jim then leaves to meet Ella and as he does so, Moses arrives.

Moses has been able to think of nothing but Sulamai since her "self-expression." When she tells him about her pregnancy he is even willing to accept Jim's baby and to take her away on the same "matrimonial special," provided he can get Tongola's permission to leave the Pilgrims. Sulamai is impressed by his generosity and his persuasion. She is strongly attracted to Moses and recognizes that she is about to lose Jim, so she finally promises to go with him if he will meet her at midnight at Hope Baptist Church. But Sulamai bitterly resents always being subject to outside authority so she also lays down the condition that he must ask no one's permission and Moses is horrified since he fears for her safety if Tongola is angered.

At the Hope Baptist Church Reverend Jones is conducting the revival service, assisted by Reverend Allen and a visiting woman evangelist, Sister Strong. Among the many participants giving testimony is Ella, who has been fasting and praying for the return of her husband to the fold. She is the center of attention as she confesses a voice has assured her that this night her prayers will be answered, and at this point, as if in direct answer to those prayers, Jim enters and takes his place beside her. Reverend Jones starts his sermon which is, appropriately, on the Lord's loving forgiveness of sinners, but Sulamai now enters and he quickly switches to a vehement condemnation of tempters.

A tremendous storm has been brewing throughout the service, both outside and inside the Church, and Sulamai, unable to stand Reverend Jones' direct assault on her, dashes out of the church, with Jim following. Reverend Jones is shaken by this turn of events. He resorts to fervent prayer for Jim's salvation, and then for Sulamai's forgiveness, and immediately Jim dashes back up the aisle proclaiming his victory over the devil, to the hysterical joy of the entire congregation. But Sulamai, who is now ready to leave with Moses, also runs back up the aisle, throws her arms around Jim in a quick, farewell embrace, and once more retreats. Before she can reach the church door, however, she is struck dead by lightning, and Brother Moses, accompanied by strains of Pilgrim music, appears at the church window as the final curtain falls.

This is the bare plot of *Run Little Chillun'*, but the plot is by no means the dominant element in the play; it is the vehicle of spiritual truth. What is of major importance is Johnson's theme, God is One, and the metaphysical conflict which the plot dramatizes, explores the very meaning of the universe, and of religion, in terms of the traditional African and Christian theologies.

To dramatize this conflict of philosophies, Hall Johnson uses a two-act structure with each act containing two scenes; the arrangement of the acts and of the theologies they present broadly parallel each other, and the theologies also interweave with the effect and precision of motifs in a musical arrangement. In act I, the first scene dramatizes a disruption of the Baptist community's moral and religious harmony and contrasts Christian morality with African morality; it is enacted outside the worship situation. The second scene, the Pilgrim worship, dramatizes the African theology in action, introduces the dominant theme both of the African theology and of the play, and ends with the disruption of African moral and religious harmony. In act II, the first scene interweaves and personalizes the religious and moral problems of protagonists from both communities, and contrasts the effects of the two moralities on their practitioners; it is also enacted outside the worship situation. The second scene, the Hope Baptist worship, dramatizes the Christian theology which, in action in the black Church, is a synthesis of Western and African formal elements. It ends dramatically fulfilling the dominant theme of the play and restoring both Christian and African moral and religious harmonies. Both acts build to spectacular climaxes but with the finale of the second—the restoration of harmony—far surpassing that of the first—its disruption. In this play Johnson's thematic dominance, repetitive structure, and techniques of presentation combine to achieve the dramatization of philosophic truth. [Note that thematic dominance and repetitive structure are techniques of the African oral tradition, while the structure of the play itself reflects African polyphony.] But let us examine some of the African elements in the play.

We are first greeted by the fact that Jim has kept two women for the last year. He has also done so without feeling sinful [he is polygamous, not promiscuous] and Sulamai has explained to him the direct relationship between his natural feelings and the African beliefs of the Pilgrims [both are devoid of inhibitions] and Moses has assured Sulamai that sin is not a natural phenomenon, it has only been determined to be so by arbitrary decree. As the major exponent of African philosophy, he is not at all disturbed by the relationship between Jim and Sulamai.

In Hall Johnson's instructions for the playing of the Pilgrim scene we also find that no idol worship is intended; it celebrates man's oneness with nature (I.ii.1), and the object of reverence is the moon [a natural symbol of divine beauty and of black ideals (I.ii.5); this symbolism is similarly reflected in the poetry of Langston Hughes[3] and other black poets]. The worship is not scheduled to occur on Sunday at 11 a.m. but coincides with the rising of the moon [thus it is event-oriented] and increases in intensity of expression as the moon sails up into the sky.

We also find that Moses is poetic and that his oratory, in spite of his Oxford education, is dotted with concrete and kinetic imagery [the hallmarks of the African action-oriented culture which also expresses the spiritual physically]. He begins the religious celebration with a recitation of the legendary and heroic past, [a major purpose of the African oral tradition]. He introduces nature as a harmonious creation and proclaims its relationship to the spiritual and physical well-being of man:

Many thousands of years ago, there lived on this earth a race of people which enjoyed the harmonious manifested blessings of Nature, which always go hand in hand with the steady growth towards spiritual perfection. They had riches, wisdom and beauty. (I.ii.3)

[This universal harmony is pure African cosmology, the natural order that insures all well-being.]

But, Moses continues, the ancient heroes eventually retreated from the earth to a higher plane [they moved from Sassa to Zamani time] yet they remain concerned for man's welfare [being the spirits of guardian ancestors] and in every age they send a messiah in human shape, to guide man's steps. [Here the visible and invisible worlds perpetually interact.] The present messenger is Tongola, and Moses is Tongola's medium, his spiritual voice [Moses therefore further unites the physical and spiritual world and serves as a vital communication link in the universal harmony].

Moses then tells the people of his mission: he has been instructed by Tongola to "set them free with your high gospel of joy . . . teach them the enduring spiritual qualities of laughter, dancing and song" (I.ii.3). [Note the non-separation of spiritual and physical elements in man; here the physical manifests spiritual qualities, which insures the ultimate in man's freedom, his uninhibited, total expression of life, of joy] for

> the very chains that once bound your feet securely have also taught them how to dance the rhythm which sets the Universe in motion. (I.ii.3–4)

[This universal rhythm, expressed in dance, is also a manifestation of the inseparability of the physical and spiritual elements; even the chains of sorrow have contributed to creativity] for "out of the deep-throated cries of your most bitter anguish you have created the song that makes articulate the soul" (I.ii.4). [Here, combined with rhythm, is Nommo, the creative power of the word;] Nommo, which Arthur L. Smith maintains is still the essential ingredient—the soul—in black drama.[4] In Hope Baptist Church this articulation will have blossomed into the spirituals.

Moses continues: "the Black man's God . . . has never meant that his children should suffer in his name." He is not a God of malice, but of peace, joy, and well-being [and here is part of the cosmic foundation that justifies immediate gratification and the joy of living life on earth fully; it is in diametric opposition to the Christian doctrine practiced in Hope Baptist Church—the joy of suffering and of gratification delayed until the harvest is ultimately reaped in heavenly rewards]. Moses then summarizes the whole philosophy and simultaneously proclaims the dominant theme of the play, "God is One," and then, "God, and Nature, and Joy is One" [and this doctrine proclaims that

God is not only transcendent but also immanent; unlike Descartes' ghost in the machine it also proclaims the indivisibility of total man].

Moses next calls on the worshippers to be as "one soul having many bodies" (1.ii.4) [this cosmic communion and communality is based in the cosmological Oneness of God and Nature] and he delivers the Credo Tongola has brought from the Harmonious ones [the Orisha— the personified, harmonious qualities of God—and perhaps also the legendary heroes who have retired to Zamani time]. The Credo is couched in the language and melodies of ten thousand years ago [the heroic past], and all of the ritual is performed in the communal call– response form [a traditional African mode of manifesting the insepa- rability of God, nature, man, and man's institution, the state]. Johnson's instructions read, "Brother Moses leads off each section with a solo phrase in the ancient tongue, the congregation responds with answering phrases" (A.1.ii.38), and it ends in an antiphonal chorale. [Since this rhythmic African structure also generally de- scribes the structure of the play, as a musician, and a black musician, Hall Johnson's roots are unmistakable.]

Moses now delivers Tongola's command to the people: "Rise, oh black peoples of the Earth! Tell the nations what you have learned past the possibility of any forgetting" (1.ii.5). The vital thing they have learned, the theme that Hall Johnson will so spectacularly dramatize at the finale, is "God is One." [Note that its African expression extends beyond Christian theology to "God and Nature and Joy is One" which not only underwrites the brotherhood of man, and the brotherhood of man and the rest of nature, but also makes man spiritually eternal— the uncreated—and a partaker in the object of his worship. This pinnacle of human dignity and divinity will be lost in the final syn- thesis in Hope Baptist Church.] Moses then announces Tongola's imminent departure for "higher planes" in a storm, but assures his flock that Tongola will continue to communicate with them through him. [This is a reiteration of the indivisibility of the spiritual and physical worlds, an assurance of the continued beneficence of the departed, and an acknowledgment of a form of spiritual possession, since Moses will act as medium. It also specifies Tongola's vehicle of transcendence, thunder and lightning, the vehicles of God, so there is no doubt where Tongola is going when he leaves the Pilgrims.]

The welcome of the Pilgrims to the rising moon can only be cate- gorized as an African cosmic communion. The music, song, and dance reflect the poem of rhythmic coordination which was described by Sithole as expressing the vital life forces[5] and it is, indeed, sheer living drama for it reflects the African's total physical, spiritual and emotional expression of his relationship to the deity. It begins with a slow, antiphonal, ritual chant that swells into the dance of Reba, which also starts slowly, with languid grace, and gradually increases in speed and abandon while "the people chant, clap their hands and gesticulate wildly" (I.ii.6). [This living dance drama is also highly reminiscent of Sallymae's dance in *Turpentine*, that similarly starts slowly and mounts to a frenzy of rhythmic motion (II.i.51); this suggests how pervasive was the traditional African influence on the black playwrights of the thirties.] Reba is pre-empted by a band of young people who rush in, taking possession of the clearing. Guitars expand the vocal interpretation of the chant, and drum rhythm controls the entire performance. [The rhythm proclaims, harmonizes, spatially defines, and underscores its cosmological quality.][6] The dance grows wilder and wilder until Sulamai, possessed and unable to restrain herself, "throws off her robe and hurls herself among the dancers" (I.ii.6).

But the seductiveness of Sulamai's uninhibited abandon creates a real crisis. Jim scoops her up and carries her off, when he notes that the Pilgrim preacher is fascinated by her performance, but he is not the only one present who observes Moses' enchantment. Kanda, too, has been watching intently, and when Moses springs to his feet as if to follow Sulamai, Kanda restrains him. The startled eyes of Reba, who until this moment has been in a trance-like state, also note his disruptive performance, and only Tongola is unmoved. The author suggests, symbolically, that perhaps Tongola [whose spiritual sight needs no eyes] is physically blind.

For the New Day Pilgrims, the implications of Moses' unexpected reactions are enormous [the African culture, based on the African cosmology, accents duties rather than rights], and Moses is committed to Tongola and to the Pilgrim community. But a medium whose mind is in a ferment of sexual passion is hardly likely to be either receptive to Tongola's thoughts, or mindful of his duties to the community. That such a disruption has indeed occurred is later confirmed at Toomer's Bottom by Moses' willingness to forsake his religious mission for Sulamai. Moses had been dedicated and trained and it is unthinkable that he could now be so affected as to put personal desire before communal well-being; to make matters worse, his emotional upheaval is ill-timed since it has occurred on the eve of Tongola's planned departure.

By this time it is clear that Sulamai has become a thorn in the gardens of both the Hope Baptist congregation and the New Day

Pilgrims and she is welcome in neither. But the problems she has created are by no means the same for both sects. Her sin, according to Hope Baptist doctrine, stems from self-gratification; she is a harlot and a seducer, and as such has placed her own soul and also Jim's in jeopardy. These sins, however, do not exist in the doctrine of the New Day Pilgrims [self-gratification is part of the physical and spiritual joy of living, polygamy is an honorable estate, and man's spirit is eternal] therefore no one's soul is in jeopardy. Tongola's problem with Sulamai, then, is not one of sin; it is more serious than that, for through her "self-expressing" she has succeeded in disrupting the cosmic harmony, and Tongola's problem is one of cosmic necessity. Although Jim is a Christian preacher, he admits to Kanda, when she brings him the note that bans Sulamai from Pilgrim worship, "I felt something was wrong, the night I was there" (II.i.7), and Kanda assures him that unless he takes Sulamai away quickly, Tongola will take her away with him. Clearly, the restoration of cosmic harmony is imperative and will be achieved by the departing prophet.

Later, when Moses meets Sulamai at Toomer's Bottom, it is his desire to protect her from Tongola's wrath that underlies his insistence on asking the prophet's permission to leave the Pilgrims. He is overwhelmed by his desire to touch her, but dares not, and when Sulamai states that she "ain't never gointer be 'fraid o' no dead" (II.i.21), lightning flashes and thunder rolls [the voices of God] and Moses implores her to stop talking. [Note that he is not concerned with her unexpressed thoughts; it is the power of the spoken word he fears since good or bad is expressed only in action, and words have the creative power of action.] He is also aghast at her demand that he "don't ask nobody nothin'" and bursts out, "little fool, you will destroy yourself" (II.i.22). But Sulamai, in her ignorance, is adamant.

It is also interesting that in the black Christian community it is only Sulamai who is ostracized as a harlot while Jim is excused. He is considered to be a "good boy" except in regard to this sin of adultery. Several factors no doubt contribute to this, his socioeconomic position as the minister's son and as a preacher himself, his own popularity and that of his suffering wife, and established Western religious and cultural sex discrimination. The community's judgment of him also suggests the survival of African ethics in Afro-America [a definition of good and bad, not in the abstract but solely in terms of performance]. This does not however extend to Sulamai who is considered to be a seductress—an instrument of the devil.

The last scene of the play, which takes place entirely during revival service in Hope Baptist Church, contains both effective contrasts and similarities to the Pilgrims' worship scene. The Christian worship occurs in the man-made temple of God while the Pilgrim worship takes place in the natural temple of God; there is a terrific thunder storm whipping itself up throughout the entire revival service, which is in sharp contrast to the soft, clear moonlight that enchants the joyful pagan worshippers in the woods; and ritual dance has been eliminated from the Christian form of worship. On the other hand, there are striking similarities in structural composition and progression, in the repetition of motifs, in the techniques of the pagan and Christian preachers, and in the survival of many African cultural elements in the black Christian worship.

In the Pilgrim scene, Moses had stood on a raised platform before the worshippers, flanked by Tongola and Kanda, with Reba seated submissively at her mother's feet. In the church, Reverend Jones is also on a raised level, flanked by Reverend Allen and Sister Strong, the lady evangelist who, like Tongola, is "packing them in" with her message. At the foot of the platform before the mourners' bench, Reba's counterpart, the absent, wayward Jim, is replaced by a sinner who lies prostrate on the floor, praying submissively for spiritual guidance. The church, like the woods worship, is well attended and the congregation similarly mills around in relaxed, communal friendliness until the service begins. The flappers' row in the church reflects the group of young Pilgrims who eagerly awaited their turn to dance, and Moses' call for converts has its counterpart in Reverend Jones' call for testimony; even the motif of blindness is twice repeated, once in the initial hymn, and again when a blind man is led to his seat.

Corresponding to the initial ritual chant of the Pilgrims, the hymn lined out by Reverend Allen is *Amazing Grace:* "I once was lost, but now I'm found, was blind, but now I see" (A.II.ii.2), and the call–response participation of the congregation is immediately launched and continues throughout the service. After Reverend Jones welcomes the congregation and announces the achievements of the revival in terms of souls saved, he requests Sister Strong to begin by approaching the throne, which she does in song and prayer, reflecting another Pilgrim motif: Tongola is to depart at midnight in a storm while Sister Strong [using the same divine vehicles as the African God] sees Jesus "Comin' in de lightnin' / Comin' in de thunder" (II.ii.3). She lacks Tongola's power of direct thought transmission, and perhaps the author intended to suggest some loss of the force vitale in the process of Westernization, but she is a powerful talker. She, like Moses,

thanks God for life, but in contrast to his cosmic, joy-of-living doctrine her entire preoccupation is with death—that time of reckoning,
of rejoicing, and of reward for delayed gratification. In the Hope
Baptist congregation all effort is directed toward acquiring the
strength to fight the devil's temptation for the purpose of achieving
heavenly reward, thus the time for rejoicing differs radically from that
of the Pilgrims [whose African doctrine supports immediate gratifica-
tion]. Sister Strong's imagery is also about as concrete as it can get: her
thanks for continued life are that her "bed was not [her] coolin' bo'd"
and her "kivver" her "windin'-sheet"; they are all "graveyard
travellers" (II.ii.3), but look forward to a "mornin' of everlastin' re-
joicin'" (II.ii.4).

After her down-to-earth prayer, Reverend Jones calls for testimony
from his congregation and he, like Moses, has his legend and his
stylized, heroic imagery as he addresses "the old members, those
warriors in the fiel'—true an' tried soldiers—battle scarred heroes of
many a bloody battle with Satan" (I.ii.4). The theme of the testimony
is, of course, individual salvation, but it is enacted with the same
spectacular abandon as the Pilgrims' worship. A steady stream of
testifiers, together with the rest of the congregation, sing, pray, hum,
sit, stand, walk around, applaud, greet, congratulate, shake hands,
scream, gesticulate, laugh, wave their arms and rock rhythmically,
proclaim brotherly love, shout at the devil, throw fits, faint, fan each
other, holler hallelujahs, and achieve several spiritual possessions.
Brother Abergail flies like a bird down the aisle and around the
church, and the prostrate sinner, who suddenly finds religion, is
ecstatically resurrected—his spiritual possession foreshadows Jim's
rebirth. [Here individual, Christian salvation, African communality,
and multiple African modes of reflecting total man in his relationship
to his God, combine with spectacular vitality; spirituality is physically
reflected, and spirit possession is multiply achieved.]

When Ella testifies about her three days of prayin' and fastin' for
Jim's salvation she is the focus of excited attention. Her testimony and
that of the other testifiers are psychological titillators, every bit as
effective and as dramatic as the seductive dances at Brother Moses'
meeting. When Jim enters the church, as if in answer to Ella's prayer,
the excitement is so high that someone starts a song to save him
embarrassment. The song, composed by Hall Johnson, reflects the
title of the play, "Oh run little chillun' run / 'Cause de devil done loose
in de lan'" (II.ii.8), and it reflects the degree of emotional turmoil in
the congregation; but as an added, almost clandestine, recognition of

the sacred centrality of African rhythm in worship, someone in the
Amen corner rises and vigorously taps out the song's rhythm!

Reverend Jones' sermon, which follows, is, like that of Moses, an
unmistakable product of the African oral tradition. His initial theme is
forgiveness of sinners, as clothed in the parable of the lost sheep; its
topicality and applicability to the existing situation [requirements
in the African oral tradition] are unquestionable. His dialogue is a
rhythmic, poetic vernacular and he immediately engages his congregation in the communal experience with a question.

> Do y'all think, when the shepherd lef' the ninety an' nine safe
> in fol' and went on out into de chilly hills to fin' de po' little lam'
> that had gone astray—I say, do you think he was so made that he
> felt like jumpin' on the hepless creatur and stompin' half to death?
> (A.II.ii.9)

The responsive "no indeeds" and "God forbids" of the congregation
are positive indicators of his success. [Note also in this short excerpt
his picturesque turn of phrase, his concrete, kinetic imagery, his
dramatic pause for deliberation, and the emphasis he achieves by
repetition, all African oral techniques.] Reverend Jones is indeed a
veteran of the oral tradition and soon has a chance to prove it, for
his intended sermon is just getting under way when Sulamai, accompanied by the rising storm, makes her unexpected entry. With the
improvisational virtuosity of his ancestor, the raconteur, Reverend
Jones makes an immediate switch from the forgiveness of sinners to
the damnation of tempters, continuing almost without a falter.

"When a speaker possesses visionary ecstasy," Arthur L. Smith
points out in his discussion of Nommo, "he is far more effective than
syllogistic reasoning."[7] Hall Johnson's preacher possesses both
visionary ecstasy and the African based expertise of the black gospel
preacher, and he battles the devil for the soul of his son, assisted by an
enraptured and responsive congregation. Sulamai is now his primary
target:

> An o-o-oh you women, who ain' satisfied unless you runnin'
> from one man to de other . . . try-y-yin' to lead him astray.
> (Worshipper shakes her finger at Sulamai "Tha's you!").
> O-o-oh you big-breasted daughters of Babylon, who ain' never
> learned to respec' the sanctity of the marriage bed . . .
> (Shakes finger).
> O-o-oh you filthy spawn of Jezebel, you black blood-hounds of

Satan who . . . brings the foul stench of yo' deeds . . . into the very
Holy of Holies . . . to make God's house yo' cruisin' groun'.
(Tha's you!)
How do you think, you gointer face a jus' an' angry God in that
mo'nin'? (A.II.ii.11)

Reverend Jones' charismatic outburst [his sustained thematic dominance; his concrete imagery; his exaggeration, coupled with the
alliterative intensity and rhythmic quality of his language which rises
almost to a scream, accompanied by gesticulation; and his direct,
interrogative involvement of Sulamai—all African oral techniques]
creates a performance of overwhelming virtuosity, seldom matched
in sermons under lengthy preparation. Bursting into sobs, Sulamai
rushes out into the storm, followed by a compassionate Jim, whereupon Reverend Jones, shaken by his own effectiveness [the divine
creative power of Nommo] resorts to prayer for divine intervention.

Tongola also intends divine intervention to restore universal rhythmic harmony.

Reverend Jones now prays for Jim's salvation with fervent communal support, and he prays for mercy for "dis little Magdalene dis
po', hepless instrument of Satan" (A.II.ii.13), and the moment his
Christian charity includes Sulamai divine intervention he gets and
Jim, miraculously released from sinful urges, comes charging up the
aisle proclaiming his rebirth amidst song, hallelujahs, and general
pandemonium. Reverend Jones' inspired performance would now
seem to be crowned with success, but the spectacle is not yet over, for
the dramatist's major concern is not with Jim's salvation but with his
theme [the dominant element in the African oral tradition], Jim has
made resolutions before to reform and has wavered in his determination, and the little Magdalene is still at large.

Sulamai now makes her last mad dash up the church aisle, embraces
Jim, and retreats as a momentary hush envelops the scandalized
congregation. But before she can reach the church door lightning from
the smashing storm that brought Jesus to Sister Strong and will take
Tongola to higher planes strikes Sulamai dead in the aisle, while
Moses is silhouetted in the church window, *in an aura of Pilgrim music
which blends and harmonizes with the Christian song within.*

At this point the author footnotes his finale with the question:
"Who is revenged Jehovah or Tongola?"

Hall Johnson's opposition of the African and European philosophic
elements that comprise the Afro-American culture is stunning; each is

stated, and they are then synthesized in Hope Baptist Church. *Run Little Chillun'* is truly the story of the sorrow songs which "from the accumulated torrents of your tears of sorrow . . . the deep throated cries of your most bitter anguish . . ." pour forth to swell the church to the limit of its rhythmic spatial content.

But the ultimate synthesis that is sheer, thematically controlled genius is the finale which so spectacularly fulfils Moses' early proclamation that "God is One." Whether the lightning has spoken for Jehovah or for the God of Africa, the response is the same, and Hall Johnson leaves us with the burst of recognition that God is, indeed, One. It has not been possible to determine whether the Federal Theatre's audience was aware of the dramatist's final question, but whether it was or not his intent is clear for it is inherent in the dramatization. Johnson's last question, however, phrases his synthesis for the reader in its most thought-provoking form [the interrogative technique of the African oral tradition] and undoubtedly it contributed a valuable key for the effective dramatization of his play.

To be sure, Hall Johnson was not the only black playwright to dramatize either the survival or the seductive appeal of African cosmological elements in Afro-American culture. In *The Divine Comedy*[8] black playwright Owen Dodson brilliantly dramatized the creative power of Nommo used by the charismatic evangelist, Father Divine, at the height of the Depression to unite the deprived and disillusioned of both races in an enormous illusion of Heaven on earth. Father Divine's blending of illusion and reality is also highly reminiscent of Pirandello, and Dodson's selection and dramatization of it suggests that perhaps he saw common ground between the roots of black drama and the commedia del' arte that were well worth exploring. Nevertheless, no black playwright of the thirties so spectacularly dramatized the fusion of the African and Western elements that comprise the Afro-American culture as did Hall Johnson. With his play, the Afro-American playwright achieved the dramatic internationalism that is his heritage.

It is remarkable that Hall Johnson's play was not generally recognized as something highly experimental that far surpassed the dramatization of "perennial voodoo." Of its New York critics, Kenneth Burke probably came closest to a glimmer of its dramatic achievement as "an insight into a way of life."[9] Los Angeles was enchanted with it in 1938, but critics there came only a shade nearer to understanding its experimental signifiance.[10] Yet this is perhaps not so remarkable, since the recognition of experimental theater as such, or even of realism as such, depends largely on the orientation of its interpreters. Aristotelian philosophy, which generally defines Western art as an imitation of life based on probability, separates art from life and imposes limitations on the dramatization of life's infinite possibilities; it also states what manipulation of the possible is necessary, namely the achievement of a semblance of probability, and experimental manipulation in these terms would be the expectation of a Western audience. But African art and life are not separable and African art is bound by no such limitations; it is a dynamic manifestation of life qualities, regardless of probability. To an uninformed Westerner, therefore, dramatization in African terms might violate the expectation of probability and might well be unbelievable. But in addition, a manifestation of life qualities in action that did not happen to violate probability, although highly experimental as drama, might well be viewed as pure realism, precisely because its total and spontaneous mode of expression might give the impression that it really lives.

Evidence that this type of experimentation by black dramatists was not fully understood comes unexpectedly from Hallie Flanagan, the muse of Federal Theatre experimental drama. Her comment on the production of Gus Smith's *Turpentine* is intriguing. "While the writing lacked fluency," she wrote, "the production possessed breathtaking fervor . . . in this production the Negro is not exotic. Plain working people and their problems are movingly dramatized."[11] Hallie Flanagan here echoes a disposition of the past—and one which still persists—to glorify the black performer while underestimating the creative ability of the black dramatist. If the dialogue lacked fluency by educated Western standards, it was wholly appropriate to Smith's characters, who had been denied education, and uncharacteristic perfection in the dialogue would have been a technique scorned by the best African raconteurs. What it did reflect was many characteristics of African thought and speech, such as the concrete, kinetic, poetic, rhythmic, picturesque elements that have given black English its great vitality. Other elements, such as Smith's sophisticated translation of African drum rhythms into the beat of his hoopers' hammers, were quite exotic. It is significant, too, that Smith included in his script brief character sketches for his actors, and that when he directed his own play he insured that the quality of spontaneity dominated. Both in his script and in production he avoided crossing the vital boundary of encroachment on "the breath-taking fervor" of living drama, and perhaps Hallie Flanagan—at least through her familiarity with the commedia dell' arte[12] if not with African cosmology—should have recognized the playwright's intention to achieve character assimilation and spontaneous interpretation, rather than imitation. The final product was so effective and memorable, Hallie Flanagan also reported that repercussions "were heard in Congress, where two years later on February 27, 1938 Senator Russell of Georgia . . . criticized [the Federal Theatre for staging] the production."[13]

There is no doubt the black dramatists of the thirties were engaged in a form of dramatic experimentation that was not familiar to Western culture, and it was this experimentation, rather than the proficiency they achieved with the Euro-American dramatic modes and techniques, that was their greatest achievement. They introduced and synthesized elements of their African heritage with those of the West to create an Afro-American idiom which expressed the living qualities of the Afro-American experience.

Natural Man.
John Henry (Joseph Straton) at extreme right, observes with growing disgust the idleness of the hoboes.

The Trial of Dr. Beck.
George Doolittle (Slim Mason) prayin' and shuckin' to the Judge (Clifford Dempsey) as District Attorney Madison (Frank Harrington) prepares to question him.

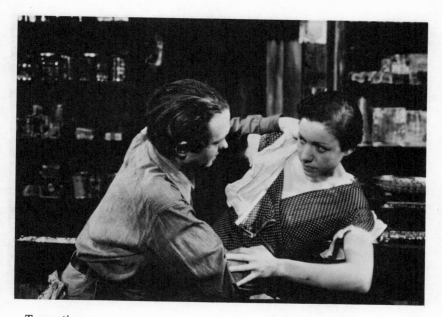

Turpentine.

Cap'n Sap (Thurman Jackson) attacks Sissy Jones (Muriel Mc Crory) in her cabin. In a moment the women of the camp will enter, and rout Sap's attack.

Run Little Chillun'.

Sula Mae (Florence O'Brien) refuses Jim's (Alfred Grant) offer to carry her North on the "matrimonial special." She intends to stay here in Toomers Bottom and flaunt Jim's baby in the faces of the good Baptists.

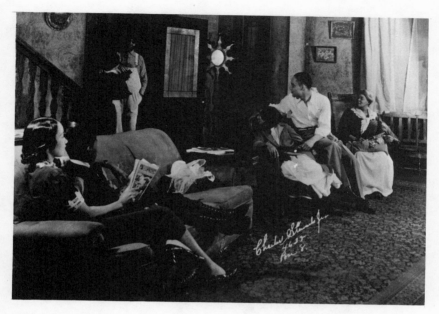

Big White Fog.
The Mason family. Vic Mason (William McBride) is greeted at the door by his wife, Ella (Gladys Boucree). On the left, Wanda (Alice Brooks) and Philip (Woodrow Wilson). Right, Caroline (Helen Howard), Les (Thomas Preston), and Mrs. Brooks (Isabell Futrell).

Black Empire.
Rigaud (Joseph Albert Smith) threatening the life of the crippled Emperor Christophe (Joseph Straton). In a moment the Frenchman Jacques will relieve Rigaud of his pistol with a sword thrust.

TEN

IDENTITY, OR BLACK RACISM IN BLACK DRAMA

OF THE THIRTIES?

I N THE FIRST three decades of the twentieth century, racism in American drama had been the exclusive prerogative of the white stage. The white superiority myths that had dictated the inferior roles to be played by blacks in real life had also established the stage images, and black dramatists who had either the financial need or the hope of getting their plays produced had no opportunity to indulge in overt racism. In the thirties, the economic support of the Federal Theatre and its professed dedication to artistic freedom did relax this straightjacket; while some of the black-authored plays still failed to reach the footlights, both these and the plays that were produced certainly projected very different images than had been established by the white stage.

There is no denying that the black playwrights' departure from established white standards did, at the very least, challenge the singularity of those standards, while some of the plays exposed, even ridiculed white ethical practices; the author of *Natural Man* even went so far as to create a revolutionary hero who challenged their superiority—a challenge that was also unmistakable in *Big White Fog*. As we have noted, critics interpreted John Henry's anger as being directed at the "forces of mechanization," no doubt because of the ambiguities of the dual communication system, but one reviewer of *Big White Fog*, while staunchly supporting the author's right to "free speech on stage or off," also recorded that there had been serious efforts made to persuade the mayor of Chicago to stop the production, and one of the reasons stated was that it was believed to incite "race prejudice."[1] A review, written in the same vein, reported "weeks of backstage whispers concerning the play's subversive influence and its tendency to fan into white heat again embers of racial strife";[2] and Sterling Brown noted that "because of Mr. Ward's frankness in discussing the race problem, policemen and censors were on hand prepared to quell a riot."[3] To be sure, the term racism was not actually used by the white reviewers, for the days of such direct confrontation had not yet arrived, but their method of suggestion parallels the style

113

noted by Doris Abramson in which white critics denigrated the work of black playwrights through "tone" and "innuendo."[4]

But could such challenges to white racism by black playwrights of the thirties be considered, by any stretch of the imagination, black racism?

Actually, W. E. B. Du Bois had accurately pinpointed the black dilemma—which included the dilemma of the black dramatist: "Can I not be both a Negro and an American?"[5] and the answer to his question, of course, depends entirely on the definition of *an American*. America does not comprise a homogeneous population which is either, all white, or even white oriented; yet the definition of an American has traditionally been dominated by the white superiority myth, and black recognition of this deficiency in the national image is powerfully reflected both in Du Bois' question and in the words of Malcolm X, "everything that came out of Europe, every blue-eyed thing is already an American."[6]

The dilemma of the black dramatist of the thirties was very real. Could he not project his non-white identity and cultural orientation without being, by definition, "unAmerican"? Could he not, instead of reflecting the white aesthetic that black was ugly and evil, project his belief in the beauty of blackness without being considered racist? It seems that we must now attempt to separate those elements that reflect black racial and cultural identity from those that might be defined as racism, so that we can place the images projected by the black-authored plays of the thirties in their proper perspective. While I do not presume by any stretch of the imagination to offer a definition of Afro-American identity, I shall attempt to enumerate its major sources and show something of the experiences and the synthesizing process which have produced that identity; the vital components of racial identity—or of racism—may then become clear in the plays.

Certainly, the Afro-American is no longer the pure, seventeenth- or eighteenth-century African who was panyared and brought to American shores. In addition to a liberal injection of non-African blood— and indeed the blood of all the world's continents flows in Afro-American veins—his orientation has undergone considerable modification; it is therefore no idle claim that his twentieth-century cultural identity has been derived from many sources. The most basic of these is the common human heritage; the second, his African cultural inheritance; the third, the Western modifications it has undergone, whether through force or through choice; the fourth, his Afro-American experience; and these are still further modified by the

Afro–West Indian influence, considered in Chapter Twelve, and by a host of minor influences, too numerous to explore in detail.

The first of these, the common human heritage, is the capacity of the human self for rational deduction and self-appraisal, and its flower is the recognition of human right to human dignity and equality. This is well expressed in the words of Le Roi Jones (Imamu Amiri Baraka), who was speaking on the Black Arts Movement: "we are preaching virtue and feeling and the natural sense of the self in the world. All men live in the world, and the world ought to be a place for them to live."[7] Today, this conviction is being proclaimed and fought for by oppressed peoples worldwide, but it is as old as man's ability to evaluate his relationship to nature and to other men. Thirteen hundred and eighty years before Jesus of Nazareth commanded brotherly love, the Pharoah, Ikhnaton, sacrificed an empire to teach that Egyptians and Asiatics were all children of the same benevolent father-creator; in Africa, it was expressed cosmologically by belief in the divinity of the human spirit; it was proclaimed by Christian abolitionists and slave orators in the Western hemisphere; and in this century, it has been preached from the black American pulpit and demanded by black intellectuals like W. E. B. Du Bois, Marcus Garvey, Alain Locke, and Baraka. In his *Foreword to Panyared*, Hughes Allison applied this doctrine to drama, to lay upon the black dramatist the function of an educator and the responsibility of insuring audience understanding through the projection of Afro-American genesis.[8] In *Panyared*, his African slave–prince placed such a value on his white owner's daughter that he jeopardized his own life to save hers. In *Natural Man*, Theodore Browne dramatized this doctrine through his legendary steel-driver, who declared that God "meant for every man to be a king" (375). It is a vision of human dignity and equality that is directly opposed to racism.

The major elements of the second source of Afro-American identity, the traditional African heritage, have already been enumerated, and their survival in black American culture was recorded by several black dramatists. It was brilliantly dramatized in *Run Little Chillun'*, but Hall Johnson's play also acknowledged that many of the African elements had been modified while others had been almost entirely replaced by Western customs—the third source of Afro-American identity.

Among the major modifications to the African heritage has been the replacement of the African languages with English, but with the words still dynamically structured within the African mode of thought and expression.[9] Afro-American English has also retained the rhythmic quality of traditional African speech, the concrete and kinetic imagery,[10] the asymmetry in prose and verse—readily identifiable in the spirituals—the liberal use of verbal nouns and nouns created from verbs,[11] and many African words which, conversely, have been adopted by American English.[12] In black English, traditional English has also been modified by inversion, inflation, and other such means of negating its inherently white racist definitions.[13]

For literary purposes, the written word has replaced the African oral tradition although many of the traditional techniques are still used. The black epic is now the product of individual creation, not of accretion, and theme, plot, characterization, and dialogue are locked in to a specific environment, time, and set of circumstances by the finality of the written word. The Afro-American dramatist, one of the heirs of the African raconteur, is thus no longer the dramatic projector of his own story but, like the Euro-American dramatist, must work through actors—dynamically defined as "liberators" by Barbara Ann Teer—to create his communal experience. Since his creation can no longer be spontaneously altered by him in immediate response to audience reaction, audience participation is now also partially controlled and the Western stage technology and props that accompany this form of drama have also been adopted.

Afro-American music, which has probably retained more of the African spirituality and force vitale than any other Afro-American art, has nevertheless experienced modifications. Western musical instruments, with emphasis on percussion instruments, have been added to the African, and are used as extensions of the vocal and drum rhythms.[14] But written music has also taken its place beside the soul-releasing improvisation that still basically characterizes black music, and it imposes on its creators limitations similar to those of written literature.

Afro-Americans were also forced to accept drastic modifications to their African cosmological orientation as they became increasingly involved in the industrial complexes of a scientifically rather than a metaphysically based world.

It is noteworthy—because it stresses the inevitability of change when science and cosmology clash—that the same problems of industrial reorientation that had to be worked out by Afro-Americans are currently being experienced by emerging African states. Many of those states, whose population explosions have largely resulted from the disruption of their natural order by Western medical technology, have of necessity embraced Western industrial technology to feed their increased populations, and John S. Mbiti has pointed out some of the effects of this. Separation from the land—which to the traditional African ranks next to God in cosmological importance—has been a major dislocation; it has also entailed separation from the ancestral spirits and the loss of pre-established function both in the rhythmic universal harmony and in the communal agrarian society that reflects it. The concentration of displaced people in an impersonal, urban atmosphere, far from communal controls, has resulted in widespread anomie, while the adoption of time as an impersonal, saleable commodity has caused a disruption of the process of creative living.[15] In some African states where industrial dislocation is accompanied by the added burden of white domination, the crisis has been even more acute and a sense of hopeless entrapment has promoted both drunkenness and crime. Paul Bohannan has recorded that even the impact of the introduction of money as a means of exchange among the Tiv of Nigeria took its toll of their scale of values, and of the rights and dignity of their women; it nullified the traditional form of marriage exchange that set on Tiv women the very highest value, for formerly "the only 'price' of one woman [had been] another woman."[16]

All of these problems, caused by the encroachment of Western science on African cosmology, have been experienced by Afro-Americans, who have endured double cultural fragmentation, first through their displacement from the freedom of the African homeland and its cosmological associations to the debasement of slavery on American plantations and then by their compression into industrial and urban ghettos. The acceptance of three-dimensional time, which was forced more by the second upheaval, made the Afro-American no longer its creator, yet it also permitted, even necessitated, future planning—to the extent of revolution and nation-building.[17] Event-oriented time, or c.p.t.[18] does still exist in black America, particularly in rural areas and in the world of the ghetto hustler,[19] but to twentieth century Afro-Americans time is predominantly an impersonal commodity to be sold, rather than a cosmic, creative act.

The encroachments of Christian theology, which date back to the early period of black enslavement, preceded even these exacting industrial demands. For the majority of Afro-Americans who have accepted Christianity—even for most of those who have rejected it, but who have been reared in its value system—man's spirit is no longer divine; man no longer partakes of the object of his worship—the uncreated which becomes temporarily incarnate in living man—but has become a lesser creature, dependent on the good will of his creator. The Christian concept of godly love paved the way for a host of other abstractions, such as the concept of good and evil as distinct from their practice, while the concept of personal salvation introduced and fostered introspection, individuality, and egocentricity. Stemming from the individuality of Christian salvation and its derivative political system of individual rights rather than communal duties, vocations are no longer subject to communal approval or common welfare, they result from personal choice.

In spite of these disruptions, the black Church has miraculously succeeded in retaining much of the African form of communal, creative expression in its worship, and this has left its stamp on black politics, art, and culture in general. Afro-Americans have become increasingly aware of the dangers of fragmentation and inhibition that accompany Western Protestantism and that threaten their natural sense of self in the world, and as a result concerted efforts to guard against further encroachments by Western ideologies have been made through renewed emphasis on traditional African values.[20] But even if a wholesale repudiation of Christianity and its value system occurred, as long as Afro-Americans continue to live in a scientific, techno-logical, competitive system based on individual rights, those modifications which it entails will be irreversible.

The range of African beliefs and customs that have been affected by this reorientation is immeasurable; those mentioned by no means represent an exhaustive list, but they may give some indication of the magnitude of the synthesizing process that has produced twen-tieth century Afro-American identity. Under the conditions of American slavery, and later in urban industrial centers and ghettos, most of the customs of the African inheritance could not survive in their pure forms: what did survive to a remarkable degree was that sense of cosmic spiritual harmony and creative vitality that pro-jects the essence of the black man's being in all his forms of expression.

Perhaps the most painful element in the synthesizing process that has produced twentieth-century Afro-American identity has been the imposition of white Western aesthetic standards, for not only the doctrine of white supremacy, but even the English language pro-claimed the aesthetic superiority of white over black, and this had a devastating impact on the black American's self-image. The "Black is Beautiful" movement, which has achieved such spectacular success, was a direct response to the derogatory white aesthetic; but the slogan can hardly be considered racist, for unlike the white aesthetic, it makes a positive, not a comparative, statement.

Another painful element in the Afro-American synthesizing process has been the continuing conflict of ethical systems. The Black Arts Movement of the sixties proclaimed "that your ethics and aesthetics are one"[21] but while his African ancestors reflected abstract qualities in traditional African art and the Afro-American himself has generally accepted abstraction for scientific, educational, and such utilitarian purposes, he still rejects the notion that right and wrong have any real meaning as abstractions separated from practice: for him, equality and brotherhood are ultimately equality and brotherhood only if they are practiced. This conviction is also at the core of the contemporary effort to stimulate black consciousness of traditional values, but such efforts did not originate with the Black Arts Movement; this doctrine has been preached in the West as long as there have been black intellectuals to deplore white double standards.

But African ethics have been as distasteful to white twentieth-century Americans as Western ethics have been to Afro-Americans, for they force the white American into a defensive, often untenable, position which he resents since they expose the inherent conflict in Western ethics between the separation of the abstract from the concrete and the ethics actually taught by Christ, in terms of performance. The Westerner's defense then is often attack; for example, the classic white defense of the Western enslavement of blacks is, "But didn't the African, in Africa, also practice slavery? And didn't he sell his own brothers into slavery? Was that ethical?" There is, however, an implicit presumption in this question that is very misleading. It does not judge the white enslavement of Africans by white ethical standards, and the African enslavement of Africans by African ethical standards, it presumes identical ethical standards—the white—in both cases.

Certainly slavery was practiced within the African states. This was acknowledged by Allison in *Panyared* when his prince hero, Bombo, was seized together with his slave, Kito. But slavery in Africa could result from a number of entirely ethical causes based in the religious cosmology: conquest, default of payment of various forms, voluntary bondage contracted in time of famine or other want, exchange as family collateral, and legal or ethical retribution,[22] which were one and the same. It could also result from unethical causes, which in African metaphysics, however, was an error in spiritual judgment that demanded moral and legal retribution. In the ethical forms of African slavery, the master assumed all legal responsibility for his

slave and his slave's actions, except for the performance of his servi-
tude. Even after he was transplanted to the American plantation,
Bombo, Allison's African prince, never ceased to feel responsible for
his slave Kito, and he pleaded for his slave's release from white
bondage when he was granted his own freedom. The slave in Africa
played a specific role in the cosmic harmony and could and often did
achieve wealth, fame, or leadership.[23] August Meier points out that
the children of slaves were often adopted into the master's family,
thereby achieving free status, and "among the Dahomeans, kings
sometimes selected the son of a favorite slave wife to succeed to the
throne."[24] Thus, regardless of the hardships that occurred in some
African slave systems, the professed ethics and practices were not at
odds. In addition, the Africans on the other side of "the water that
never ends" had no earthly concept of what Western slavery entailed,
and into what total dehumanization they were selling their brothers.

On the other hand, the white men who fomented African tribal
warfare, who seized and bought blacks, who transported them to the
West in the stench of filth and death, and who owned and worked
slaves on their plantations, were bound by a different ethical standard, that of Christianity, which even God-fearing Christians succeeded in separating in the abstract from their actions. Western
slavery was hardly ever interpreted as moral error and it was protected
and enforced by laws passed by Christians and was even sanctioned
by the church. The basic conflict between the abstract and the concrete
in Western ethics then proliferated into a myriad of other conflicting
beliefs and actions. For example the black was categorized as intellectually deficient, yet the slave-owners feared to allow him to learn to
read; he was treated like an animal, yet the church was anxious to save
his soul; black females were used in their human capacity for their
masters' sexual gratification, yet white owners deliberately, even personally, impregnated them for the purpose of increasing their property, and this gave rise to the ultimate in Christian moral perversion,
for the white masters then owned, repudiated, and sold their own
sons and daughters, all strictly within the law.[25] This immoral and
debasing practice, in its own ethical terms, was dramatized by Frank
B. Wells, whose play, *John Henry*, was produced by the Federal
Theatre in 1936, and Sterling Brown commented on the "surprising"
insight of this young white Southerner.[26]

Clearly, the basic difference between Western ethics and Afro-
American ethics—the separation or non-separation of good and evil
in the abstract from their practice—is not academic, it is real and

far-reaching, and it would be unrealistic to expect the black dramatist to reflect the two ethics as identical, or even compatible, but this could hardly be interpreted as racism.

It would also be unrealistic to expect him to reflect what he has experienced of the West's practice of its professed Christian ethics as superior, and it is experience that is the fourth source of twentieth-century Afro-American identity.

Even in post-slavery America the myths and ethics of white superiority supported various forms of black oppression and debasement and most major black problems, both inside and outside the black community, stem from them. As a result no authentic dramatization of black identity could ignore their consequences.

The myth of white superiority demanded that black males show the correct subservient attitude to whites. In *The Trial of Dr. Beck*, Inspector O'Malley is outraged by what he considers the ''smartness'' of Beck's colored defense attorney while questioning him, and in *Turpentine*, this is reflected in Sap's complaint that Forty-Four and Shine are not to be trusted since they never drop their eyes. Black males were prohibited from hitting back, either in self-defense or to protect their women. Big Sue's father and brother were lynched for doing so, and it is the women in *Turpentine*, who, en masse, route Sap's attack on Sissy although her husband was carrying a gun. Inferior education for the express purpose of maintaining a low-paid labor force also made it impossible for black males to support their families. Writing about conditions in the ''Black Belt,'' W. E. B. Du Bois states

> young men marry between the ages of 25 and 35, and young women between 20 and 30. Such postponement is due to the difficulty of earning sufficient to rear and support a family and it undoubtedly leads, in the country districts, to sexual immorality.[27]

This condition is reflected in the suffering of the blacks in *Turpentine*, and in their determination to achieve a livable wage and an education for their children. Du Bois further notes, ''the unwritten law of the black districts and small towns of the South [is] that the character of all Negroes unknown to the mass of the community must be vouched for by some white man,''[28] and the overall effect of these various forms of degradation and oppression was a virtual state of black male castration. Loss of dignity, self-respect, and confidence did promote servility, but they also nurtured frustration and mounting anger, which were devastating to black family and community relations.

This bottled anger sometimes exploded in self-destructive forms, such as drunkenness—in *Big White Fog*, which will be discussed in detail, this anger keeps Uncle Percy a perpetual cabaret bum. Often it exploded against available members of the family, or in forms that jeopardized black or white communities. Joseph Cotter's Caleb, violently resentful of God, fate, and the social order, steals, sniffs cocaine, slays his father, drives his mother to her death, and destroys himself; in *St. Louis Woman*, Biglow's anger and violence bring about his murder; while in *Go Down Moses*, Harriet Tubman, who is leading Cumbo north to freedom, is tragically forced to shoot the angry mulatto giant, when he rebels against her leadership and jeopardizes the safety of her other passengers. The violence of castration thus bred violence, and a deep psychological need for black males to prove their manhood.[29] Black intellectuals were greatly concerned with this problem, and this need motivates Thea Dugger, in *Bad Man*, and a host of other heroes of black drama.

But the black male's inability to support his family had other devastating effects. Black wives and mothers, driven by dire economic necessity, became both breadwinners and homemakers, and thus the dominant figures in black households, and this further affected the male self-image and promoted bitter family resentments. The father image was also debased and distorted, which had its effect on future generations, for male children grew up with an intensified need to prove their manhood and reject their fathers' subservience. The effects of these needs are poignantly reflected in *Big White Fog*. Yet the breaking of the mold was an almost hopeless venture, for the white superiority myths not only established racist criteria of excellence, but imposed restrictions on their attainment by blacks. In *The Trial of Dr. Beck* Hughes Allison dramatizes the fact that in spite of his brilliance, Dr. Beck is forced into a loveless marriage and is motivated to advocate race dilution for the sake of race survival—a doctrine that makes him a prime murder suspect.

In the words of W. E. B. Du Bois, white America had established "eternal segregation in the Lord!"[30] and it was a pattern of the black experience that not even the industrial demands of two World Wars was able to break. Black labor, recruited throughout the South, poured into the Northern industrial centers, but soon found itself compressed into segregated ghettos where The Man continued to dominate the quality of black life. Here, white property owners charged their captive tenants exorbitant rents for cramped, unsanitary, rat-infested housing devoid of privacy; white merchants engaged in every known form of exploitation;[31] and in these cauldrons of thwarted ambition and seething anger there was no escape, and no physical, psychological, or cultural outlet, except in the black churches or in violence. Streets and alleys were the only places where the young could fraternize, and the formation of gangs and the pursuit of warfare and other antisocial behavior was inevitable.

Inevitably, too, this was interpreted as evidence of the black's inferiority and lawlessness, and the result was increased police activity and more discriminatory laws and law enforcement. Penalties for theft in the ghettos generally depended on who committed it, exploiters or exploited; landlords, merchants, and other white hustlers squeezed and thieved the black out of existence, while retaliatory theft on his part was punished severely. Theft, therefore, became a moral and justified method of retribution and equalization, and a necessity to survival, for the black ghetto male was now engaged in a fight, not only to prove his manhood, but even to preserve his right to existence, and he soon came to look upon the law enforcement officer as the living symbol of injustice.

All of these elements—the oppression, the exploitation, the anger, the frustration, the retaliation—were reflected in the black plays of the thirties because they were authentic dramatizations of the Afro-American experience, not because their authors chose to counter racism with racism. The authors of *Liberty Deferred* and *Big White Fog* even dramatized the fact that Afro-American males had fought in several wars to protect the very freedom and equality that were still denied them, and they dramatized the effects of such injustice and rejection on the black self-image.

Even today there are white Americans who are loath to accept responsibility for white America's historical actions and who would exclude from black plays all the effects of past oppression, on the ground that those conditions no longer exist. The justification goes something like this: "I have never oppressed anyone. We have now given the Negro freedom, protective laws, education, social welfare, and all sorts of other costly support, what more does he want? Why can't he begin now from scratch and make his own way?"

But what is scratch to the white American has not been, and still is not, scratch to the black. Is it scratch, even today, when blacks swell the ranks of the unemployed in disproportionate numbers? Is it scratch when a white middle-class population, already firmly established culturally and economically on the fruits of black labor, enters the job market with superior skills, money, and family backing to tide over

the rough spots, and the proverbial Anglo-Saxon school-tie contacts?
Is the housing prejudice, that still largely pins blacks to the protective
safety of the filthy, overcrowded ghettos, scratch? Perhaps these questions will emphasize that it is not just the angle or mode of the
Afro-American's perception that differs from that of the white American, but the very reality that is perceived.

Dramatization in the thirties was in terms of the reality perceived
and lived, and even the few blacks—like Dr. Beck—who were shown
to cross the social or economic lines to success, served as reminders to
their communities that the lines still existed; often, they also served as
reminders of the penalties extracted for success, and the price was
high in terms of the black self-image since it included, at the very
least, an admission of aesthetic inferiority. For Afro-Americans, as Du
Bois observed, "the price of culture is a lie."[32]

Actually, there was hardly a theme the black playwrights of the
thirties could dramatize that did not involve the effects of the white
superiority myths on black identity, and this was true even when their
plays were set entirely within the black community, dramatized the
problems of all black characters, or were written for presentation to
all-black audiences. Consequently, almost every serious play by a
black dramatist contained some awareness of injustice, some degree
of anger, and some inherent form of protest, direct or indirect. These
essential elements of the black psychology and experience of the
thirties were conspicuously absent in white plays that were adapted
for black actors and in plays about black life that were authored by
white playwrights. Of The Green Pastures Hughes Allison stated:

> I do know that if The Green Pastures is Negro folklore . . . then, I am
> Hitler! . . . as authentic Negro religious belief [it] is definitely
> phoney! It's the sort of thing that keeps Negroes, each and every
> Negro, 'Sambo' and 'Liza' in the minds of the American white
> public.[33]

Although Sterling Brown did praise the "pioneering" plays about
black life written by Ridgely Torrence, who "obviously knew a great
deal about folk life and cared deeply for his characters,"[34] and stated of
Frank Wells, white author of John Henry, "it was surprising that a
young white southerner could catch the idiom and character of these
folks without any traces of condescension,"[35] he also pointed out that
"the intimacy with Negro life requisite for the types of drama still
necessary is in the main to be expected from Negro playwrights."[36] In
the white-authored plays, generally, the entire Gestalt was that of

whites performing black roles according to white standards, white motivations, and the white experience—and for that reason, if for no other, white racism was inherent in the white-authored plays about black life while it was precisely this distortion that the black playwrights aimed to correct.

But a comparison of the black Gestalts reflected in a white-authored and a black-authored play can now best reveal the difference between racism and identity in black drama of the thirties, and *Return to Death*[37] and *Big White Fog*,[38] which are discussed in the next chapter, are historical records of this difference.

ELEVEN

IDENTITY IS THE SOUL OF DRAMA

RETURN TO DEATH, a play on black life which was produced by the Federal Theatre in 1938,[1] was written by white author P. Washington Porter and revised by white playwright John Wexley. Copies of Porter's original script and of Wexley's revisions are in the Federal Theatre Collection and they record the white on black orientation of that era. The play is about black sharecroppers in the lower Carolinas, and all three acts take place at the two room shack where Irma and Alex Herman live with their small son, Dewey, and Irma's father, Old Jim.

As the original play begins, Irma is deeply worried: Alec, her worthy and hard-working bridegroom of a few years back, has become a drunkard, for no apparent reason; he idles away most of his time in the village, and Old Jim, who is long past his prime, is forced to work the cotton fields alone. Dewey is very ill and has to take expensive medicine, but the doctors at the county hospital have been unable to diagnose his disease and the child's condition is deteriorating rapidly; he now sleeps most of the time and even has to be roused to be fed. Evelyn Berl, the paternalistic and humanitarian daughter of the white land-owner, is concerned about Dewey and comes to the cabin to tell Irma that she is bringing her fiancé, Dr. Bert Brockman, to see him later that evening. But Evelyn is also concerned because Dr. Brockman, who now has a brand new medical certificate to his credit and is en route to New York to specialize in some branch of surgery, is suffering an attack of humility and is not sure he will ever become the great doctor he would like to be; Evelyn is anxious that his confidence be restored in himself. Irma remembers "Mr. Bert," who used to hunt with Old Jim when he was a boy, and is eager for any help he can give her sick child. Since it is dusk and Evelyn is afraid to walk home alone, Irma leaves Dewey in the care of Old Jim and escorts Miss Evelyn, and while she is away Alec arrives at the cabin.

Alec has been drinking, as usual; he is broke and in search of money, and is little concerned over his son's condition. He almost dismantles the house in search of money, which he eventually finds in one of Irma's hiding places. Old Jim tries to stop him from taking

Irma's cache, but Alec knocks the old man down and departs with the family's last five dollars until the cotton can be baled and sold.

When Irma returns and sees the condition of the shack, she is dumbfounded, but she excuses Alec's behavior and blames it all on "likker"; Old Jim, however, considers his son-in-law a good-for-nothing "nigger." Evelyn and her fiancé now arrive; Brockman examines Dewey and diagnoses the disease almost immediately as Cushings syndrome—rare indeed. The doctor states that an operation is imperative to save the child's life but he has neither the experience nor the facilities to perform it, and the boy is also too weak to stand an operation. Evelyn, however, points out that he has little choice for the boy will die without the operation and she encourages him to do a transfusion first. She offers to assist him with her nurse's aid training and Brockman is persuaded. Now, a suitable blood donor must be found and Irma is sent to persuade the villagers that the doctor is in need of volunteers. Next day, when Brockman tests the villagers to find an acceptable donor, Alec is among them, and he turns out to have the only matching blood. By the time this is determined, however, Alec has disappeared for he has, in the interim, strangled a white widow in her home.

While the doctor is combing the village in search of Alec, Alec arrives once more at the shack, filthy from his flight through the swamps. Irma informs him that only he can save their son's life and pleads with him to await the Doctor's return, but Alec is willing to give his blood only if it can be done immediately, for at this point he is bent on self-preservation. Irma attempts to detain him with a shotgun but he manages to evade her and darts out of the shack into the woods to attempt a getaway, while Irma, to Old Jim's disgust, cannot bring herself to fire the gun. Actually, the townspeople do not yet know who the murderer of the white widow is, but they are already tracking his scent with bloodhounds, and soon the baying dogs nose past Irma's door and follow Alec into the woods. Both Dewey and Alec now seem to be doomed and Irma is frantic with worry.

The following day, while Irma and Old Jim are praying desperately for a miracle, Alec, filthy and exhausted and now overcome by paternal love, returns to the cabin to save Dewey's life. Irma knows the terrible danger her husband is in, but she is determined that the child must come first, so Dr. Brockman and Miss Evelyn are hurriedly fetched from the big house, and the transfusion is successfully performed. Alec is now not only exhausted from running but also weak from loss of blood, and before he can recover enough to resume his flight the dogs are once more heard coming in the direction of the shack, followed by the sheriff and a "blood-thirsty" mob. As Irma and Old Jim now attempt to figure a way to save Alec, the doctor and Miss Evelyn learn, to their horror, that Alec is the murderer the whole village has been tracking. The doctor hurries Evelyn off in his car to safety, but he insists on remaining at the cabin to gather up his medical equipment. Old Jim hastily hides Alec in a manure pile to cover his scent, then he ties Alec's shoes behind a horse and slaps it to a trot through the woods to make a false trail.

As the inmates of the shack brace themselves for the coming ordeal, the dogs reach the cabin, nose around for a while, and then follow the horse into the woods. But the sheriff is not so easily hoodwinked, for the dogs have now led them here twice and he and the mob are sure that the dogs are after a false trail. When the sheriff receives evasive answers as to Alec's whereabouts, and notes the transfusion equipment in the cabin, he decides to take Dr. Brockman with him, hoping to extract more information from him, and Irma and Old Jim are left in an agony of suspense. It is not long, however, before the Hermans' neighbor, Harry, arrives with news of the latest impending disaster: the mob has become "fighting mad" for they believe it was Brockman who tricked them, and they have seized him from the sheriff and are talking about lynching or tar and feathering. Jim tries to assure Irma that there is nothing "niggers" can do about a mob like that, but Irma does not dare to let the doctor die, for not only is he Miss Evelyn's fiancé and her benefactor but Dewey's life also depends on Brockman's survival. She makes the heart-rending decision to sacrifice Alec to the mob as the final curtain falls.

Undoubtedly, the plot of this play has considerable dramatic potential for it is packed with fast-moving and suspenseful action. But the author's orientation toward his black characters reduces them to nonentities and robs most of their actions of meaning. Here, to start with, are some of his character descriptions, which are certainly gems of enlightenment: "Irma . . . a negro woman of close to forty. . . . Her nose is a little longer and not quite as flat as a typical negro's" (I.3); when Irma wanders around the cabin in a state of anxiety over her husband and son, "she partly talks and partly sings in a monotone to herself, as only a negress can, who is in deep trouble" (III.5); and when Alec first enters the cabin, he, too, is described by the author: he is drunk, his eyes are shifty, he is a large "muscular Negro" with "heavy eye-brows and narrowly spaced eyes, flat nose and wide thick lips and mouth" (I.9). Certainly the aesthetic standards used in the author's descriptions differ markedly from W. E. B. Du Bois' black aesthetic which maintains that the generous, softly undulating contours of the Negro face are far more attractive to blacks than sharp European features, and they also differ greatly from Alain Locke's view that "art must discover and reveal the beauty which prejudice and caricature have overlaid."[2] The description of Harry, too, is that of a popular stereotype of the white stage: "his face is the most notable part about him, beaming with a good natured smile," and Harry is also "very slow in talking" (II.4), which reveals the level of intelligence the author intended to be projected.

In contrast to the author's orientation toward his black characters is his view of his white characters. Evelyn needs no description; she is the white land-owner's daughter and is appropriately dressed. Brockman is clean-cut, his mouth denotes his good humor, his posture is erect and his movements effortless. The sheriff, who enters "carrying a shotgun with two sawed-off barrels . . . one pocket stuffed full of shotgun shells" and "a revolver strapped to his waist," is described as "a large man with iron-grey hair, [and] honest deeply lined face . . ." (II.20). Certainly this view of a heavily armed Southern law enforcement officer, at the head of a mob, does not project either the black orientation or the black experience. It is in marked contrast to the sheriff portrayed in *Turpentine*.

The orientation reflected in the above character descriptions permeates the whole play: Irma had been educated as a school teacher; she had wanted to do great things for her race, but in spite of her aura of education and the fact she is equipped by the author with a straighter nose, she cannot understand when Dr. Brockman explains to her that for a blood transfusion the blood of donor and recipient must match. As dramatized by Porter, listen to her own description of her plight:

> I, a common negress . . . wanted to raise their plane of understanding . . . I threw away my chance in order to marry Alec, I forgot my race in order to be one of them . . . time has tied my tongue with the words of the 'nigger.' (I.4)

And here is Old Jim, who tries to comfort her that she really couldn't expect to help the colored race because he knows "dat er nigger is er nigger and we is as de good Lawd done intended us to be" (I.4). From the mouths of blacks, this is a pathetic projection of the author's own orientation toward his black characters.

Another remarkable distortion of Old Jim occurs after Alec steals

Irma's last five dollars in the world and knocks the old man down to get it. Here is Old Jim, watching anxiously over the dying child who needs expensive medicine and wondering how he can tide the family over financially, when his neighbor, Harry, stops by on his way to the village. Old Jim now extracts a quarter from his pocket and gives it to Harry to buy him tobacco and peppermint candy. A quarter—in 1938—in a black sharecropper's shack—where there is nothing between morning and starvation—and for candy—for this deeply concerned grandfather's personal pleasure? This is a distortion not only of black economic reality but also of black family values.

And then there is Alec, who is a complete mystery. Nowhere in the original of this play is Alec's abrupt change from worthy bridegroom to a man with an unquenchable thirst for liquor and violence motivated; one is simply expected to believe that he is just another "nigger who took to likker." Unexplained, too, is his second character reversal, in mid-flight from the law. When he returns to his cabin for the transfusion, he has suddenly become the loving father who heroically jeopardizes his life to save his son's, yet only hours before he has robbed his wife and child, knocked down his father-in-law, murdered a white woman without any stated motivation, and deserted that same son in his hour of need.

In the final act, the switch that places Brockman in jeopardy of being lynched or tarred and feathered by the mob also stretches credibility considerably. Had Brockman been black, his danger would have been very real indeed, but he was a white man, a doctor, and the prospective son-in-law of the local white land-owner, and it is highly unlikely that the sheriff would have insisted that Brockman leave his scattered medical equipment immediately to accompany him for questioning and even less likely that he would have been seized by the mob. Certainly, none of these character discrepancies, value distortions, or situation contradictions would have come from the pen of a black dramatist, writing about blacks and the black experience.

But the dialogue in *Return to Death* is another revelation: it is liberally interspersed with "sno'nuffs" and "so'ises," and the like, which are intended to suggest the black Southern dialect, but the thought processes are entirely European in structure. There is a total absence of black native wit; there is only one approach to concrete imagery in the play, when Old Jim threatens to skin the cat for "gaiter bait," and there is not a single kinetic image in spite of the fact that everyone is continuously, often frantically, in motion. There is also no evidence of the rhythmic speech quality in the choice and structuring of words, and there is a dearth of sustaining black spirituality. While the cabin is symbolically supplied with both Bible and shotguns, Irma's crooned snatches of dialogue and song are quite meaningless since her "monotonous" tone, rather than the spiritual quality of her anguish, is repeatedly stressed.

Equally damaging to the play as an authentic black experience is the fact that there is absolutely no evidence of oppression: the share-croppers' economic condition is treated as a natural phenomenon, and consequently there is no resentment or anger on the part of the blacks; they accept their lot as the natural order of things, and no wonder, for all the white characters are entirely admirable. The sheriff is an honest and upright citizen and Dr. Brockman and Evelyn devote all their time and efforts to saving the sick child. Although the story is supposed to be that of the Hermans, it is the white characters who dominate the play as the good guys. The incensed mob does not choose another black to substitute for Alec, as in *Bad Man*, but the admirable white doctor, and even Irma's final, tragic sacrifice seems of secondary importance to the doctor's deliverance. There is indeed racism drama-tized in this play, but it is the white racism inherent in its author's own attitudes toward his characters.

The revision of *Return to Death* by Wexley is undoubtedly a great improvement on the original play. Evelyn becomes the niece of the white land-owner and while her humanitarian attitude is unchanged, her uncle, Mr. Berl, does not share it; he is interested only in money. Her fiancé becomes a Northerner who finds it difficult to understand her fondness for the sharecroppers, but he is still interested in helping the child from a medical point of view since his disease is so rare, and he arranges for the child's transfer to a New York Hospital after the transfusion so that the disease can be studied while the operation is being performed by an expert. It is also obvious that Wexley recog-nized the need for black motivation in a black play: he partly accounts for Irma's ignorance by marrying her to Alec before the completion of her education, and Irma, Old Jim, and Alec show a vague awareness of the futility of effort when working for a man like Berl, although Irma and Old Jim still describe themselves in much the same aesthetic terms. The greatest change is that Berl becomes the murder victim, instead of the white widow. Berl had got Alec fired from his job in the village so that Alec could return to working the cotton fields, and Alec had apparently responded by loitering in the village and taking to "likker." But this attempt at motivating Berl's murder is still far too vaguely defined to be effective. Neither Irma nor Old Jim see or admit any connection between Berl's exploitation of the blacks and his murder—Old Jim still defines Alec's problem as "likker an de big head"; Alec's presence at the Berl house is unexplained—the sheriff rules out theft to buy "likker" by admitting that nothing was touched —and Alec himself admits to Irma that he doesn't know why he murdered Berl. Certainly if his motive had been revenge, it is highly unlikely that Alec would have been unaware of it, thus he still more or less remains one more "nigger who took to likker" and violence for what his family sees as insufficient provocation. Alec's abrupt switches in attitude toward his sick child also remain unchanged.

At the finale, Wexley also heightens the drama by having Irma shoot Alec herself, rather than surrender him to the mob, but the focus is still predominantly on Brockman's deliverance, and the mob's seizure of the doctor is even less credible than in the original. Brockman leaves the shack immediately after sending Evelyn away. He is accompanied by Harry, who has been very helpful, but it is still the doctor, rather than Harry, who is seized directly by the mob on suspicion of complicity—a most unlikely occurrence, in view of Brockman's race and status, and Harry's availability as a victim.

In spite of the improvements in Wexley's revision, the orientation of the play remains basically unchanged. The superior white tone, the white aesthetic standards, the dominance of the white characters, the disorientation and complacency of Irma and Jim, and the structure of the dialogue are some of the deficiencies that still mark *Return to Death* as a product of white supremacy rather than as a product of the black experience.

But the lack of an authentic black identity image in *Return to Death* was not an isolated occurrence in white-authored plays; its absence in *The Emperor Jones*, whose author was no amateur, has been noted and it is not difficult to recognize the racial orientation of most of the plays on Negro life in the collection of Federal Theatre scripts. One of the few exceptions is *Turpentine*, where the orientation of black author Gus Smith clearly dominates the contribution of his white collaborator.

No doubt all of these playwrights had hoped to capture both white and black audiences. *Return to Death* and *Turpentine* were both first produced by the Federal Theatre, whose policy was to encourage integrated audiences, and although O'Neill's original experiment with the rich realm of African religious beliefs was first produced in Greenwich Village, the lead was played by Charles Gilpin. Yet Harlem audiences ridiculed *The Emperor Jones* while the exposé of the exploitation of black laborers in *Turpentine* excited the anger of white industrialists and politicians.

In marked contrast to the image that dominates *Return to Death* is that projected by *Big White Fog*, which was written by black playwright Theodore Ward and produced by the Federal Theatre in 1938.[3] *Big White Fog* was also written in the conventional three-act structure, and, like *Return to Death*, it is starkly realistic drama. The whole play takes place at the height of the Depression in the living room of one family in Chicago's black community, and the cast includes only one white supporting actor. The main characters are all members of the Mason family, which consists of Vic Mason, a dignified, intelligent, and well-educated black; his wife, Ella; their son, Les, who has earned a scholarship to a college in Maine; their daughter Wanda, almost eighteen; their two younger children, Caroline and Phillip; and Ella's mother, Martha Brooks. Percy, Vic's brother, completes the household, and Ella's sister, Juanita, and her husband, Dan, who is a college graduate with a Kappa key, are frequent visitors at the Mason home.

In this play, the racial orientation of Ward's characters is an important factor in the black experience: Mrs. Brooks is a light-skinned woman who considers herself a Dupree, she "ain't no African" (i.i.6), as she expresses her own racial bias. All of the other members of her family are also light-skinned except Phillip, who is dark like his father. Vic Mason is a Garveyite leader who works for the return of the black race to Africa because his experience has convinced him there is no future for the black man in capitalist America. On the other hand, his brother-in-law, Dan, has adopted the capitalist philosophy: Dan believes that if you can't lick them, you must join them and beat them at their own game, and in the beginning his efforts are crowned with temporary success. After the financial failure of the Garvey movement contributes to the ruin of the Masons, the collapse of Dan's capitalist enterprise follows, and the impoverished families face ejection from their homes. Vic's son, Les, who, in his own disillusionment at having his college scholarship repudiated on racial grounds, has embraced socialism, then offers socialism as a third alternative to relieve the destitution that is slowly engulfing the entire black community, and while Les' comrades are helping to prevent the court-ordered eviction of the Masons, Vic is shot and killed by the police.

At the time this play was presented by the Federal Theatre few critics took it seriously enough to examine in depth the authenticity of the black experience it dramatized. Some of them admitted that the playwright knew his subject, while others saw the play either as confirmation of the black's inability to provide for a rainy day[4]—a doctrine stated by white-oriented Mrs. Brooks, who one critic found to be "a loveable old mammy"[5]—or as a dramatization of "an idealistic plasterer with a smattering of education and a natural gift for eloquent statement of his race's problems."[6] None of these interpretations begin to capture the essence or significance of the play.

It would also be a mistake to presume, from the socialist note on which the play appears to end, that its author intended it as a communist propaganda vehicle. On the contrary, *Big White Fog* is the stark tragedy of a black family in a black community which was unable to find either opportunity or security under any of the systems available to it in America. By exploring all the political alternatives of the period, Ward succeeded in showing that the tragedy of the Mason family was the tragedy of the Afro-American experience: strangulation by the big white fog of oppression. One could accurately interpret the play's title as a synonym for the white superiority myths which circumscribed the entire scope of the black socio-economic potential. The myth-fog even dominated black thought and black identity in the play, and Ward's dramatization is an impassioned plea for that brotherhood of equality inherent in the American constitution.[7] In a letter to this author (25 July 1979) Mr. Ward stated:

> The title *Big White Fog* reflects a folk image [of] the condition of the life of the black man in these United States. . . .
>   . . . what *Big White Fog* sought to accomplish was the dramatization of the idea that, both internally and externally, the impact of these conditions amounted to a Big White Fog through which the black American could see *no light anywhere*, including his rejection of the wave of the future, known as Communism.

Unlike *Return to Death*, the motivations of Ward's characters are dramatized and based in dramatized fact. Vic, who is a real humanitarian with African-based communal concern for his entire race, acts for the deliverance of all blacks, including the millions "down South living on corn bread and molasses and dying like flies from hookworm" (II.i.8). Vic personally experiences the futility of black education in this "godforsakencountry," for although he was well educated, he starts as a hod carrier in the play and ends up unable to get any kind of work to support his family—six bits represent his full day's earnings shovelling snow on the day it is obliging enough to fall. He loses the respect of his wife for his inability to provide for the family and she lashes out at him in anguish for all their ills—Caroline and Phillip's illness because of holes in their shoes, Wanda's dropping out of school, even the lack of fifteen cents a week for a newspaper. Vic even reaps the ultimate reward of learning that his daughter has turned prostitute so that the family can survive.

Vic's brother, Percy, is a cabaret bum who lives for today in a general haze of inebriation, but, unlike Alec in *Return to Death*, Percy's drinking and lack of ambition are well motivated: he had fought for democracy in World War I but, upon his return to America, an angry group of white men in a bar had ripped the uniform off his "nigger" back. This incident and its devastating effect reflected a factual part of the black experience.

Vic's son, Les, is an A-student who earns his scholarship by hard work and who looks forward eagerly to his college education, but his experience with the big white fog is no less disillusioning than Percy's, for he receives a letter from the college which regrets that the scholarship has been withdrawn since it is not open to members of his race. In spite of his rejection Les is determined to get an education, so he enters a college in Chicago where he is acceptable, and goes to work for his Uncle Dan to pay for it himself. He is again frustrated, this time by the economic impotence of his father, for the now-impoverished Mason family desperately needs the money he works for, and Les is forced to drop out of college. It is little wonder that when Piszer, an unprejudiced Jewish classmate with socialist leanings, introduces Les to a doctrine of interracial brotherhood, and backs it by calling on the brotherhood to assist in preventing the Masons' eviction, Les repudiates both his father's and his uncle's philosophies. Socialist interracial cooperation and protection appear to him to be the only glimmer of hope in the big white fog for the black community.

Theodore Ward projects through the home life of a family in a black community what Hughes Allison dramatized in the court. Mrs. Brooks' distorted self-image and inverted standards parallel those revealed in *The Trial of Dr. Beck*, and both are the devastating result of the white superiority myths. Mrs. Brooks expresses nothing but contempt for Vic, Phillip, or any dark-skinned person, a fact of which Vic is not initially aware since Ella has succeeded in keeping from him her mother's continuous, withering criticism. But Ella is constantly torn between love for her mother and love and loyalty to Vic, and when Mrs. Brooks finally steps over the line, in Vic's hearing, and tells Ella he is an "evil, black, good-for-nothing nigger" (II.iii.10), the result is disastrous. Vic retaliates by going to the heart of her problem with slashing and unforgivable accuracy: he is too black for her white

Dupree blood, and her twisted soul that glorifies her badge of shame, and this outburst creates an unhealable breach between Ella and Vic, while Mrs. Brooks, who precipitated it, hastily leaves the Mason home and migrates to the safety of Juanita's house.

Through Martha Brooks, Ward also dramatizes the effects of the multiple cultural upheavals endured by blacks. She recalls the devastating effects of her upheaval from the South to move to Chicago with the family, and states that she could not survive another move to Africa if Vic and his family should ultimately succeed in going there with Garvey (1.17).

But Mrs. Brooks, who considers herself a Dupree, is also not Africa-oriented in the first place, and Ward, like Allison, shows that her color prejudice also permeates the black community. When Aunt Juanita tries to persuade Wanda, who has lost faith in education as a means of making a living, that going back to school would at least insure her a respectable job teaching, Wanda retorts angrily that the blacks in the community are already kicking against colored school teachers.[8]

Dan's college education and Kappa key have also oriented him toward the white man's philosophy of individual success in the competitive capitalistic system, and he pleads with Vic to join him in his business venture and to abandon his Garveyite notions of black economic autonomy for the good of the whole race. In his letter to this author (25 July 1979) on the meaning of *Big White Fog*, Mr. Ward also wrote:

> It is a summary, on the one hand of the former slave psychology that self-preservation required an acknowledgement of the idea that resistance to oppression was futile because 'you couldn't win.' This outlook, on the other hand, was, and continues to be, reinforced by mis-education and the black man's exposure to the ideology of the dominant group—to the extent that the black middle class continues to advise its offspring that it is the better part of wisdom *to keep one's mouth shut*, regardless of the predicament of the race.

Dan believes that as a slum landlord he can adjust to white prejudice and outwit the white man at his own game, thereby achieving his primary aim—to make money. But again Vic hits the heart of black disorientation as he informs Dan that his education has become a pair of "knee pads" that enable him to "crawl through the mud of white prejudice without the least sense of pain or dishonor" (1.ii.10). Dan, however, is unconvinced; he emulates white business practices by preying on his own people,[9] and flaunts the early fruit of his success, a new Cadillac. When there is nothing left for him to squeeze out of his destitute black tenants, and when even eviction of them does not produce payment, he, too, dives to bewildered disaster. His wife, Juanita, is then forced to take in "roomers" and run a house of "sin" which sends the self-righteous Mrs. Brooks dashing back to the Masons for refuge.

The portrait that Theodore Ward paints—of the tragic effects on the black identity and experience which are caused by the white myths and all their derivative forms of oppression—is stark, and it was clearly his intention to present the black reality, for when Dan assures Vic that superiority is the white man's temporary illusion, Vic responds emphatically that what he is concerned over is its effects, and they are no illusion. Indeed, the black reality is the essence of the play's tragedy.

The dialogue of Ward's characters, unlike that of characters created by Porter, Wexley, and other white authors writing about blacks, reflects the concrete and kinetic black mode of thought and expression. At the opening of the play Ella inquires of her visiting sister, "what storm blew you to Dearborn Street?" (i.i.1). When Wanda becomes sassy, Mrs. Brooks threatens to take her "down a button hole lower" (i.i.13), and when Mrs. Brooks tries to convince Vic that Garvey is a crook, these are the words she chooses: "If I tell you a chicken dip snuff, jes look under her wing and you'll find the box!" (i.ii.18). After Garvey is arrested, Dan tries to get Vic to sell his shares in the foundering movement, and brother Percy too throws in his word of advice: "a smart flea knows when to hop" (ii.ii.26).

Theodore Ward's own orientation toward his characters is also in sharp contrast to that in *Return to Death*. Vic, like Alec, is a black man, but Ward does not find it either necessary or useful to describe his physical and facial characteristics in terms of white aesthetic standards. Wanda and her friend, Claudine, who are young and extremely attractive, are also not described in terms of nose length. It is clear that the author and his characters do not inhabit different worlds, and there are therefore no discrepancies in characterization, motivation, or experience.

In black Chicago, too, the law is reflected as no paragon of virtue in the eyes of the community: when Vic appears in court to plead for a stay of eviction, he is dressed in the worn uniform of the now defunct Garveyites because he possesses nothing else to wear. But the uniform is enough to provoke scathing sarcasm from the judge, before which Vic is helpless. Vic relates this experience to Dan on his return home:

"Oh so you're one of the Niggers who thinks this country isn't good enough for you, eh? Well, well, and you've got the nerve to appeal to the court for leniency?" and as that wasn't enough, he went on to rub it in by telling me how thankful we ought to be because his people brought us out of savagery—But I couldn't say anything. (III.i.22)

Needless to say, the eviction stay was exceedingly short. In the final scene, when the unarmed Vic is shot while carrying his furniture back into his house with the help of Piszer's brotherhood, he is shot by a law enforcement officer who arrives on the scene to the music of sirens which "rise in diabolic accompaniment, leading an atmosphere of menacing terror and high riding death." This chase to the Mason home terminates with "screaming brakes which is followed by deadly silence" (III.iii.15). Characteristically, there is no mention in the black community of "honest-looking" law enforcement officers.

One of the most characteristic elements of the Afro-American culture which is dramatized in *Big White Fog* is the self-sacrificing solidarity of the black family, and this is also a marked contrast to *Return to Death*. While Porter shows Old Jim practicing self-indulgence in the face of penury, Ward shows the sustaining solidarity of the Mason family in spite of its desperate economic plight and tragically fractured dreams. Ella heroically endures the searing criticism and racial bias of her disoriented mother until she fears that Mrs. Brooks' attacks on the dark-skinned Phillip threaten her son's self-image. When Mrs. Brooks flees Juanita's "house of sin" with her bundle of belongings, Vic, who is a victim of her prejudice and himself on the verge of economic disaster, takes her back into his home. When Les loses his scholarship, Dan, who is still enjoying temporary success, gives him a job to help him earn the money to pay for his education, and Percy depletes his cabareting wardrobe to insure that Les is well turned out for college. Juanita helps with the childrens' clothes, and Les, in his turn, sacrifices college when his earnings are needed to feed the family. Wanda, who has no inclination toward promiscuity, prostitutes herself to house the evicted family, and when she fails to heed Les' warning that "when a white man begins to take a Nigger girl riding it can't mean but one thing" (III.i.14), and she lands in jail, Les tries valiantly to protect her from the shame of family discovery. Even Dan, who urgently needs to vindicate his own judgment by achieving a decisive victory in his ideological conflict with Vic, and who has been adamant about lending Vic money unless he renounces the Garveyites and sells his shares in their business ventures, offers his home to the Masons when they are to be evicted, although he faces a like disaster in the none too distant future. And finally, Vic, crushed by the weight of economic oppression and prejudice, instructs his family while he is dying:

> I want you to stick by each other and never let nothing come between you. . . . You'll all find it pretty hard, for like Les said, "This world ain't nothing but a Big White Fog," and nobody can't see no light nowhere! (III.iii.19)

In spite of the flurry of civic concern that preceded the production of *Big White Fog*, it is difficult to see what black racism it may have been thought to project. To the extent that white racism, and its effects on black identity and well-being, were part of the black experience, these are reflected, for the play is an authentic dramatization of the black, urban image and the black reality of its day, but this by no means constitutes black racism. On the contrary, the play shows that the black community was in urgent need of justice, equality, and brotherhood, and both Sterling Brown and Langston Hughes considered it the greatest social play of the black theater.[10]

The comparison of *Return to Death* and *Big White Fog* also shows why, in the thirties, Ward's type of image came only from the pens— from the souls—of black dramatists.

And soul is what drama is all about, for ultimately identity is soul.

There is no doubt that there were also black playwrights in the thirties whose plays were white-oriented and white dominated. Under the prevailing limitations, this was inevitable and Ward acknowledges in *Big White Fog* that the black community included its Martha Brookses and its Dans who were determined to achieve economic success at any price. But there were black playwrights who were dedicated to, and who achieved authentic dramatizations of, the black identity and experience; their goal was not the promotion but the elimination of racism in America.

TWELVE

THE WEST INDIAN INFLUENCE

I T IS A NOTABLE testament to the enduring and sustaining qualities of the African cosmological mystique and culture that wherever Africans have been subjected to the rigidly enforced reorientation of Western slavery their spiritual vitality, and in some cases even their traditions and customs, have survived.

Because of the varied laws, customs, religious beliefs, and military capabilities of the colonizing European nations, the conditions of slavery varied greatly throughout the Caribbean and American colonies, yet recent field studies—such as those done by Roger Abrahams of the University of Texas[1]—have recorded parallel survivals and even some similar developments in the West Indies and in Afro-America. In both areas, the expertise of the African oral tradition is still highly prized: it licenses the "broad talker"[2] to perform the anti-ritual of the community, while stories of the tortoise, Anansi the spider, and the signifyin' Monkey still clothe the timeless wisdom of Africa with infinite variety, and on street corners of Island towns and villages, as in Harlem, young males still learn to manipulate the rhythmic, imagistic, and other qualities of language in that most exacting of linguistic competitions, the "dozens."[3]

To those who are familar with both areas, other survivals and developments are apparent. At cane-field crossroads, or on the quays of West Indian fishing villages, black youths speak their silent greetings, strike their rapping stances before dark beauties, and advertise their social and sexual desires in the very rhythms of their walk much as they do in black American communities.[4] At dayclean,[5] Island fishermen hoist their sails and glide out to sea with the same rhythms of Africa on their lips that vibrate over the Sea Islands of South Carolina and Georgia, and at sundown, in informal groups, Islanders translate religion, politics, sex, the rigors of yesterday's labor, or the kiss of the golden moon on whispering, blue-black waters, swaying palms, and cane arrows into the poetic imagery of Africa while a guitar plucks the spiritual mood into existence, or fingers and feet tap it alive just as those of Gus Smith's hoopers did in a Florida turpentine camp.

Everywhere in the Islands, the generative power of Nommo and the

140

dynamic force vitale translate thought, desire, and emotion into words and action—and often in a purer form than in Afro-America since the Islands still tap the spiritual wellspring of the African religions.

Because conditions in many of the Islands—particularly in those that were under early Spanish or French domination—were more favorable to the survival of African customs than in America, African religious forms flourished; in fact, they expanded, for while efforts by the Catholic colonial powers at slave conversion did result in attendance at Christian worship, Christianity remained superficial and Catholic saints were simply incorporated into the African pantheons.[6] Elements from the different African religions were fused to meet the needs of the many tribes that were thrown together in the plantation communities: generally they merged the strong pantheon of one dominant tribe, such as the Dahomeans, with the ancestor cult of another, often Akan or Bantu, and with the ritual or magical practices of others, usually Ashanti.

These synthesized religions still survive in most of the islands: Cumina in Jamaica is predominantly Akan and Dahomean, and includes the magical practices of the Ashanti; in Haiti, Vodun, which acquired its name from the Dahomean word for "spirit," is predominatly Dahomean and Arada; Santeria, in Cuba, is dominated by Yoruba customs; in Trinidad, Shango, which is named for the god of war, is predominantly Akan and Dahomean; and there are other derivatives both in the Islands and on the mainland.[7] In contrast to Christianity, the entire orientation of these religions is toward joy, gaiety, and the fullest expression of life, and this religious joie de vivre dominates the outlook of the black Island populations. Hall Johnson reflected this superbly in the New Day Pilgrims whom he created and contrasted to his Baptist congregation in *Run Little Chillun'*.

The synthesis of African religious customs in the various West Indian colonies was also a manifestation of the spiritual unity that was possible, and that was achieved between these different speaking African peoples in the Western world. Although best known in Vodun, this spiritual unity was achieved in all the derivative religions and was highly effective in bridging other tribal differences. In the practice of Shango in Trinidad, for instance, on certain festive and ceremonial occasions "The Drums of the Nations" poured forth, and in this unique prototype of a United Nations the rhythmic languages of every tribe that experienced slavery in the Island were spoken by the expert drummers. It was of seminal importance that at a time when

African cultural customs were being rigorously stamped out in America, these religious practices preserved all the forms of African expression: ritual, drums, dance, the word, spirit possession, and a remarkably effective degree of magic and sorcery—or obeah, as it is called in the Islands.

In many of the Islands—particularly in those under Spanish domination—family life was encouraged for religious reasons; but this was also practiced under other colonial powers for the benefit of the plantation owners since land was allocated to families for the cultivation of their own produce to minimize the cost of feeding. African markets were soon established for the exchange of produce between slaves of neighboring plantations, and although these were suppressed from time to time they survived and assisted immeasurably with the preservation and fusion of tribal customs. They also provided common meeting places for the hatching of innumerable plots of revolt.[8]

The continual warfare that existed between the English, French, and Spaniards for control of the Caribbean also made total suppression of African customs, such as the drums and dance, impossible and each of these European nations found it necessary at various times to come to terms with Cimaroones—slaves who had escaped to establish free communities in the jungle wildernesses. The Ashanti-led Maroons of Jamaica, who were found to be virtually unconquerable in mountain and jungle strongholds,[9] inspired revolts in the other islands as well.

Patrick Hylton has pointed out in "The Politics of Caribbean Music" that the spirit of protest that underlies the spirituals, the blues, and the jazz of Afro-America is also present in the songs of the Islands.[10] However, the degree of protest and its effectiveness as a political weapon differed in the Island songs, for while the reggae of Jamaica, and the calypso, which developed to its highest form of expression in Trinidad, combined the same African elements as Afro-American music, it was the fearless spirit of the Ashanti warrior that dominated the Island music, and a look at the development of the Trinidad carnival art form reveals this.

In Trinidad, African rhythms and rituals were first translated into the original form of the calypso, the Caiso Mas'. This consisted of groups, led by a chantwell, "a man gifted not only in writing songs but in extemporizing on any given subject,"[11] and the songs were sung in French patois until the turn of the century. Rival groups of carnival celebrants, who encountered each other as they danced, sang, and paraded through the towns and villages, engaged in speech contests and in the deadly art of stick fighting, and this latter practice generally kept white spectators, who were usually enthralled with the oral, musical, and physical prowess of the performers, at a safe distance.

As the overriding need for violence diminished through the years and the more dangerous aspects of stick fighting gradually disappeared, first the descendants of the French creoles and then other white residents became more involved in the street carnival. The emphasis shifted from speechmaking toward the calypso, or protest song, and gradually calypsos emphasizing sex and immorality became popular and were included in the carnival repertoire. But even in these the same fearless spirit dominated, for the calypsonians publicized the indiscretions of white officials and socially prominent white residents in such songs as "Brackley Behind de Bline" and "The Young Footballer."

By this time, the calypso had become the dominant factor in the carnival of Trinidad, one of the greatest spectacles of living drama in the Western world. The best songs each year became the carnival "road marches" for all those in the Island population who could stand the physical strain; black and white residents poured forth into the streets each year in increasing numbers, either in the anonymity of rags and masks or the splendor of the costly and spectacular, and for the two days preceding Lent they totally and spontaneously "self-expressed" to the accompaniment of drums, stringed instruments, and song.[12] In the forties, this integrated celebration was a revelation to both white and black Americans who witnessed the drama of Trinidad carnival: some of the white Americans who were engaged in building the American defense bases in the Caribbean and who were not accustomed to being the targets of black wit were astounded at the audacity of the unexpurgated versions of such calypsos as "Rum and Coca Cola," while black Americans found it difficult to believe that such songs—often directed at prominent white residents or prominent white visitors—could not only go unpunished but be appreciated and enjoyed by the local whites.

In the two decades that followed World War II, the ingenuity of black musicians added a new feature to the carnival celebration. Based on the African prototype, a group of instruments was created out of oil drums, each of which was tempered to produce its own distinctive mellow tone, and the steel band, which is entirely made up of these drums, was born.

The twentieth century calypso has gradually lost some of its impromptu nature as the calypsonians have increasingly spent their time throughout the year composing their songs to burst upon the coming

carnival season; thus, like the Afro-American composers and dramatists, the calypsonians have partly become locked into form, words,
and music. The competition between the calypsonians, the West
Indian heirs of the African troubadours, is enormous. The aim of each
is acclamation as "King of the Carnival," and this status is achieved by
the creator of the most popular song of the season: this achievement is
never in any doubt, for as the celebration draws to a close almost
everyone, black and white, will be singing the most popular calypso.
In spite of this gradual trend toward prestructuring, the call–response
form is still vigorously maintained, with the leaders of the bands
singing the verses and their masses of followers responding with
the choruses; and improvisations, both instrumental and vocal, are
liberally interspersed.

In the thirties and forties improvisation was best preserved in the
carnival "tents" which mushroomed overnight each year as much as
six weeks before carnival. Here the new crop of calypsos was introduced to unsegregated, biracial, capacity audiences. An unwritten
law was observed whereby each calypsonian sang his own creations,
and each tent performance culminated in "war," a breathtaking
dramatic experience in which the calypsonians competed for the
honor of creating the best spontaneous verses. These were accompanied by dramatic gesticulations and flowed in a brilliant, continuous stream on any subject that appealed to the singers, with each in
turn trying to top the preceding verses. Direct involvement of the
audience, in the African tradition, was also an integral part of the
drama of the tent; impromptu verses on specific individuals present in
the audience might be complimentary, but they were just as likely to
be embarrassing. This tent drama is probably the nearest lay equivalent to the spontaneous religious experience in the black church; it is a
highly developed art necessitating quick wit, poetic imagination, and
above all a fearless disregard for established authority.[13]

Certainly, relations between the West Indian songwriters and the
authorities—both under white and subsequently under black rule—
have not always been harmonious. So potent have the songs been in
all phases of life that through the years there have been several unsuccessful attempts to suppress or to censor them on grounds ranging
from fomentation of political unrest to obscenity. The native wit of
the calypsonian, however, has risen to match each occasion. In the
thirties, after one such attempt at censorship for profanity, in Trinidad, "Attila the Hun" (Raymond Quevedo) responded with the following calypso:

To say these songs are sacreligious, obscene, or profane
Is only a lie, and a dirty shame.
If the Calypso is indecent, then I must insist
So is Shakespeare's Venus and Adonis;
Bocaccio's tales, Voltaire's Candide;
The Martyrdom of Man, by Winwood Reid;
Yet over these authors they make no fuss
But want to take advantage of us. [14]

And in 1973 Prime Minister Manley of Jamaica was publicly censored
by one of his partisan supporters in the reggae "No Joshua, No," for
"forgetting" some of his pre-election promises, and was advised to
"forward and start anew."

Thus the reggae and the calypsos were not confined to spiritual
freedom and heavenly deliverance like the Afro-American spirituals,
which were created under far more stringent conditions of slavery.
They have been potent and effective forms of protest that have been
delivered under highly dramatic circumstances to maximum partici-
pating audiences. In this respect they also exceeded the effectiveness
of early Afro-American protest drama, since they spoke for the vast
majority of the population and provided a continual spur toward all
types of reform. They are still the voice of freedom that will not be
intimidated and will not be silenced. Yet most of the calypsonians
achieved their goals through witty and humorous ridicule—similar to
that later practiced by Redd Foxx and "The Jeffersons" on American
television—for this is often a more memorable and effective means of
influencing public opinion than flagellation.

This brief outline of the development of the carnival art form in the
West Indies reveals several important points: that it helped to preserve the arts of Africa and encouraged the creativity of Afro-West
Indians in developing those arts into a native West Indian form of
expression; that it fostered the fearless warrior spirit and provided a
valuable political forum for its expression; and that it demonstrated
the cooperation and fraternization that was achievable and that was
achieved even before the thirties between the white and black races.
But even more significant is the fact that this integrated celebration
was not expressed in Western terms, but predominantly in African
terms. Certainly the initial choice of the two days preceding Lent for
the performance of this anti-ritual in Trinidad was governed by the
Catholic calendar of its Spanish colonizers, and the custom of setting
aside that period for the performance of anti-ritual had been adopted

by the early Catholic church from even earlier pagan practices; but beyond the establishment by the Spaniards of the time and the right to such freedom of expression, both the Spaniards and later the English had as little control over its form and content as they did over the synthesized religions that flourished in the Islands. Nor could the calypsos be confined to the carnival season, and they were sung throughout the year.

Above all, the indomitable spirit of the Ashanti warrior which is expressed in the West Indian carnival and protest songs characterizes the Afro–West Indian influence that has contributed to the Afro-American experience and identity and this influence has a long history: Afro–West Indians reinforced and reinvigorated the African heritage in America; they demonstrated throughout their turbulent history in the Islands that the white master was not invincible and that respect and cooperation between the races was achievable, while Afro–West Indians in America have often spearheaded black attempts to break the white monopoly on economic opportunity.

For more than seventy-five years before the Louisiana Purchase the French and Spanish planters in America, becoming increasingly fearful of slave insurrections, had fallen in line with the oppressive practices of the rest of slave-owning America and had passed laws forbidding gatherings for dancing, or any other purpose, and one of the last strongholds of African cultural practices was in danger of annihilation. But at the time of the French Revolution the mass migration of royalist planters from the French West Indies, which flooded Spanish Trinidad with French settlers,[15] also brought the French planters, with their African slaves, to America. These slaves had preserved the vital elements of their culture, and the practice of voodoo, with all its accompanying arts, was revitalized.[16] Agitation for the reinstatement of dancing in the Louisiana territory then resulted in controlled assembly on Sundays in Congo Square, New Orleans. The most popular dance was the calinde, a variant of the dance performed in the voodoo ceremonies, and a description of its performance, although recorded by a white observer, will give some idea of the multiplicity of the African forms of expression it preserved.

As Herbert Asbury wrote, it was performed to the rhythm of the bamboula, which

> the negro who wielded the bones maintained without a pause and with no break in the rhythm until sunset . . . they pranced back and forth stamping in unison, occasionally shouting "Dancez

Bamboula! Badoum! Badoum!" while the women scarcely lifting their feet from the ground swayed their bodies from side to side and chanted . . . the entire square was an almost solid mass of black bodies stamping and swaying to the rhythmic beat . . . , and the frenzied chanting . . . and the clanging of the pieces of metal which dangled from the ankles of the men. [17]

In *Genesis, Juba, and Other Jewels,* a CBS black bicentennial television show in April 1976, the influence of the dance calinde was very clear and the same words punctuated the dancing.

Asbury further reports the account of an American journalist who, with a police escort, witnessed a voodoo ceremony in 1884. It incorporated the dance calinde and a bold defiant song in French patois, thus not only the voodoo arts but the warrior spirit was revitalized, and by this time a fiddle had been added to the drums.

Romeo B. Garret states:

The African group said to have contributed most of the basic nature of jazz was the Dahomeans of West Africa. Their musical tradition merged with those of the French and became the leading influence when the *'roots' of jazz were still forming in the West Indies.* [18] (Italic added.)

These roots, which also dominate the Trinidad calypso rhythm, were brought to Louisiana by French West Indian creoles: "a group of Negroes [who] were wealthy, and as well educated as Europeans." [19] Since the French were not race-conscious, interracial marriage was not uncommon in the French islands and the mulatto children of such marriages inherited their fathers' property under French law.

In *Black New Orleans 1860–1880,* John Blassingame quotes the writer Lafcadio Hearn as stating in 1878 "creole music is mostly negro music," [20] often modified by French composers. Indeed neither creole patois nor creole melodies could have developed either in America or the West Indies without the French- and Spanish-blooded slaves. This creole music transmitted that extension of rhythmic vocal and drum sound that was first expressed in brass bands and that was later to be expressed in the trumpet solos of American jazz. By 1879 there were several brass bands in New Orleans, the most famous of which was Sylvester Decker's Excelsior Brass Band. Initially used for funeral processions, these bands marched to the cemetery to "muffled drum and mournful dirge," but they always returned home to the joyful rhythms of jazz. [21]

But New Orleans was not the only area of Afro-America to feel the early impact of Afro–West Indian influence: the successful Haitian revolution was a source of renewed hope and inspiration to slaves all over America, and a living example of the fact that the white colonial powers were not invincible. Haitian volunteers later fought in the American Civil War and increased the impact of their message through personal contact.[22]

In the nineteenth century, due to the increase in population, there was an almost unbroken stream of black West Indian immigrants entering the United States. As early as 1820 West Indian Shakespearean actor James Hewlett spearheaded the formation of the African Grove Theater in New York City,[23] and in 1826 John Russworm, a Jamaican, was one of the first two colored men to be graduated from an American college, Bowdoin. He established and edited the first black newspaper in America and was later one of the founders of Liberia.[24] In the 1840s, Peter Ogden, also a Jamaican, established in New York City the first Odd Fellows Lodge for Negroes, and as W. A. Domingo records:

> Prior to the Civil War, West Indian contributions to American Negro life were so great that Dr. W. E. B. Du Bois, in his *Souls of Black Folk*, credits them with main responsibility for the manhood program presented by the race in the early decades of the last century.[25]

Domingo further points out that:

> Coming to the United States from countries in which they had experienced no legalized social or occupational disabilities, West Indians very naturally have found it difficult to adapt themselves to tasks that are, by custom, reserved for Negroes in the North.[26]

They have consequently refused to accept inferior categorization or defeat, and have often been trailblazers in new areas of employment. In the 1890s John W. Shaw of Antigua performed the unique feat in segregated America of invading the white supervisory job preserve: he passed the civil service examinations and became deputy commissioner of taxes for Queens County.[27] But the most important Afro–West Indian contribution to Afro-American experience has been their "insistent assertion of their manhood in an environment that demands too much servility and unprotesting acquiescence from men of African blood."[28]

In the twentieth century, West Indian contributors to the Afro-

American experience have not diminished: they include the greatest black vaudeville comedian on the American stage, Bahamas-born Bert Williams, who, blazing a brilliant trail across segregated footlights, performed with the Ziegfeld Follies for ten years;[29] Claude McKay, poet and herald of the Harlem Renaissance, was a Jamaican;[30] playwright Eulalie Spense, whose *Undertow*, written in 1929, is in James Hatch's black drama anthology, was also a West Indian. Hatch's comment on her play is significant: "not many black playwrights attempted what Eulalie Spense did: to write a play whose characters were undeniably black, but whose problem within the play was not ethnic";[31] it underscores Domingo's contention that West Indian blacks, unaccustomed to the degree of ethnic oppression practiced in America, did not envisage it as the only dominant factor in their experience. J. A. Rogers, for fifty years one of the foremost black historians in America, was a Jamaican;[32] Sidney Poitier "came to New York from Florida with a West Indian accent so thick you could cut it with a knife,"[33] and the influence continues up to the present, for Shirley St. Hill Chisholm, congressional representative from New York, was born of Barbadian and Guianese parents and spent her early years at school in Barbados.[34]

In *Black Drama*, Loften Mitchell had this to say of the early decades of the twentieth century:

> We knew, too that Harlem was Africa-conscious. Anyone who states otherwise is ignorant and insulting to the nationalist leader Marcus Garvey, to J. A. Rogers, Claude McKay, Richard Moore, and the whole West Indian group that revitalized the black American's interest in Africa.[35]

But of all the West Indians who have influenced Afro-American culture and identity, none can compete with either the immediate or the lasting impact of Jamaica-born Marcus Garvey.[36] Son of a Maroon, and claiming descent from the proud Ashanti warrior, Garvey developed his oratorical prowess through the heirs of the African raconteurs; he studied the style of black preachers in the churches of Kingston. When he broke upon the Afro-American scene in 1916 with his doctrine for black unification and self-determination, "One God, One Aim, One Destiny," he fired the Afro-American imagination beyond the achievement of any previous leader, and his charismatic leadership and appeal remained unmatched by any black in America until the advent of Dr. Martin Luther King. Afro-American membership in his Universal Negro Improvement Association and African

Communities (Imperial) League (UNIA) was over two million—which exceeded that of the NAACP.

As might have been expected, Garvey's doctrine of black economic autonomy and nationhood greatly displeased white America, while his phenomenal appeal to the masses displeased those black intellectuals whose leadership he usurped. He was naive in the business arena and had less financial ability than creative genius, so he handed his political opponents the opportunity to bring about his downfall by buying—from the white shipping industry—ships for his Black Star Line that turned out to be unseaworthy. Thus, his enormous effort at black commercial autonomy failed, and he was tried and convicted of mail fraud in what most blacks still believe to have been a gross miscarriage of justice. His deportation brought to a close the activities of the UNIA, but of the influence of his prophetic vision, there is as yet no foreseeable end.

He caressed with the creative magic of his words the spiritual rhythms that slept in black memories, and lo! the heart of African America sprang to life. He lashed with the fury of his anger the perpetrators of the inverted and fragmented black self-image, and lo! black once more became shining, and beautiful, and dignified. So profusely did he shower his visionary ideas on black America that several different black groups and organizations have since emphasized different elements of his doctrine: his demand for the teaching of black history has become a major issue in all black educational planning; his call for renewed respect for black women was echoed by the Black Muslims along with his dream of African repatriation. His doctrine profoundly influenced the thinking of Malcolm X, and he also showed the way for the black American community to achieve political and economic justice through consumer pressure. His call for the unity of black peoples everywhere lives in contemporary Pan Africanism[37] and his call for racial autonomy was later picked up by the Black Power movement, the slogan-title of which was provided by Stokely Carmichael, another militant black Trinidadian. This slogan has now circled the globe, and is being currently heard in the African homeland. In short, Marcus Garvey initiated the greatest black mass movement for freedom, dignity, self-respect, and unity that has ever occurred in Afro-American history, and the failure of his repatriation movement, and his deportation, did not lessen the frenzy of Afro-American interest he had stirred up in the African heritage.

It was inevitable that some black playwright of the thirties who was dedicated to projecting the black image and black experience should dramatize the enormous impact of his doctrine, and that playwright was Theodore Ward, whom we have already met. *Big White Fog* properly belongs to the drama of ideas, for, as we have already noted, each of Ward's major characters speaks for one of the prevailing sociopolitical philosophies, and he dramatizes the effects of these ideas on the black community. The play's critics, however, were so busy magnanimously defending the dramatist's right to freedom of speech, or recalling the financial failure and conviction of the discredited Garvey, that little if any attention was focused on the play's dynamic dramatization of Garvey's tremendous impact on Afro-American culture,[38] a dramatization that Ward made as prophetic as the doctrine it projected.

Ward starts by showing the scope of Garvey's appeal as Ella Mason informs her sister that the UNIA has attracted "over four million paid up members."[39] Ella's daughter, Wanda, then announces her disenchantment with the job prospects afforded by black education in America, and her determination to go to work as a soda jerk instead of returning to school; but when her father, Vic, is asked to exert his authority, he refuses to force her to return because "they're only filling her head with a stack of white folks' lies anyhow" (I.i.18). Vic is a Garveyite leader and this is his paraphrase of Garvey's denunciation of Western historians for falsifying history by excluding all mention of black achievements,[40] and of the inculcation of blacks with white aesthetics and ethics.

Vic's leadership in the UNIA is the subject of much criticism by his mother-in-law, Mrs. Brooks, who is white-oriented, and his brother-in-law, Dan, who is capitalist-oriented, but he wears the elaborate Garveyite uniform proudly because he understands that it is a direct effort to promote black pride and to rehabilitate the black self-image, and in spite of the criticism the Mason family is very proud when it hears of Vic's appointment as Lord of Agriculture of Garvey's proposed African Republic. Although the family is in dire financial straights, Ella spends her last money to buy eggnog for the committee that comes to confer this honor on her husband, and the children, and even Dan, are impressed by the paper he prepares to present to a Black Congress in Harlem on communal agricultural experimentation in the Republic. It is also clear from Ward's dramatization that while lack of economic opportunity has made Vic a hod-carrier, his intellectual capacity is impressive, and this reflects Garvey's deep concern over the terrible waste of black talent that occurs under the prevailing socioeconomic conditions: the exalted titles he bestows on his followers are an effort to counteract the effect of this demoralizing rejection on the black self-image.

Garvey's efforts to rehabilitate the image of black women is also reflected; his Black Cross Nurses are among those present at the ceremony honoring Vic, and Garvey's effectiveness in promoting black consciousness is reflected in the black doll that Vic's daughter, Caroline, and her grandmother are dressing. Characteristically the black doll incites the contempt of Mrs. Brooks, which further points up the fact that Caroline's fondness for it is the result of her father's attitude.

Garvey's aim, stated by Vic, is black economic independence and the brotherhood of all black peoples. He is convinced that only total effort by the black community to achieve that independence will break the yoke of white oppression, and Vic, who is committed to the economic betterment of all blacks in America including the millions "down South living on corn bread and molasses and dying like flies from hook worm," rather than his own, individual betterment, invests his savings in Garvey's Black Star Line, although the news has already broken that the Black Star ship, the *Republic*, manned by a crew of seasoned West Indian seamen and ready to sail for Cuba on her maiden voyage, has been stopped in harbor because of unseaworthiness. When the financial ruin of the UNIA leads to Garvey's conviction for mail fraud, Vic refuses to abandon his cause, stating that "it's a mighty poor slave that'll give up trying to break his chains just because there's a knick in the hammer" (I.ii.26), and when Garvey's sentence is upheld by the Supreme Court, the depth of Vic's commitment overrides his terrible disappointment: "It's a mighty blow, Son. But it's all right. No man is indispensable. We may not find another as great, but we'll carry on" (II.iii.7). Vic's words were indeed prophetic, for the stone in Garvey's sling had smitten black consciousness and his doctrine has inspired every black leader who has succeeded him.

Big White Fog ends on a socialist note when the Masons' financial ruin drives Vic's son, Les, into the arms of the brotherhood and his comrades help prevent their eviction. A touch of exquisite ambiguity is injected by the author, however, and at the 1977 convention of the American Theater Association Mr. Ward replied to this author's question that this ambiguity was quite intentional. As Vic is dying from his gunshot wound, received during the eviction, he is eager to believe that his son's socialist brotherhood is possible. Vic begs Les to show him his black and white comrades standing together; he feels for them with outstretched hands as they press forward, but is unable to see them. "I guess my sight is gone" (III.iii.21) are his last words before he sinks back, dead, on the couch. Was it Vic's dying vision that was faulty? Or was his inability to see the black and white brothers standing together his recognition of the futility of his son's expectation in the thirties? Certainly no one in the Mason family had experienced any interracial brotherhood until the advent of Les' Jewish classmate, Piszer, and the intervention of Piszer and his socialist brotherhood brings only an aborted hope and a bullet for Les' father.

On the other hand Vic had stated about Garvey's conviction: "We may not find another as great, but we'll carry on" (II.iii.7), and one is led to speculate whether the dramatist deliberately sabotaged Les' socialist solution, prophetically suggesting instead that although Garvey's repatriation movement, and Vic, were historically dead, the forcefully dramatized doctrines of Marcus Garvey were not.

White critics of the play generally agreed that it was Garvey's financial failure that caused Vic's economic destruction, and ultimately his death. But was it? Although Garvey's financial failure did wipe out the Masons' savings, this does not alter the fact that Vic, a well-educated black who was intellectually and physically capable of supporting his family, was ultimately unable to find under the capitalist system a job that paid enough wages to support them. His only alternative to investing in Garvey's Black Star Line had been to join Dan's capitalist venture, but this alternative would also have wiped out his savings along with Dan's. What ultimately destroyed Vic's body was a capitalist, police bullet, invited by well-meaning socialist intervention; what destroyed his spirit was prejudice—the big white fog that denied him all dignity and thrust its deadly cancer into the very heart of the black community, including his family: "Prejudice, everywhere you turn nothing but prejudice. A black man can't even get away from it in his own house—And I was fool enough to think I could get away from it in Africa" (II.ii.15).

It would seem that with the exception of Garvey's repatriation program, which came to an end with his financial failure and conviction, Ward's dramatization projected the doctrine and influence of Marcus Garvey into the future virtually intact,[41] and as history has subsequently recorded, he was not a false prophet.

THIRTEEN

THE COMMON RHYTHMS

W HILE *Big White Fog* dramatized the influence of Marcus
Garvey on the twentieth century Afro-American, other plays
in the Federal Collection reflect other elements of the West
Indian influence. The French colony of Haiti was one of the most
prosperous and fiercely defended of European slave enterprises in the
Caribbean, and the successful black revolution, which thwarted even
Napoleonic efforts to re-establish French domination in the island,
has fired the imagination of numerous playwrights, both black and
white.[1] As a source of inspiration to the Afro-American playwright,
this historic black achievement differs greatly, however, from the
dramatic appeal its spectacular elements held for white playwrights,
and a comparison of *Black Empire*, which was written by Christine
Ames and Clarke Painter,[2] and *Troubled Island*, which was written by
poet–playwright Langston Hughes, clearly reveals this; it also shows
that drama is not black drama unless it projects the black soul, in the
black experience.

While *Black Empire* was produced by the Federal Theatre in 1936,[3]
Troubled Island was not produced by the Federal Theatre by the time it
closed and Langston Hughes, who was employed on the Writers'
Project, never specifically wrote for the Theatre. However, both scripts
are in the Federal Theatre Collection, and the setting and subject of
both are the black empire which was established in Haiti by successful
revolution. Langston Hughes chose to dramatize the rise and fall of
the slave-emperor Jean Jacques Dessalines, who led the slaves to
victory over the French after Toussaint L'Ouverture was captured
through trickery and deported to France. Ames and Painter have
dramatized the fall of his successor, Emperor Henri Christophe, who
also engaged in the historic revolution. The authors of both plays use
the historical fact that most of the intrigue that precipitated the downfall of the black empire was instigated by the highly educated free
mulatto population for its own benefit; both dramatize the black court
as a parody of the French court at Versailles; and both have chosen the
potential wealth of tropical splendor to interpret. The orientations of

the playwrights and their affinities for the black West Indian experience differ so drastically, however, that they affect every aspect of the plays.

In Ames and Painter's play, Emperor Henri Christophe and the exotic Haitian Empire provide the mysterious and spectacular background for white protagonists who are uncomfortable with the native elements of black Haiti. In *Troubled Island*, the black emperor, Dessalines, is the protagonist in an all-black cast, and all of the colorful Haitian elements form an intrinsic part of the black experience dramatized by Hughes.

The heroine of *Black Empire* is Cecile, the governess to Christophe's son, Crown Prince Victor Henri. She is a beautiful, blonde, French girl who as an infant was saved by her black nurse when her father, General Leconte, and the rest of her family were massacred in the revolution. Cecile has never known a white woman; she was raised in the black empire, was consecrated as a voodoo priestess—or Mamaloi —and all her life has practiced the voodoo sacrificial rites. At Christophe's court, where few whites are welcomed, she falls in love with Jacques Leblanc, a French officer who has entered Haiti and managed to avoid execution by Christophe through his quick wit and charm. Jacques is in search of the emperor's twelve million franc treasure, with which he hopes to buy Napoleon's freedom from the British; but Napoleon dies before Jacques can remove the treasure. Cecile is loved by both Jacques and Christophe's mulatto aide, Rigaud. Rigaud, too, is a voodoo priest—or Papaloi—and he intends to claim Cecile as his bride at the next ritual sacrifice.

Although prohibited by Christophe, voodoo is still clandestinely practiced throughout Haiti and Rigaud uses it to foment revolution for the purpose of seizing power himself. The court is a hotbed of voodoo intrigue. The Empress Marie is torn between her love and loyalty to Christophe and to her voodoo faith, and she privately pays obeisance to the Mamaloi and Papaloi whenever the emperor is not present, entreating them to pray for Christophe's safety. But the emperor's safety is not the aim of either Rigaud or Cecile; his safety would be contrary to Rigaud's plan to make himself emperor, and also to Cecile's determination to pray death for Christophe to revenge the death of her father. Unlike Cecile, Rigaud's greed prompts him to accept bribes from the distraught empress to placate the gods, while he is actually fomenting mutiny among the troops, and his efforts to promote another revolution are greatly aided by Christophe's tyrannical rule, which the emperor has imposed for the purposes of making the black empire impregnable and raising the cultural standards and dignity of all Haitians.

When Rigaud approaches Cecile with his offer of marriage, she rejects him for the white Frenchman, and in a frenzy of jealousy Rigaud then plans to capture Jacques for the voodoo sacrifice. His plan miscarries because of Jacques' expertise as a swordsman. Jacques, who has grown to admire the courage and determination of the black emperor, later kills Rigaud when he threatens Henri's life.

As the political unrest borders on revolution, Christophe's legs are mysteriously stricken with paralysis, either by the power of the voodoo death ouanga placed on his throne by Cecile or by a stroke. Thus crippled, he is no longer able to control his mutinous troops and they storm the palace, whereupon Christophe shows Jacques and Cecile how to escape through a secret passage to the beach, on condition that they take his empress and children with them to safety. As Jacques hurries the fugitives into the passage, a shot rings out; Christophe, hidden from view behind his loyal bodyguards, has taken his own life with a golden bullet and dies still an emperor and a free man.

Certainly the assembled elements of this play were exciting to a white audience of the thirties. The voodoo drums, which beat ominously and with appropriately varied degrees of intensity, form a tense background. Cecile, who is overcome by remorse for praying death to Christophe, performs a voodoo dance of intercession for Legba's mercy, accompanied by two native dancers, a chanter, and drummers. The gaudy court costumes of the Dukes of Marmalade, Orangeade, Limonade, and other nobility are highly colorful, while Christophe's brand of justice, which commands either back-breaking industry and immediate and unquestioning obedience or execution, is hair-raising. Christophe's enormous physical stamina and will-power are also spectacularly dramatized when he is shown walking on paralyzed legs in an abortive attempt to mount his horse and prove his indestructibility to his troops. But except for this historic achieve-ment, all the feats of valor and chivalry in the black empire are performed by the Frenchman. Jacques kills three stalwart attackers who attempt to capture him; he twice relieves Rigaud of his pistol with a superb sword-thrust, saves Henri's life, carries his family and Cecile to safety, and as a final romantic touch, he leaves Christophe's treasure, which he did succeed in finding, "for future generations." Beside him, Christophe never quite emerges from the secondary role of tyrant and Jacques emerges as the undisputed hero in the black empire. Even the emperor's "golden" suicide is blocked from view by his bodyguards.

There is no mistaking the fact that in this play the authors' orientation is strictly white; their descriptions of the characters not only reflect Western aesthetic standards but are unmistakably discriminatory in tone. Cecile is "a beautiful blonde white girl . . . simply but becomingly dressed" (II.i.4), and "Jacques is infatuated by her loveliness" (I.30). In contrast to Cecile, the black women are nondescript: the Empress Marie "is a plump middle aged negress," gaudily adorned (I.10), and Princesses Athenarie and Amethyste "are negresses and rather favor their mother" (I.16); they too are flashy. But since the whole court is flashily adorned and Cecile was raised in Haiti and has never even seen a white woman, it remains a mystery where she acquired her European taste in dress—unless she is supposed to have inherited it genetically. Jacques is "a manly young Frenchman" (I.3), while Christophe is described as "powerful," and Prince Victor Henri as "a frail anaemic negro boy" (I.16). Even the three minor white characters, Dr. Stewart, Pere Brelle, and Morbleu—the captured ex-slave-owner of Christophe whom the emperor executes with relish— have individual, distinguishing characteristics while the black courtiers in attendance on Christophe are just "negroes."

The authors' method of describing facial expressions and gestures also reveals their racial orientation: Dr. Stewart's face "reflects enlightenment" (I.29), and Morbleu, in agony, wrings his "fat hands" (I.25), whereas Rigaud "has a fiendish smile on his *brown* face" (II.12) and the Empress Marie reflects "abject terror on her *black* face" (I.20), or wrings "her *black* hands in despair" (I.19). When Bobo, one of Christophe's retinue, speaks, it is with "his *black* face lighting" (I.23), and when Christophe has a sinister expression, it is also coupled with his color: "His *black* face [is] covered with a diabolical sneer" (I.35), and "his face [is] in a *black* scowl of hatred" (II.9). (All italics added.)

An additional indicator of the playwrights' racial bias is grossly distorted probability: when Jacques, the epitome of everything gallant, loyal, and wise, confronts Rigaud, the treacherous mulatto has a pistol pointed directly at the Frenchman; yet Rigaud, who is the leader of the coming revolution, retreats like a coward when Jacques, sword in hand—but considerably out of sword's reach of his opponent— steps toward him.

Certainly no group of black actors and no Afro-American audience could be expected to believe that all Haitian blacks of the revolutionary period were nondescript, unbeautiful, sinister, or cowardly, but this is precisely the impression that is created by the script of *Black Empire*.

Appendices to *Black Empire* credit its voodoo elements to *The Magic Island* by M. B. Seabrook, and in the play these elements are obviously not motivated by the playwrights' affinity for the black philosophy or the Haitian culture that should support them. Like the superstitious fears in *The Emperor Jones*, they operate in an entirely negative manner, and thus stripped of sustaining power they transform both white and black characters into uncomfortable and inconsistent distortions. In spite of Cecile's life-long dedication to voodoo and her experience as a professional Mamaloi, she becomes suddenly revolted by the whole practice after she falls in love with Jacques; but she is also afraid of its power and she rejects her voodoo faith with enormous relief. The empress, who is a firm believer, is inspired only by her terror of the voodoo power which may be used against the emperor, while, for a man of his profound strength and determination, Christophe wavers with extraordinary indecision in his attitude toward voodoo.

As reflected in the play, Christophe's religious attitude cannot be interpreted as either dual religious acceptance—which was common in Haiti—or as enlightened rejection of voodoo. He admits only the anti-civilizing effects of voodoo superstition; he repudiates voodoo and forbids its practice on penalty of death, ordering his people to participate instead in Pere Brelle's Catholic worship, for its civilizing influence. He also emphatically denies any personal belief in the Christian God and refuses to attend services himself—even as a civilizing example. In spite of all these denials, when Pere Brelle is brutally murdered by the angry mob Christophe kneels to pray at the Christian shrine on his terrace—which also houses his treasure. As if in response to Brelle's earlier threat that God will punish him, he is now greeted by a vision of Brelle's battered ghost, whereupon, horrified, he is stricken on the spot with paralysis, but immediately attributes his condition to the power of the voodoo death ouanga that he had found on his throne. At the empress's plea, he then violates his own orders against the practice of voodoo and permits the white priestess to perform her intercessory dance to Legba, but while the dance is in progress his generals enter, and Christophe once more reverses his religious attitude by summarily stopping the dance.

In addition to Christophe's extraordinary religious orientation, *Black Empire* dramatizes Christophe's extraordinary racial orientation. The court is bristling with black Haitian nobles, many of whom had been the emperor's compatriots in the revolution, but Christophe, whose professed reputation in the play is that of making short work of white men, selects as his most constant and trusted companions the white foreigners, and it is to Jacques that he entrusts the safety of his family. While he is unable to read or write, Christophe's language is that of a European philosopher and is completely devoid of concrete or kinetic imagery. The authors also appear to confuse their own racial orientation with that of the black emperor. When Christophe informs Jacques that Cecile was "an infant when *the blacks* revolted" (II.6), he uses the third person, although the black emperor himself figured prominently as one of the black revolutionaries. After his stroke he also instructs his son that "the black race must rise until *they* can take an equal place in the world with other races" (III.8), and throughout this scene he separates himself from the black race and refers to it as "they" and "them." (Italics added.)

The playwrights' lack of black Haitian orientation is also reflected by their scarcity and misuse of local color; their characters are virtually suspended from their environment. The set for the entire play consists of Christophe's room, which leads out to a manicured lawn and a stone terrace that is surrounded by a parapet, beyond which is a backdrop of distant tropical hills and sky. Here the emperor holds court before his huge tree of justice—of nondescript type—which is decorated with a hangman's rope—Southern style. When he stands at the parapet and uses his telescope to survey his domain, as he often does, he does not observe the lush, tropical countryside but, always, his fortifications or his lazy subjects. On one occasion he observes a worker sleeping on the job so he immediately orders his cannon to fire on the miscreant. This, of course, blows up the worker and solves the problem of his laziness, but it does not get the work done. It does contribute immeasurably to Christophe's image as a butcher. Haiti's produce, which is enumerated by Christophe's Minister of Agriculture, is confined to cotton, cocoa, and sugar; there is no mention of the profusion of tropical fruit. One local dish is mentioned when Christophe sadistically suggests, before executing his ex-owner, Morbleau, that he might like the job of lighting the emperor's pipe and cooking his "calaloo"; the emperor, however, is not eating calaloo; by his own admission he is relishing Jacques' French dishes. There is a complete dearth of the type of descriptive imagery that a Haitian would use to bring the Haitian countryside to life; the characteristics of only one piece of tropical vegetation are mentioned, when Christophe symbolically likens himself to a huge jungle tree that is being strangled to death by the vine "loup garou." Thus the authors' negative and sinister view of the Haitian environment supports their negative and sinister view of the black emperor, and enhances the heroism of their white protagonists.

The playwrights' mode of presenting the colorful voodoo elements of the Haitian culture also divorces them from the black identity and experience, and these elements are more talked about than acted. The dominant voodoo representatives are the Papaloi, who is white-oriented, and the Mamaloi, who is a white French girl; yet Christophe tells Jacques that only a full-blooded Negro can really understand voodoo. Almost all the clandestinely practiced palace voodoo consists of ritual greetings between palace adherents, priest, and priestess, with the white-oriented characters in the dominant roles, and of warnings to Jacques of the terrible danger which voodoo represents to him and to Christophe. The three black Haitians, stalwart, white-streaked voodoo worshippers who are accustomed to the rigors of tropical labor, should make short work of Jacques when they attempt to capture him as their sacrificial "goat-without-horns,"[4] but they are all summarily vanquished by him, and except for this abortive incident the only actual dramatization of voodoo is the white girl's interrupted dance, during which her two black companions dance only secondary roles.

Undoubtedly, *Black Empire* had great appeal for white audiences when it was produced by the Federal Theatre, and its reception is no more being questioned than the recorded success of Orson Welles's spectacular voodoo Macbeth, of which Hughes Allison stated: "William Shakespeare is a good playwright, Orson Welles is a good showman. The 'Boy Wonder's' adaptation of the Bard's drama was a classic stunt."[5] Indeed, a review from the *Los Angeles Examiner* states:

> *Black Empire* continues to please Mayan audiences. The second week of this startling drama of Haiti's black Napoleon opens Monday night and all indications point to a continuation of the first seven days' remarkable attendance records.

The *Los Angeles Times* describes it as "a historical epic which unfolds three powerful acts of suspense thrills,"[6] while the production notebook for the play's presentation in Seattle also records that "audience reaction to the play was on the whole very favorable." The point here is simply that although it attempts to dramatize black history, this play is not black drama: the protagonists are white; the orientation of the play is white; the play is riddled with inconsistencies that distort the black image and the black experience, and it is not supported positively by the black West Indian culture and environment in which it is set. Clearly, white-oriented drama for black actors no more projects black identity than would an Englishman, equipped only with an Oriental mask, project the philosophic and cultural bases of the Noh stage.

Of the white-authored plays on the Haitian revolution which are in the Federal Theatre Collection, *Haiti*, which was produced by the Federal Theatre in 1938, is probably the least dominated by its author's race. William Du Bois did treat his black characters with a respect and sympathy that is totally lacking in *Black Empire*; they are the protagonists, while the occupying French officers are portrayed as spineless villains, almost to a man. But as black drama *Haiti* too has serious flaws. Du Bois's effort to "think black" backfired, for his dramatization of the French is far too extreme to be believable in the black experience and tends to rob the victory of the Haitian revolutionaries of much of its significance. In contrast, black playwright Hughes Allison did not make the mistake of undervaluing or underestimating the capabilities of his white antagonists in *The Trial of Dr. Beck*, with the result that the victory of Beck's black defense attorney was impressive. Fannin Belcher, who in 1940 chose six white-authored plays as the best on black life to date, described *Haiti* as "a good show, not a good drama,"[7] and Sterling Brown, who has often been kind to white authors of black plays, noted that it was melodrama, not history, and that "it was an attempt to capitalize on the vogue of Macbeth . . . with the lines somewhat inclined to ranting." He also noted that there was a "trite" situation when the "heroine who thinks she is white discovers she is black."[8]

This situation, where the heroine, who has lived all her life in France with her aristocratic white mother and has never before been in a black community, refuses to leave with the retreating French general and places herself under Christophe's protection, parallels the one in *Black Empire* in which Cecile, at the drop of a hat, renounces her entire Haitian upbringing. In *Haiti* the races are reversed, but the effect is just as unbelievable, possibly more unbelievable to a black audience of the thirties which had established a social hierarchy based on education and skin color. Yet Brooks Atkinson praised *Haiti*, stating that "nothing so good had exploded in the midst of Harlem since the racy nights of Macbeth,"[9] and McDonald considered it "excellent," but he also recorded and bemoaned the fact that only twenty five percent of its audience was black.[10]

In marked contrast to these visions of the black Haitian revolution were those of Langston Hughes. This subject obviously inspired and fascinated him for he worked on it for many years and, like Hughes Allison in *The Trial of Dr. Beck*, one of the messages he delivered to his black audience was that there was a pressing need to re-evaluate the hierarchy based on skin color which had been established in the black community.

We may recall Langston Hughes' almost overnight assembly—from many of his previously written poems—of *Don't You Want To Be Free?* for presentation by the Harlem Suitcase Theater. Indeed, he had an infinite capacity for "mix and match" or as Fannin Belcher stated, "Mr. Hughes' comedies have been constructed on the cook-book principle: a teaspoon of this and two tablespoons of that."[11] But this recipe has also given us tragedy by this poet-playwright in three closely related works, two of which he entitled *Troubled Island*. One of these works is *Emperor of Haiti*, which play he copyrighted in 1936.[12] Another is the libretto for the opera, *Troubled Island*, the music for which was written by William Grant Still; it was copyrighted in 1941, presented by the New York City Opera on 31 March 1949 at the City Center, New York, and published by Leeds Music Corporation in 1949.[13] The third is the play, *Troubled Island*, which he submitted to the Federal Theatre. Understandably, his "teaspoon of this and two tablespoons of that" have resulted in conflicting reports on the evolution of these works.

In his dissertation, Fannin Belcher does not list *Emperor of Haiti* at all; he lists *Troubled Island* as having been produced by the Gilpin players at the Karamu theater, Cleveland, Ohio, in 1936, and as having been first titled *Drums of Haiti*.[14] In *Black Drama in America: An Anthology*, Darwin T. Turner, however, states:

> Hughes worked on *Emperor of Haiti* for more than one quarter of a century. He first produced it in 1935 as *Drums of Haiti*, revised it in 1938 under its present title, adapted it into an opera, *Troubled Island* (1949), and completed his revisions of it as a drama in 1963. (p. 48)

Thus Turner does not mention *Troubled Island*, the play, at all, nor does he list it in his bibliography of Hughes' plays. In her dissertation, *From Shadows to Selves: Developing Black Theater* (University of Toronto, 1978), Leslie Sanders, who saw the Hughes papers at Yale, states that drafts in the *Drums of Haiti* file are variously titled *Drums of Haiti*, *Emperor of Haiti*, and *Troubled Island* (footnote 42, p. 230), but she does not record that these drafts were dated. She does record, however,

Langston Hughes' statement in an interview, *Chicago Defender*, 25 March 1954, that *Drums of Haiti* was directed by Elsie Roxborough in Detroit in 1934, and was revised by him the following year for the Gilpin players (footnote 44, p. 230). This would place *Drums of Haiti* in the background of the other three works and it would seem that Belcher just skipped a step in the evolution of the play, *Troubled Island*.

With regard to the evolution of these three plays, what we do know is that *Emperor of Haiti* was in existence by 1936 (copyright date), that the play, *Troubled Island*, was in existence by 1939, at which time the Federal Theatre was closed and its material stored, and that the opera libretto was in existence in 1941 (copyright date). An examination of these original scripts also indicates that both the play *Troubled Island* and the opera libretto were based on *Emperor of Haiti* (originally *Drums of Haiti*)—but not necessarily in the order suggested by the above dates.

Emperor of Haiti and the play, *Troubled Island*, are not identical, but one could certainly describe the latter, as submitted to the Federal Theatre, as a brilliantly polished version of the former. The plot, characterizations, and even much of the dialogue are the same, however parts of the dialogue have been cut, rewritten, even switched from one character to another in a highly effective manner, while several monologues have been broken up by the comments of other characters and have become more active. The result is that *Troubled Island* flows more smoothly, concentrates more sharply on essentials, and is usually more brilliantly, wittily, or poetically phrased than *Emperor of Haiti*. There are also several subtle shifts of emphasis in *Troubled Island*. There are fewer deferential references to the leaders, Toussaint and Christophe, in the act in which the revolt against the French occurs, and this enhances the stature of its hero, Dessalines, as the liberator of Haiti. In the scene between Dessalines and his slave-woman, Azelia, which immediately precedes this revolt, Dessalines is less harsh with her in *Troubled Island*, and his greater tenderness heightens the tragedy of her later rejection and of his own fatal choice to enthrone a beautiful mulatto girl in her place. The explicitly stated expectations of the mulattoes in *Emperor of Haiti*, of the manner in which Dessalines will inevitably react when he hears that the country is in revolt against him, are eliminated in *Troubled Island*, and this shift—from inevitability to freedom of choice on the Emperor's part— heightens the suspense and greatly enhances the quality and immediacy of the dramatic action. As she kneels beside his dead body in the final scene, Azelia's reminiscences over her slave life with Dessalines, and her rejection by him, are also more sharply focused on her agonized outpouring of love for the dead emperor than on his sins, which have already been fully dramatized; thus the finale is more positive and less diffused.

The story of the opera libretto is also essentially the same as that of the two plays, and so are the names and functions of all major characters. The dramas, and the opera libretto, however, have their own distinctive characters since music, which dominates and controls the scope of the libretto is, in the plays, confined to drums, which, conversely, support and reflect its various dramatic moods. There are also several scenes and incidents in both plays that are not included in the opera—undoubtedly because of the demands of musical dominance—but these dramatic interludes in the plays relieve, in Shakespearean fashion, the tension of this stark tragedy. The dialogue of each of these works also differs somewhat from each of the others, but in those scenes that are common to all three, the dialogue of the libretto is much closer to that of the copyrighted *Emperor of Haiti* than to the brilliantly polished play, *Troubled Island*. It seems likely, therefore, that while both the libretto and the play, *Troubled Island*, were based on *Emperor of Haiti*, and in spite of the above dates, the libretto was actually written between *Emperor of Haiti* and the play that was submitted to the Federal Theatre as *Troubled Island* by 1939. But there is always the possibility of alternatives with Langston Hughes. He may have chosen, deliberately, for instance, not to incorporate in the libretto the improvements he made in the play, *Troubled Island*, although this seems unlikely, or the music for the opera may already have been written by William Grant Still with the dialogue of *Emperor of Haiti* in mind.

Certainly, the opera merits far greater attention in its own right than it has received here, but since our present concern is with drama, further discussion of *Troubled Island* will be confined to the script of the play as submitted by Hughes to the Federal Theatre, and a look at what he has done with the same elements used in *Black Empire* will show how the Afro–West Indian influences that reinvigorated black American interest in its African heritage inspired a black playwright.

The first act of *Troubled Island* dramatizes the gathering of the Haitian slaves for the historic revolt. Dessalines has been elected to lead, and his adoring woman, Azelia, is at his side. Here the blacks are joined by the free mulattoes, who have grievances of their own against their white fathers. The mulattoes, represented by the poet Vuval and his cousins, Stenio and Beyard, are not liked or trusted by the slaves, but

Dessalines recognizes the blacks' need of their superior education, so he defuses a racial confrontation that threatens the crucial gathering and chooses Vuval as his aide. The mulattoes are disappointed by the choice of Dessalines as leader since they had expected to be elected to lead the revolt, and subsequently to rule; but Vuval is awed by the ferocity of the slaves' pent-up emotions and takes his place beside Dessalines. The slaves gather, the moment of action arrives, and they pour forth to the intended massacre of their masters.

The second act takes place several years later in Dessalines' palace. The nobles of the court generally parallel those in *Black Empire* in their fantastic titles and barbaric splendor of costume, but they are thoroughly enjoying the fruits of their successful revolution. Dessalines had been a great warrior leader, but, as Old Martel says, he is no statesman, and a giant conspiracy by the mulattoes to overthrow the emperor is about to come to a head. Dessalines has been reluctant to tax the peasants for schools and other public improvements and for the fortifications which he, like Christophe in *Black Empire*, considers necessary to insure Haiti's liberty and well-being. He has instead taxed the nobles—black and mulatto—to whom he has given land, and who should be making handsome profits. Many of the blacks do not yet fully understand that freedom does not mean that they no longer have to work. Some of the mulattoes are living lavishly in Paris instead of helping to build and educate Haiti, while those that remain in the island are sending huge sums to Paris banks. They are pleading poverty to the emperor and lack of markets for their produce, while they themselves are taxing the peasants out of existence with the apparent approval of the unsuspecting emperor, for Vuval has taught Dessalines only to sign his name, and the emperor is dependent on his Most High Grand Keeper of Records and Seals, Count Vuval, for all communication with his empire. Vuval's correspondence with Dessalines' generals is designed to promote distrust of the emperor and to incite them to join the increasingly dissatisfied peasants in revolt and, to complete the mulattoes' well-laid plans, Dessalines has been seduced. To accomplish this, they had sent to Paris for Claire Heureuse, the beautiful mulatto cousin of Beyard, who had lost her land and fortune in the revolution and was eager to regain them.

Claire Heureuse is the most beautiful and cultured girl Dessalines has ever seen, and he is immediately infatuated by her and abandons Azelia with the offer of a handsome pension or a job in the palace— both of which the distraught Azelia refuses. He makes Claire Heureuse his empress, but Claire is Vuval's sweetheart and she plays her part well in the conspiracy to overthrow the emperor while she too is bilking the court of all she can lay her hands on. Dessalines, who does not trust his Most High Grand Keeper of Records and Seals, has Claire Heureuse read for him the letters Vuval writes in his name, but she reads what Vuval instructs her to read and Dessalines remains in fatal ignorance of their treachery and the explosive conditions they have promoted throughout Haiti. Dessalines, like Christophe, has forbidden the practice of voodoo at court because the Paris-acculturated Claire Heureuse is a Catholic and detests the drums—although they were "good enough for her mother"—and this suppression motivates the priests too to stir up the peasantry against him.

While a sumptuous court banquet is in progress, the revolt is triggered. The mulatto nobles excuse themselves early and set out for the fishing village where Dessalines' Royal Haitian Army, Division of the South, has been quartered. The general and his troops have joined the mulattoes and have vacated the village, as ordered by Stenio, and the mulattoes' yacht rides at anchor in the bay, ready for the coup. The trap for Dessalines has been well laid and when he hears, at the banquet, that the island is in revolt, he immediately reacts in character: he orders his horse and, accompanied by only two faithful attendants and contrary to the advice of Old Martel, he dashes off toward the fishing village to take command of his "loyal" army. At the village, Vuval and Stenio await him with a squad of hand-picked soldiers, and as the emperor dismounts and strides up on the quay he is surrounded. On orders from Stenio the soldiers seize his attendants, but they dare not touch the legendary Dessalines for they are convinced he cannot be killed by bullets. "The Tiger," Dessalines, draws his sword and moves toward Stenio, whereupon Vuval shoots him in the back and is hailed by Stenio as the new liberator of Haiti. Stenio takes Dessalines' sword as a souvenir, and he and the rather shaken Vuval retire to the barracks to await the empress's arrival, while wandering Azelia finds Dessalines lying face down on the quay. He is surrounded by scavengers who are stripping him of his finery and as she chases them away she recognizes the old welts from the slave whip that stand out like cords on the emperor's bare back. Azelia falls to her knees beside him.

Claire Heureuse now arrives at the quay, laden with palace booty. The empress glances with a shudder at the welts on her husband's back—a sight she will never forget—then she and Vuval board the yacht to leave for the bright lights of Paris, while Stenio goes to join the army and set up the new government. Only Azelia is left to croon her agony over her dead love as the play ends.

Now what does Langston Hughes do with this tragic plot and the resources of black, tropical Haiti? Certainly, there are no character contradictions. Dessalines had been a veritable "Tiger" during the revolution, but as he acknowledged, an uneducated one, and as emperor he pays the ultimate penalty for this deficiency. The mulatto rebels, whose superior education and untrustworthiness the dramatist had established in the first scene, perform characteristically and efficiently to precipitate his tragedy. Azelia goes a little crazy when she is rejected by the emperor in what should have been her hour of triumph, and Claire Heureuse is also true to the character which was foreshadowed for her. In addition, every black in the play is an individual, not by description but by dramatization.

Langston Hughes' language is also a delight. Often beautifully poetic, it is also thoroughly characteristic of the black form of rhythmic expression, of black wit and of black kinetic imagery—both Afro-American and Afro–West Indian. Here is Popo informing the emperor that his regalia is ready for the banquet: "I've done laid out your robes. . . . I put the ruby crown out, too, and polished up the scepter. It shine like a lightning rod" (II.i.4). As the banquet table is prepared, two old serving women discuss Baron Congo's infatuation with the Lady Celeste, who is mistress of the banquet arrangements. Both Congo and Celeste had participated in the revolutionary massacre in act I, and the old women are uncertain about the protocol involved in the grandiose titles bestowed on the revolutionaries.

> Second Old Lady. Congo's a baron, and she's a Lady. If he marry her, what title do that give 'em both?
> First Old Lady. What you mean, 'em both? Celeste gonna run him just like she do everything else, and he'll be a Mr. Lady Baron, that's what! (II.ii.2)

When Lady Celeste and Lady Lulu, High Grand Keeper of the Linens, enter, Lady Lulu announces that she is getting ready to "give that Jean Jacques a piece of [her] mind"; she wants time off to go to Port au Prince "to look up a new husband" because "these men around here's too banana bellied to suit [her] taste" (II.ii.3–4), and when Baron Congo steals a kiss from Lady Celeste and proclaims that "it tastes sweeter'n a honey bee," she immediately retorts "wait till you feel the stinger!" (II.ii.11). The First Old Lady then collars a ragged boy and instructs him: "boy, scramble up there and light that big lamp over His Majesty's head. He likes plenty light" (II.ii.12)—and Dessalines is not even anywhere in sight. One does not need to search

Troubled Island for this type of wit and imagery, it rises in the flesh from every page.

But the most striking contrast between *Troubled Island* and *Black Empire* is what Langston Hughes does with the colorful West Indian elements. In his play black identity, the black experience, and the environment support, rather than contradict, each other. In act I the slaves collect for the revolt at an abandoned sugar mill, where the moon shines through the broad open door, silhouetting tall coconut palms against the stars and the distant, green wooded hills. Josef carries the curve of a cane knife in his hand, and Azelia balances a flat wicker basket on her head, that feat that gives West Indian peasant women their magnificent carriage. Beneath an overlay of bananas are concealed machetes, an axe handle, and whips, and she swings the basket down with an easy grace and rests it on the cane grinder. When he arrives at the mill, Jean Jacques' back is raw from the forty lashes he received only that morning. As the slaves await zero hour, Mars replies to the child Pierre's question about his one arm that he lost the other to Le Code Noir for striking a white man (1.ii.2). Old Martel speaks exultantly and poetically across the years to Africa: "Thy children in Haiti have thrown off the yoke of bondage and *are men again*" (italics added), and the slaves are assured by him that the spirit of Mackendal, who was burned after a previous unsuccessful revolt, walks with them through the revolution "crying the name of freedom" in the Haitian hills (1.10). Here the African heritage is not talked, it is lived; for

> when the slave Boukman lays his fingers on the great drum hidden in the cane-brake tonight, he'll beat out a signal that'll roll from hill to hill, slave hut to slave hut, across the cane-fields, across the mountains, across the bays, from Island to Island, until every drum in Haiti throbs with the call to rise, (1.6)

for "the drum's a black man's heart a-beatin'" (1.ii.2).

The Mamaloi, carrying a live sacrificial cock, and the Papaloi, with a rattle in one hand and an African drum in the other, chant their supplications to Dambala, Legba, and other Orisha in an African tongue, and are joined in their supplications by the assembling slaves. The Elders, led by Martel, proclaim, in the heroic tradition, Dessalines' worthiness, and their trust of him, to which Dessalines responds while the entire assembly joins in the call–response war ritual.

Dessalines' intent now is to whip the assembly to a pinnacle of purposeful anger. His speech is electrifying in its imagistic simplicity, as he describes how he grew up eating at the trough with the dogs and thinking he was an animal until he became tall and strong; then he was driven to the fields with whips across his back,

> and when I turned, he lashed me in the face, I cried out, he struck again. Then I lifted up my head and looked him in the eyes, and I knew I was a man, not a dog! I wanted to be free! (1.28)

The strategy for the revolt which was outlined by Dessalines was that which had been used by countless bands of Cimaroones in the Caribbean:[15] fire the cane-fields and the mansions, kill the white oppressors, poison the springs, choke the rivers, ambush the roads, and collect in the jungle-covered mountains where food supplies, marked by scarred trees and scattered sea shells, have been buried and where cannon cannot follow. Dessalines promises that there they will make powder and bullets, sacrifice the goat to Legba, and then they will swoop down on the seaports to set Haiti free. As the chanting and swaying approaches frenzy, the drums begin to signal, filling the air with urgency, and the slaves pour forth to live or die, accompanied by the Mamaloi, the Papaloi, and the Orisha of Africa.

In the second act, the banquet table is set on a covered terrace "whose arched portals are open to the sky" (II.ii.1), "palm trees and the early evening stars" (II.ii.4), and "where the air is still rosy with sunset" (II.ii.1). The table is laden with great bowls of tropical fruit, and the empress walks outside to pick a flower for her hair. Although voodoo and drums have been banished from the court to satisfy the empress, who has brought her own Catholic priest from France, an unexpected voodoo dance occurs during the banquet's entertainment. The approved European music, which accompanies a dozen dancing girls decked in precious stones and in anklets of beaten gold, is invaded and obliterated by drums, and a male dancer, "feathered and painted like a voodoo god" (II.ii.16), displaces the girls, who sink to the floor before his fierce, terrible dance. Covering her ears with her hands, Claire Heureuse pleads with Dessalines to stop the drums from driving her crazy, but when he angrily gives the order to stop them and lectures his court on the values of refined entertainment and on his intention to *impose* culture and industry on Haiti if he must, distant drums in the Haitian hills pick up the rhythm and continue until the emperor dashes out to quell the new rebellion and meets death.

The last scene on the quay of the fishing village is another banquet of supportive Afro–West Indian elements. It dramatizes the survival of African communality through the slave produce market, where everything of importance in Haiti is discussed. The women vendors line the embankment that curves down to a beach, which is fringed with coconut palms festooned with fishing nets, while the tops of the sails of fishing boats slash the sky beyond the wall. Here the barefoot vendors, their heads covered from the sun with gaily colored bandanas, hawk their wares: mangoes, melons, yams, oranges, limes, sugar canes, coconuts, red peppers, thread, thimbles, and other trinkets, set out on baskets and cloths. They chatter gaily about all the latest news, and carry on a lively repartee with the departing fishermen, who try to tempt them with the fish, sea crabs, and squid they hope to bring back. "You can smell the sea when the breeze blows" (III.2), and one vendor shares her uninhibited wisdom on how to deal with the "sweet mens": "A man is like a palm-leaf fan to me. When I feels the need, I picks one up, and when I cools off, I puts him down!" (III.4), while another declares that according to the priest "it ain't moral." The prevailing attitude toward religion is accurately expressed by one who attends both the Catholic mass and the voodoo dances of Legba: "Might as well believe in all kinds of gods, then if one fails you, you got another one to kinder help out" (III.5). Here cracked Azelia also wanders, her basket now heavy with premature age and the load of machetes she believes she is still carrying beneath the bananas. She chatters about the revolution and about her man, Dessalines—"you mean Dessalines, the Emperor?"—and is believed by nobody. Here the economic plight of the peasants who have no ploughs to produce food is discussed, and hungry urchins, who speak a strange back-country dialect, watch their chance to seize a handful of fruit and run, while no one is looking.

Here, too, graft and politics are discussed: the red sails of the "spendthrift" mulattoes' yacht stain the peaceful blue sky with prophetic symbolism, and its size is noted by the vendors "cause its anchoring way out in deep water" (III.9). "Haiti gone to rack and ruin," and "the farmers done refused to pay taxes," while "poor Jean Jacques he don't know what to do" (III.10). New rumors of wars are exchanged: the soldiers have left the fort, and "the Papaloi says there's gonna be change soon" (III.11).

As Stenio, Vuval, and their squad of soldiers invade the peaceful quay, the women beckon, hold out their fruit, and chant their enticing hucksters' melody: "Melons! Nice, cool melons!" (III.11).

Certainly this is not the Haiti that inspired Ames and Painter's dramatization of the black empire, and it becomes apparent that black drama, to have any meaning as such demands far more of a dramatist than the setting of a play—even a spectacular play—in a little understood black community. *Troubled Island* presents the historic black West Indian experience authentically and meaningfully: here is black Haiti, or almost any other island in the Caribbean sun where the proud spirit of the African warrior refused to recognize white superiority, where African communality survived, where African speech patterns and imagery still dominate, and where Christianity rests comfortably in the same hand that kills the sacrificial cock.

The melody of the words may vary slightly from Trinidad to Haiti, or from Haiti to Afro-America, but the spiritual rhythms are the same: they are the language of the African heritage and of black identity. These common rhythms make an Afro-American at home on a street corner in Kingston, or with a steel band in Port of Spain. They were the match with which Marcus Garvey fired the imagination of two million Afro-Americans. They united in a common creative flash when Stokely Carmichael, a West Indian, introduced Afro-America's most powerful twentieth-century slogan along the highways of the South,[17] for the *Black Power* mystique emphasized the ancient, spiritual oneness, the international scope of black identity, and it changed forever the direction of American race relations.

We have now explored the common human heritage, the African inheritance, the Western modifications, the Afro-American experience, and the Afro–West Indian influence and convergence, all of which have contributed to the twentieth-century Afro-American identity. We have also seen that all these components were translated into the black drama of the thirties by Afro-American playwrights whose expanded consciousness of their international and interracial heritage was seldom recognized. But as Alain Locke so aptly stated of the Harlem Renaissance, "if America were deaf, they would still sing,"[17] because "the future listens, however the present may shut its ears."[18]

FOURTEEN

BLACK REVOLUTIONARY DOCTRINE AND

BLACK DRAMA OF THE THIRTIES

I N THE THIRTY-FIVE years since the Federal Theatre era, the American stage has seen many changes. The segregation of theater artists and audiences has become a thing of the past, and the black dramatic art has become free to develop its own modes in its own manner for its own audiences. Yet two of the major problems which the Federal Theatre had done much to alleviate during its short life reappeared to plague the efforts of black dramatists and the black stage. These were lack of adequate financing and the lack of a large enough black audience. In the sixties, the lack of financing was to some extent alleviated by government and other grants, such as that of the Rockefeller Foundation; however the creation of a black audience was incomplete, and was still essential for the success of the black stage.

Since the closing of the Federal Theatre, the most influential organization in the black dramatic world to address itself to this need has been the Black Arts Movement—the Black Revolutionary Theater—of which Imamu Amiri Baraka (LeRoi Jones) was the guiding light in the late sixties and early seventies.[1] As its name implies, this theater is firmly committed to black politics and it established the "correct" ideology for the black revolutionary stage, based on what it saw to be the cultural and political needs of the black community. Two of its ideological requirements were that black plays must have spontaneous appeal for the black masses and that they must be authenticated by the black community. To the theorists, this meant that black playwrights must be committed to projecting legitimate images of the community's identity, its culture, and its experience, and, in conjunction with its political aims, it also meant that for plays to be considered valid its playwrights must be committed to nationalism and revolutionary change.

To accomplish these aims the movement dictated a complete rejection of the white commercial stage, including its ethics, its aesthetics, and its cult of stars. Black drama should and must return to being a communal expression, and the Western abstraction and separation of art from life should and must be replaced by their reunion through the dramatization of specifics—the specifics of black identity, black history, and the black experience. The movement rejected protest drama on the grounds that it was ineffective as a political medium and was demeaning to black dramatists, artists, and audiences, and it also renounced biracially oriented drama on the premise that explanations which were necessary for the understanding of white audiences were tedious to blacks.

The establishment of this ideology was facilitated by the fact that, at its inception, the Black Revolutionary Theater's playwrights and critics were one and the same. They experimented with new modes, wrote new plays, and pronounced on the validity of those and other black plays in accordance with the ideologies they had established, and there is no doubt that this unification of dramatic and critical functions was a potent factor in the establishment of Black Revolutionary Theater ideologies. The movement further insured that their criteria would become firmly rooted in the black community by attaching them to existing cultural norms and attitudes, such as the attitudes towards the function of music, ritual or religion in black life. Thus in essence the black performing arts became a function of black politics, and to the Revolutionary Theater this function represented a legitimate reunion of art and reality. Within a relatively short time, this marriage of black arts and black politics was firmly established in the black community and young blacks were acculturated with their inseparability. As one black critic later stated, the Black Arts Movement, and particularly its chief theoretician, Baraka, "embodied the complex forces of historical becoming,"[2] and there is little doubt that it had great influence in raising black consciousness.

After the advent of legal desegregation, the elimination of white prejudice and of socioeconomic inequality had not kept pace with rising expectations in the black community, and the bitter disappointment and rising anger of most blacks were reflected on the revolutionary stage, where black dramatists and critics of the revolutionary school lashed back at the rejecting white community, at white ethics and aesthetics, at white commercial stage practices, at white liberals whose efforts to promote integration were considered to have been ineffectual, and even at those black theorists, critics, or dramatists who had found any value at all in white standards. It was not long before most black critics fell in line with the new black aesthetic, and a plethora of literary flagellation of white standards ensued.[3]

Soon black revolutionary politics, which were directed toward self-

determination and nationhood, repudiated the value of integration—
a term which had become, to many Afro-Americans, synonymous
with assimilation on white terms—and the black revolutionary stage
became a political battlefield. John O'Neal wrote, "the theater (all art,
in fact) is political."[4] But as Adam David Miller stated, the great
talents of Imamu Amiri Baraka, "despite his brilliance," were devoted
to "still trying to do something with whites, either flagellating them
verbally or parading them as beasts. The results [were] often vivid but
shallow abstractions,"[5] and on both sides of the race line charges of
racism and counter-racism rent the air.[6]

Unquestionably, the Black Arts Movement, spearheaded by Baraka,
has a great many positive achievements to its credit. Socioeconom-
ically and politically, there is nothing either as solidifying or as cathar-
tic to an oppressed people as participation in the flagellation of the
oppressor and his value system, and this also helped greatly to raise
black consciousness and to solidify black determination to achieve
equality and autonomy. The dramatic images thus projected by the
revolutionary dramatists struck responsive chords in the black community and were far more meaningful to black audiences than those
projected by white-oriented plays on black life,[7] and this was instrumental in helping to increase black theater audiences, which was still
essential to the expansion, even to the survival, of autonomous black
theater.

The Black Revolutionary Theater's rejection of the standards of the
white commercial stage—whose capitalist eye continued, necessarily,
to be focused through its box office on the expectations and tastes of
the white majority—also greatly encouraged experimentation by other
black theater groups with new ideas and with traditional African
forms,[8] and interesting new modes, such as the ritual drama of Barbara
Teer, emerged. The Black Revolutionary Theater set a new tone for
black drama which was to be felt throughout both black and white
communities, while its ideologies established an effective means of
achieving this change.

In spite of its remarkable achievements, not all of the effects of its
ideologies have been positive. One fact that emerged from all its
revolutionary changes was that the white superiority myth was still a
potent factor in black life and thought for the myth continued, through
the focus and the limitations imposed by the new medium, to concentrate both the attention and the artistic efforts of the black community
on reaction rather than action, and these limitations curtailed the
freedom of black dramatists to draw on their entire interracial heritage

to create as they chose—an ironic twist for a people dedicated to achieving freedom. Much of the drama of white flagellation which Baraka and the Black Revolutionary Theater inspired bears witness to the effects of this focus and these limitations on their authors' creative potential. Not unlike the fate of Zema in *Panyared*, the fate of the black dramatist hung precariously in the balance between total freedom and the bounds set by reaction, and it was clear that sooner or later the pendulum would have to swing back to permit greater creative latitude if rigor mortis was ultimately to be avoided.

Nevertheless, the future tone of black drama was firmly established in the minds and expectations of black America, and one of its most negative effects has been in the value placed on pre-revolutionary black drama. This devaluation of early black drama has not jeopardized the status of black performers of the past, since as interpreters rather than creators they posed no threat to revolutionary ideologies, and they have continued to be greatly appreciated and glorified. It has, however, been devastating to the public image of pre-revolutionary black theorists and dramatists and the validity of this devastation we must now explore in detail.

In 1974 Abiodun Jeyifous, a highly articulate spokesman for the achievements of the Black Revolutionary Theater, summed up the effects of its ideologies on the black dramatic past.[9] Using the Black Revolutionary Theater's ideologies as his criteria, he separates the ineffectual from the effectual periods of black dramatic development, drawing the dividing line at the inception of the Black Revolutionary Theater in the late sixties. The pre-revolutionary period of drama and criticism he defines as the theater of black "sensibility" during which black playwrights were in "flight from a specific racial identity,"[10] and he states that their efforts at integrated theater were dominated by white standards. The second period he defines as the theater of "Black Esthetic Criticism," and of black "consciousness" and "commitment," which he attributes entirely to the aims and efforts of the Black Revolutionary Theater—and indirectly, therefore, also to the aims of black revolutionary politics. Since the father of black dramatic theory, Alain Locke, and the black dramatists of the Federal Theatre era whom he inspired, wrote considerably before this arbitrary date of separation, there is no doubt that Jeyifous' intention was to establish that their work is of little current value as black drama; moreover, Jeyifous was expressing the views which had become firmly established in the black community as a result of Black Revolutionary Theater ideologies.

In actual fact, Locke's dramatic vision, which like that of Max Reinhardt extended beyond "the formal horizons," was obviously somewhat of an embarrassment to the Black Revolutionary Theater and to its spokesmen; their political limitations, and their emphasis on the importance of the concentration of both the critical and creative aspects of black drama in the same group—the creators of Black Revolutionary Theater doctrine—made this inevitable, for Locke had diametrically opposed views. He refused to subordinate art to politics, stating:

> my chief objection to propaganda, apart from its besetting sin of monotony and disproportion, is that it perpetuates the position of group inferiority even in crying out against it. . . . genius and talent must choose the role of group expression, or even . . . free individualistic expression, in a word must choose art and put aside propaganda.[11]

Thus he also refused to limit the artistic scope of the Afro-American dramatist, and his numerous articles reveal that his criticisms were directed with equal objectivity at both white and black shortcomings. With Locke's view W. E. B. Du Bois was in agreement, for he also stated:

> We want everything that is said about us to tell of the best and highest and noblest in us. We insist that our Art and Propaganda be one. This is wrong and in the end it is harmful.[12]

While *Afro USA*, an impressive literary product of the new black aesthetic period, lists Locke's achievements as "his effort to make the general public aware of the Negro's aesthetic achievement—from the art and artifacts of Africa to the poetry and novels of the American writer,"[13] and Locke's own book, *The New Negro*, published in 1925, exultantly informs the public of the emergence of a new black self-image, Locke's dramatic foresight and theories far exceeded these services credited to him. He was deeply interested in the development of black drama and his critiques in this field were visionary and penetrating; he also warned Afro-America of the past effects of "the pathetic over-compensation of a group inferiority complex"[14] and of the necessity for objectivity to insure dramatic growth.[15] Creation in terms of reaction to white oppression Locke recognized to be self-limiting and ultimately self-defeating.[16]

In view of this major conflict between the theories of Locke and those of the Black Revolutionary Theater, if Black Revolutionary

Theater ideologies were to flourish, the theories of Locke obviously had to go—and with them, inevitably would go the works of all those dramatists who had written for what Jeyifous established arbitrarily by date, rather than by individual content, as the theater of black "sensibility." After this firm dividing line between the theater of black "participation" and the theater of black "consciousness" had been established by Jeyifous all that any revolutionary theoretician or critic then needed to do, to relieve the Black Revolutionary Theater of the embarrassment of the scope of the father's vision, was to link it inseparably to rejected white standards. And that is exactly what Jeyifous, himself, does.

Jeyifous' thinking is typical of the flaws inherent in the Black Revolutionary Theater's ideology, so the method of argument by which he discredits the black dramatic past merits close attention. First, he dismisses several pre-revolutionary critics with little comment, but admits that Locke is a special case since Locke's critiques were "energized, in Walter Benjamin's phrase 'by vibrations of the future'"[17] and he begins by commending the father of black dramatic theory for his bold attacks on the shoddy practices of the white commercial stage and for other visionary and valuable critical services to the development of black drama. Then he proceeds to discredit the breadth of Locke's vision by a chain of vague associations and selects a few of Locke's own words, taken out of context, for this purpose. According to Jeyifous, "he advocated experimentation, imaginative boldness, and a return to 'the roots of drama (which) after all are action and emotion,'"[18] and these words are intended to demonstrate Locke's relationship to those black critics who advocated integration and to prove his domination by white Western standards which separate art from life and ethics from the realities of socioeconomics. This connection, according to Jeyifous, also being "through the private emotions of responsive and sensitive individuals," created a conceptual impasse for Locke, which, Jeyifous maintains, Locke "acknowledged," and which was "responsible for the general redundancy and mediocrity of the criticism."[19] Thus he sweeps away with one hand the bouquet he held withering in the other, and by so doing, establishes as unassailable the doctrines of the Black Revolutionary Theater.

But let us now look a little more closely at the components of Jeyifous' chain of association.

As we have already discussed, it is true that Aristotle, who laid the foundation for Western dramatic standards that prevail today, defined drama as the imitation of an action, and its audience appeal as intellectual and emotional: he also posited imagination to be one of the vital ingredients of the creative process. However action and emotion are also the core of African ritual expression: dance, for example, is a physical manifestation of the entire range of man's emotions. In addition, the efforts of the raconteur of the African oral tradition were directed toward engaging his audience intellectually and emotionally, and Grace Sims Holt has recorded these survivals in the techniques of the black preacher who must reach both intellectual and emotional segments of his congregation and who slowly tries one approach and then another until he captures both, and eventually plucks the emotional strings of his entire congregation.[20] Furthermore, since the raconteur, like the black preacher today, did not use prepared scripts, the fleshing out of his themes demanded the utmost imagination. Even at the core of black revolutionary ideologists, no one who has had any exposure to Baraka's *Black Mass* could eliminate imagination as one of its most vital ingredients,[21] and one is forced to conclude that action, emotion, and imagination are among the roots of drama in both traditions, and that Locke's recognition of their centrality is hardly evidence of his exclusive affinity for white standards. As we also noted, *Afro USA* has acknowledged his extensive efforts to publicize the "arts and artifacts of Africa," therefore it can hardly be presumed that Alain Locke was unaware of these African roots of black drama.

Aristotle's definition of drama as the imitation of an action certainly has no counterpart in African tradition, in fact it is contrary to the African philosophy of the inseparability of art and life and presents a problem to those Afro-American writers who face the reality of their dual inheritance and experience. But for Afro-American dramatists this distinction has become far more academic than real: a synthesized product, prestructured Afro-American drama cannot be considered either to be the pure form of spontaneous African religious ritual expression or the spontaneous manifestation of the raconteur's art. John O'Neal admits that "the theater, as a discrete form, is largely foreign to the cultural experience and heritage of the black audience,"[22] and by the very act of prestructuring, Afro-American, like Euro-American, drama requires imitators, or actors—notwithstanding Barbara Teer's imaginative definition of the actors of her ritual drama as liberators, which they undoubtedly also are—who must practice their imitation and liberation to perfection before performances. The African heritage alone has been unable to offer an alternative solution for Afro-American dramatists, and imitation of an action has inevitably invaded and defined prestructured black drama, whether revolutionary, or pre-revolutionary.

But, Jeyifous' argument continues, "Locke remained fixed in endless imaginings and ratiocinations in the esthetic estate," and he states that Locke admitted a theoretical quandary. Jeyifous now uses the following quotation from Locke, to prove both Locke's quandary and his admission of it:

> Negro dramatic art must not only be liberated from the handicaps of external disparagement, but from its self-imposed limitations. It must more and more have the courage to be original, to break with established dramatic convention of all sorts. It must have the courage to develop its own idiom, to pour itself into new moulds; in short, to be experimental. From what quarter this *impetus* will come we can not quite predict; it may come from the Negro theater, or from some sudden adoption of the American stage; from the art theater, or from the commercial theater, from some home source, or first as so many things seem to have come, from the more liberal patronage and recognition of the European stage. But this much is certain — the material awaits a great exploiting genius. [23] (Italic added.)

Ah! those self-imposed limitations that Locke so firmly rejects; and surely this quotation admits no domination, and certainly no quandary except for those who do impose self-limitations. On the contrary, it is a strong statement of Locke's conviction that black drama must break with all established or limiting conventions, of his faith in the enormous potential of black drama, and of his readiness to accept experimental breakthroughs, regardless of the source of their impetus.

If, however, it was Locke's unwillingness to predict the possible source of this impetus that Jeyifous is attempting to use to discredit Locke's vision, this statement was written in 1926, at which time no one, not even the visionary Locke, could have foreseen such a specific future event as the formation of a Federal Theatre in 1935—which did furnish unprecedented impetus to black playwrights; although even on this Locke's vision was prophetic for he did envisage "an endowed artistic center where all phases vital to the art of the theater are cultivated." [24] Much that the European stage has pioneered has also affected the development of black drama, and, although black audiences could not empathize with the superstitious fears of Brutus Jones, an original excursion by an established and popular American playwright like Eugene O'Neill into the traditional African arts did spark public interest in them as a rich source of dramatic material, and could very well have furnished the impetus for a major breakthrough by a black dramatist.

What Jeyifous was actually condemning Locke for was not foreseeing the eventual arrival, forty years later, of a Baraka on the black dramatic scene, but this would also be an inaccurate and irrelevant interpretation of Locke's words, for Locke was not in any way questioning what race would create black drama, merely where the impetus for a breakthrough might come from, and even the post desegregation rejection of integration, by white America, acted as a spur to Baraka and the black revolutionary stage.

In all of his writings Locke was fully aware of the fact that he was not talking to the African worshipper or the African raconteur, but to the Afro-American dramatist whose identity is no longer exclusively African, and whose individual creation, the play, is locked in by the finality of the written word. He also recognized that the Afro-American dramatist must eventually utilize all of his multiracial cultural resources and all of his imaginative power for the full realization of his potential.

This vision was reflected by the black dramatic pioneers of the thirties who imposed no self-limitations and who experimented with all available dramatic modes, including those suggested by traditional African ritual forms.

But Jeyifous could not confine his attack on the past to Alain Locke, since it was intended to encompass the entire period of black dramatic "sensibility," and his distaste for Owen Dodson's reference to Western dramatic achievements is cut from the same mould and directed to the same purpose. As he states, Dodson, poet and playwright, was also Professor of Drama at Howard University for many years. He is another of those black intellectuals of expanded consciousness who is thoroughly familiar with both black and white cultures and limited by neither, and he was also an able drama critic. Dodson's article, "Playwrights in Dark Glasses," criticizes some of the elements of the prevailing black dramatic trend, and this is the excerpt from it with which Jeyifous similarly attempts to illustrate Dodson's domination by white Western standards:

Most of the Negro playwrights seem to think that the suffering of Negroes is only the suffering of Negroes and although, in Shakespeare's words, they give this suffering "their own local habitation and a home" they are hardly giving it a universality that will command artistic distinction and lasting power. . . . LeRoi Jones certainly has daring, ironic thrust, and shocking power. However, he has none of the qualities listed above in his play *The Toilet*. . . . In the *Dutchman*, he goes far beyond bounds of any artistic law to shock and disgrace an audience into his way of thinking. His use of four letter words in these plays seem to be put in to make life as real as he thinks it is. Playwrights with winning and timeless power have been able to create the same atmosphere that Jones wishes to create with their special language that conjures up our imagination because we have not heard these things before. In Shakespeare's *Hamlet*, Hamlet says of his stepfather ". . . remorseless, lecherous, treacherous, kindless villain. O Vengeance," instead of saying as LeRoi Jones might say, "my stepfather is full of shit."[25]

Here, it is quite obvious that Dodson too was trying to point out to black dramatists who are *not* African oral raconteurs working from and toward the fruits of accretion, and who cannot over the coming years alter their written word with the passing of every phrase into oblivion, that a dramatist's immortality depends on his foresight and his ability to choose lasting words and images. He is discussing qualities, the qualities of "timelessness" and "universality," and he illustrates how one playwright's language achieved them. It is a fact that Shakespeare has achieved immortality, and his imagery is still much admired world-wide; that he incidentally happened to be born to Western culture does not lessen the validity of the example and one is forced to wonder whether Jeyifous is not here flirting with a double standard, rather than a different standard, for standards may differ in different cultures and still be of comparable quality. Dodson could with equal effectiveness have chosen to quote the timeless words of Confucious. Furthermore, Jeyifous' attempt to imply Dodson's affinity for exclusively white Western standards by implying Shakespeare's reflection of them is faulty, since probably no playwright in the history of Western drama broke more of its established rules than did "the hallowed cultural heirloom of the West."[26] In direct conflict with Jeyifous' objection to Dodson's comparison of the work of LeRoi Jones with that of Shakespeare is the complaint made by black author John A. Williams in 1971 that black authors are never compared to white.[27]

In a 1971 interview Dodson again points out the attributes of greatness, and here his touchstone is a black author. He then stated of revolutionary playwright Ed. Bullins' work to that date:

> Here is a man who is presenting or thinks he is presenting a whole race and that race is doing nothing but cursing, fucking, and farting. And that's what he writes about. . . . What he is doing is feeding garbage to people when that's what they've been brought up on. . . . playwrights and writers like Richard Wright know that even in the degradation there is something golden in everybody's mind.[28]

But of far greater importance than such semantic games is the fact that Dodson, like Locke, saw clearly that the Afro-American playwright would ultimately have to reject all self-limitations for the realization of his full creative potential including his achievement of timelessness and universality. And these are two terms which this revolutionary critic erroneously suggests belong exclusively to white Western dramatic theory.

But the underlying motive of Jeyifous' attack on these great black theoreticians is political rather than aesthetic, and the real issues are not those of timelessness or universality as the exclusive prerogatives of Western culture, for they are equally applicable to the African oral tradition and to the other arts of Africa, and there are other black critics who recognize their validity in Afro-American terms: "While there is a sense in which all good plays/art are relevant to universal human experience, each of us finds reflection of our own experience most useful,"[29] is the wisdom of John O'Neal, and Adam David Miller offers the black dramatist the ideal solution to the question of universality:

> The Negro playwright must reach the 'universal' through race. He should write in such a way that he makes sense to his Negro audience. If this playwright addresses himself to the needs of his Aframerican audience, their need for an understanding of both their African and American history, their need for heroes who look like themselves, for women who are not abstractions or neuter, their need to see themselves in their *complexity*, then the question of 'universality' will be answered, and the question of audience will be academic.[30]

Simply stated, timelessness and universality know no racial boundaries and do not confine themselves to any given set of ethical or aesthetic standards. Universality, if it has any meaning at all—which

Western theory claims that it does—must include the experience of all men. That it also has meaning for Afro-Americans is supported by no less an authority than African cosmology, for if the universe is a harmony of interlocking rhythms then all rhythms must also have a place in the universe. And the same is true of the value of timeless-ness, which is specifically emphasized in the thematic dominance of the African oral tradition.

Paradoxically, some of the Black Revolutionary Theater's greatest strengths have also been its greatest weaknesses. The same elements of its ideology that have so successfully promoted black consciousness have also motivated this downgrading of the black theoreticians and dramatists of the past, and while they have undoubtedly increased the black audience, they also threaten the long-range development of an objective black audience. As the Federal Theatre learned four decades ago, in a marriage of art and politics, political expediency dominates, and the Black Revolutionary Theater's doctrine, which became firmly established because the attachment of its ideologies to black cultural attitudes had enormous mass appeal, has been powerful enough to dictate which components of the black dramatic past in its view foster black consciousness and black political aims and which do not. Until very recently its tremendous influence had forced off the black stage almost the entire range of images that were projected by vaudeville, minstrelsy, and similar dramatic forms in which black actors of the past have excelled, and few plays from the pre-revolutionary period have been re-produced in the context of their time. If it remains unchallenged, this influence will not only distort black dramatic history, but the black audience's view of what that history was, and even black audience expectations of how that history should be dramatized.

The ideologies of the Black Revolutionary Theater have become so diffused and imbedded in the minds of black Americans that they have in fact already influenced audience expectation, and even some talented young black directors have expected to find little of cultural value in black-authored plays from the period of black dramatic "sensibility."

The New Federal Theatre in Washington, D. C., with the financial assistance of a grant, has been re-staging theatrical material from the Federal Theatre Project of the thirties at the Coolidge Auditorium in the Library of Congress, and there has been considerable public interest in its exploration of the American dramatic past. On 11 October 1977 Frederick Lee, who has excellent and successful contemporary black productions to his credit, directed a presentation of excerpts from the long lost black Federal Theatre plays. In this production Lee merged excerpts from black-authored plays of the thirties, which dramatized the stark realities of the black experience, with excerpts from plays about black life by white authors, who certainly had distorted views of the black experience. These excerpts slid from one into the other with musical transitions, and the merger of the two categories of plays made little difference to the finished product, for in his dramatization they combined to accomplish what Hughes Allison described in his *Foreword to Panyared* as forever keeping all blacks Sambo and Liza in the eyes of the public. How this feat was accomplished is highly suggestive of what the director saw in the black-authored plays of the past, for which reason we must examine his interpretations.

One excerpt from *Liberty Deferred* was the opening scene of the play, in which a white Southern couple invades a Harlem night club in search of a thrill and sees there all the stereotypes they had expected to find. This nightclub fragment was well presented, but it left a totally erroneous impression with the audience of what the play was all about. What was not shown was that the entire rest of the play is devoted to shredding those stereotypes and replacing them with an authentic and tragic picture of black American history, from the landing of the first black slave cargo to the National Negro Congress presided over by A. Phillip Randolph. Only the jazzy Harlem nightclub with its Sambo and Liza stereotypes were seen by the New Federal Theatre's audience. A second excerpt from *Liberty Deferred* did much the same thing. It was a jazzy glimpse of Lynchotopia, the fantasy heaven of lynch victims, but the fragment entirely disregarded the play's stark dramatization of the tragic experiences of those victims.

The scene that was selected from Theodore Browne's *Go Down Moses* was the one in which Harriet Tubman shoots Cumbo. The angry, rebellious giant of a mulatto had escaped from a slave mart by knocking out a white slave trader, and had forced Harriet to include him among her underground railroad passengers. By the time Cumbo arrives at this scene he is through taking orders and challenges Harriet's authority by refusing to follow her into the icy river; he intends to leave the group and make his way North alone. But Harriet can not chance his recapture; it would jeopardize the safety of her other passengers, for the woods are crawling with slave catchers. This scene is stark tragedy, and is dominated by the heroic action of Harriet as she reluctantly chooses to shoot the rebellious Cumbo to save her passengers. As the scene was interpreted, however, the angry giant became a small, snivelling, cringing coward who was afraid of the cold water. This was highly amusing to the audience, but the heroic action of Harriet Tubman was reduced to comic anticlimax.

The selection from *Troubled Island* was also from the first scene of that play, in which the Haitian slaves gather in the abandoned sugar mill and await drum signals to begin the massacre of their masters. The entire emphasis in this scene is on the fact that the slaves have been dehumanized and robbed of their manhood; their leader, Dessalines, relates that he grew up eating at a trough with the dogs and thought he was an animal until his first whipping, when he looked his slave-driver in the eye and knew he was *a man*; freedom was a condition necessary for the restoration of that manhood. Old Martel, who remembers Africa, croons in poetic ecstasy to the rising moon that will soon carry the news of the revolt back to the motherland and he closes emphasizing that "thy children in Haiti have thrown off the yoke of bondage *and are men again*" (I.ii). Black manhood was a major concern of the black intellectuals of the thirties, but in the fragment of Old Martel's communion that was dramatized, his words are changed to "and are *free* men again," which altered and diffused the entire emphasis of Langston Hughes' beautifully poetic scene. (Italics added.)

The Trial of Dr. Beck is also starkly realistic drama in which its author sets up and destroys the stereotypes and myths of the white culture, one by one. Above all this play emphasizes the dire need in the black community for a re-evaluation of the black self-image; it was a daring assault on the fact that a social hierarchy based on skin color—the direct result of the myths—had been established in the black community. But the complete levity with which fragments of this court trial were re-enacted entirely distorted its author's intent and the truth of the black experience in the thirties.

Even the excerpt from Hall Johnson's brilliant *Run Little Chillun'* was a travesty. Here was Ella, agonized by the fact that she was on the verge of losing her husband to a seductress from Toomers' bottom; here was a devoutly religious Christian woman who was also agonized that the soul of her husband, who was a Baptist preacher, was in jeopardy of hellfire for adultery and for abandoning his religious teaching to attend the voodoo rites of the "heathen" New Day Pilgrims, yet her testimony in the Hope Baptist Church was staged with the gaiety, the swing, the levity of musical comedy.

It was with eager anticipation that this author attended the New Federal Theatre's presentation of excerpts from the black Federal

Theatre plays, and certainly it was with the expectation that they
would be authentically and proudly staged in the context of their era.
Their distortion, however, can only be described as analogous to a
contemporary staging of a play on American history in which the
director decided to land George Washington on the White House lawn
in a helicopter—or beam him ashore from a starship. This type of
dramatization of the work of the black Federal Theatre dramatists by
the contemporary black stage is a direct result of the nationwide
diffusion of the doctrine that has pronounced pre-revolutionary drama
from the theater of black "sensibility" and "participation" to be irrelevant to the contemporary black experience. But what was even more
disturbing to this author was the fact that blacks in the audience,
perhaps because their expectations were fulfilled, accepted this interpretation of their dramatic past and learned nothing of the historic and
seminal values of the black drama of the Federal Theatre era.

In an article in *The Washington Star* of 17 June 1976 Thomas Sowell,
Professor of Economics at the University of California, stated:

> Messianic movements of whatever place or time tend to denigrate
> the past as a means of making themselves unique and their vision
> glorious. . . . The picture that emerges from these visions is
> of an inert, fearful and unconcerned Black leadership in the
> past—leaders only recently superceded by bold men of vision like
> themselves. This is a libel on the men and women who faced up
> to far more serious dangers than our own generation will ever
> confront. . . . .[31]

In this article, Sowell was specifically referring to the denigration by
blacks of past achievements in black education, and pointing out the
fact that "history must be dealt with—if only to counter the fictitious
history that has become part of current stereotypes,"[32] nevertheless,
his words are equally and profoundly applicable to the field of black
drama for here, too, history must be dealt with by a people who have
consistently demanded historical truth, and for the same reasons
stated by Sowell.

Most of the ideas—that is, the positive, non-restrictive ideas—that
form the nucleus of the Black Revolutionary Theater's dramatic theory
were the fruit of intellectual giants of the past, and were pioneered by
men and women who faced real dangers, economic and other hardships, often disappointment and heartbreak, not only to disseminate
them but to practice them in their dramatic art in a hostile environment. These pioneers are the unsung heroes of black dramatic

development, and no more deserve to be libeled than do the black educators to whom Sowell refers.

The great contributions of the Black Revolutionary Theater's theoreticians to black drama, moreover, are capable of standing on their own merits. Primarily these were their recognition of the receptivity of the era in which they presented the ideas they adopted from the past, and the originality of the techniques they used for their dissemination, such as their attachment to existing black mores. Certainly they hit the cultural jackpot and stimulated enormous interest in the black arts, and it is tragic that they should also have thought it necessary to "denigrate the past," and to convince Afro-Americans that they are—to paraphrase Alain Locke—foundlings, without a worthy dramatic history.

FIFTEEN

BLACK DRAMA OF THE THIRTIES,

THE PAST OR THE FUTURE?

T HE TWENTIETH-CENTURY black playwright who has committed himself to dramatizing a legitimate Afro-American image has had to cope with all of the problems of racial prejudice that have been spawned by the myths of white superiority and that have plagued America. Lindsay Patterson, in his introduction to *Black Theater*, describes their psychological effect on black Americans: "I mean by lost innocence that specific moment when a black discovers he is a 'nigger' and his mentality shifts gears and begins that long uphill climb to bring psychological order out of chaos."[1] Of the black author, James Weldon Johnson stated that "the moment a Negro writer takes up his pen or sits down to the typewriter he is immediately called upon to solve, consciously or *unconsciously*, this problem of the double audience,"[2] and we have seen that in the thirties there was hardly a theme the black playwrights could dramatize that did not involve the effects of the white superiority myths on the black community. W. E. B. Du Bois expressed another aspect of the problem in terms of the heroes of black fiction as "one of synthesizing [their] African heritage with [their] life in America. [They] must somehow combine two cultures, seemingly forever at odds with one another,"[3] and Adam David Miller pinpointed yet another aspect, that of racial self-integration, when he stated that "even such a playwright as Langston Hughes . . . who proclaimed at the beginning of his career his rejection of the self-denying 'urge to whiteness' and was proud to use his 'racial individuality' was an integrationist at his core."[4]

Miller's statement is particularly interesting because his term integrationist here points at two distinct problems in the biracial dramatist's dilemma; it acknowledges the internal, self-integration problem that is experienced by many biracial Afro-American writers, and it reveals the change in attitude that has occurred in the black community toward integration which change directly affects its view of such dramatists, for Miller is chiding Hughes for being a believer in racial integration in spite of his rejection of his "self-denying urge to whiteness."

In the early decades of the twentieth-century, the "self-denying urge to whiteness," and consequently the black community's social hierarchy that was based on skin color, were directly spawned by the myths of white superiority, and the most visionary of the black intellectuals—Du Bois, Locke, and others—recognized their destructive potential and the urgent need for a more equitable synthesis of the multiple heritage. Locke implored black artists and writers to explore their African heritage, to reject "truckling imitation," and to create in their own image; but at the same time he also warned that true art stems from "self-expression," not from reaction,[5] and the dramatists of the thirties strove to achieve such a goal. Hughes Allison, convinced of the value of the black dramatist as educator, directed his dramatic efforts to promoting better self-understanding within the black community, and to fostering interracial understanding through the projection of the genesis of black-white race relations in America, an aim that is also apparent in *Liberty Deferred* and other plays of this period.

After legal desegregation had made violent waves throughout America, the reaction of the Black Arts Movement and the black revolutionary community to continued white rejection was a complete reversal of the thrust toward integration, and the biracial Afro-American, and consequently the biracial Afro-American dramatist, has continued to be caught in the middle, for at both extremes—the white rejection of black, and the retaliatory black rejection of white—he is denied the right to fully integrate himself. In the black revolutionary community, the label "integrationist"—which soon became translated to mean "assimilationist" on white terms—has become almost as deadly as the label "Uncle Tom." One biracial teacher of black drama, for example, recently commented to this author that during a discussion she had with a leading black revolutionary drama theoretician, in which she pinpointed some of the flaws she had found to exist in its ideology, he ended by chiding her that she had "too much white blood in her veins." It would seem, therefore, that all that has changed for the biracial Afro-American in this disastrous polarization which has characterized American race relations is which half of his heritage—of himself—he is expected to reject to meet the prevailing racial orientation and perhaps it is worth recalling from our brief discussion of the development of the carnival of Trinidad that in

the West Indies—a mere David on the doorstep of the American
Goliath—integration has not resulted in assimilation on exclusively
white terms. In addition, this polarization in America does not exclusively affect the self-integration of biracial Afro-Americans for, as we
have noted in W. E. B. Du Bois' statement, problems of cultural
synthesis exist for all Afro-Americans, including those who are not
biracial; indeed they exist for all Americans.

The Black Revolutionary Theater also repudiated the value of biracially oriented drama as a desirable or effective means of promoting
interracial understanding, and it directed its efforts toward building a
large enough black audience to eliminate the need for white participation and the double audience. This goal of an all-black audience has
not yet been fully achieved; the black playwright still needs a dual
audience; and it is most doubtful that when this goal is achieved, such
an extreme polarization of theater audiences would solve the black
dramatist's dilemma, for even if he could write entirely for an Afro-
American audience, that audience is itself multiracial and is by no
means united in its commitment to total separation of the races or the
dramatic and other arts.

On the other hand, the existing reality, that the twentieth-century
Afro-American is an international and interracial human being, was
fully recognized by the dramatic pioneers of the thirties. This is
reflected in Langston Hughes' acknowledgment of his "racial individuality" and in his efforts to harmonize its conflicting racial elements. The dramatists of the thirties also recognized and recorded in
their plays the fact that this problem of self-integration reflected a
conflict within the larger black community which had not—indeed,
which has not yet—been wholly harmonized. It is in the DMZ between these extreme polarizations of political-philosophical-soci-
ological-racial orientation that these dramatists of the Federal Theatre
era have been suspended: between the classification by one race
prejudice in the past as "too black" and by the other in the present as
"not black enough," and it is this suspension that has prompted our
search for applicable criteria by which the newly recovered work of
these dramatists may be fairly judged, for as Thomas Sowell stated,
"history must be dealt with—if only to counter the fictitious history
that has become part of current stereotypes."

Our examination of the black-authored plays of the thirties has
revealed that the white critics of that period, who failed to recognize
that they reflected the multi-faceted Afro-American heritage and
experience of their era, entirely missed the mark; these critics applied

exclusively white criteria which were inadequate, for as we have seen the black playwrights did not create with the dramatic bricks they inherited from the white stage the same structures as the white playwrights, and the white critics did not even understand the language of the dual communication system in which many of the plays were couched. Even those white critics who attempted to be generous by exclusively white standards committed the same error that Loften Mitchell noted of the white authors of black plays, for they "failed to realize there is also a Black standard."[6]

But our examination of this group of plays by black dramatists has also revealed that they did not suffer from the disorientation and distortion of the black identity and experience that was inherent in the white-authored plays, and if we now look at the criteria for black drama stated by Adam David Miller,[7] we find that these black dramatists of the Federal Theatre era fulfilled them in every respect. They addressed themselves to the needs of their black audience to understand their African and American history, and they created dramatic characters in its image. In *Natural Man*, Theodore Browne's John Henry, enacting a black legend, is a black hero of tremendous dignity. He unites cause with effect in a series of familiar black experiences in which the complex functions of black music, religion, and traditional African cosmology unfold in an atmosphere charged to the point of explosion by white exploitation; there is also no doubt that John Henry is thoroughly conscious of who he is, what he is, and why he is. In *Go Down Moses*, Browne dramatizes Harriet Tubman, not as a neuter or an abstraction, but as the giant among women that history has shown her to be, while the protagonist of Edmonds' *Bad Man* is a Christ whose heroic self-sacrifice, so that his black brothers may live, achieves universality through race. Georgia Johnson's *A Sunday Morning in the South* dramatizes a black experience that has historically sacrificed thousands of black lives to the lynch rope, and the agony of this victim's family is a timeless and universal reality in the lives of oppressed peoples.

In spite of Miller's comment in 1968 about Langston Hughes' integrationist tendencies, there is no doubt that in *Troubled Island* the poet-playwright fulfilled his stated criteria for achieving black drama of universal dimensions. In this play, all of Hughes' black characters are highly individualized human beings who suffer and celebrate, love and hate, like all Afro-Americans; their complex motivations include specific personal needs, strengths, and weaknesses; they also include the cosmological, religious, cultural, and traditional influences of the black heritage, and the historical imperative of the black experience to fight, if necessary to die, to regain black manhood, black dignity, and black freedom. In addition, the language, wit, and imagery of Hughes' characters are exquisitely Afro-American while also being highly poetic, and even Fannin Belcher, the most stringent of early black drama critics, found them "wholly satisfying."

In *Turpentine*, its black author, Gus Smith, also achieved these criteria despite the fact that he had a white collaborator, for all of his black characters are highly individualized, highly identity-conscious, and as highly motivated by their complex Afro-American heritage as are those of Langston Hughes. There are no uncharacteristically favorable white images dominating this play, and the coordinated rhythms of the words, music, and actions re-create the Afro-American attitudes toward their heritage and experience. All of these elements of black identity and truth are also present in *Liberty Deferred*, which is a veritable Afro-American history that powerfully dramatizes the actual case histories researched by its authors.

Of *Big White Fog* Langston Huhes stated that it was an exceptional portrayal of urban black problems ahead of its time, and this play, too, is peopled not by neuters but by warm, live, black individuals who reflect the effects of the stark realities of life in a black ghetto at the height of the Depression. In *Saint Louis Woman* Cullen and Bontemps also dramatize the tough world of the ghetto hustler, with its fear and superstitions, its violence and cruelty, its optimism, and its kindness. Both Theodore Ward, in *Big White Fog*, and Hughes Allison, in *The Trial of Dr. Beck*, projected authentic dramatizations of black disorientation, but Afro-American audiences have often been unwilling to accept such images since they are unwelcome reminders that the myths of white superiority had infiltrated the black community to produce their own color prejudices.

For successful theater in any mode, the objectivity Alain Locke so strongly advocated is not only necessary on the part of the dramatist, but also on the part of the audience, which must be able to laugh at its shortcomings while it cries over its agonies, rather than demand, as so many middle-class blacks have, idealized projections of only the best side of the black community to the white.[8] Thus the dual rejection that has been experienced by the black pioneer dramatists of the Federal Theatre era has in some instances not been because their work lacked the authenticity advocated by Adam David Miller; on the contrary, it has been because the authenticity of their plays was too disturbing to black as well as white audiences. For this reason, Langston Hughes' statement that *Big White Fog* was ahead of its time still contains more than an element of truth, for it must still await the creation of a black audience that will be prepared to accept the facts of its historical becoming.

If we examine the ideology of the Black Revolutionary Theater,[9] we also find that the black dramatists of the thirties, who were inspired by the vision of black intellectual giants like W. E. B. Du Bois and Alain Locke and charismatic leaders like Marcus Garvey, faced the brunt of white criticism to project precisely the ideas that became the nucleus of the black revolutionary doctrine—that is, those elements of its doctrine which did not impose self-limitations on black artists. Without any formal codification of their purpose, these pioneers were firmly "committed" to revolutionary change both in black drama and the black community, and they fought against enormous odds to precipitate it. The primary and most sustained of their efforts was directed against the myths and stereotypes of white supremacy through their attacks on the white stage-images that contributed to perpetuating them. Their work also reflects the criterion that Baraka called "collective" and defined as a reflection of authentic black identity in specific black historical or cultural situations. This was generally the same need which was specified by Miller, and we have already noted that the work of these dramatists did indeed reflect authentic black identity in specific black historical and cultural situations—which should indeed challenge the contemporary black stage to reproduce it authentically. Their work was "functional" to the lives and attitudes of blacks in their era, as defined in Black Revolutionary Theater doctrine, since it dramatized the centrality of the word and its relationship to music, dance, song, religion, and ritual in such plays as *Liberty Deferred, Turpentine, Natural Man, Run Little Chillun',* and others; it was also "functional" to other black attitudes of the period, such as the total distrust of the black community of white justice and law enforcement, and the community's determination to achieve freedom and socioeconomic equality. *Go Down Moses, Troubled Island,* and *Turpentine* reflect this historical determination, and Theodore Browne's John Henry is the first known revolutionary hero in black drama.

Black wit and imagery and the black form of expression—including the coded grapevine or dual communication system—were also the great distinguishing marks of the work of these black dramatists, and both tradition and contemporary mythic lore were explored and dramatized in it. The central aim of these dramatists, like that of the

Black Revolutionary Theater, was to raise black consciousness, and plays such as *The Trial of Dr. Beck* and *Big White Fog*, as we have noted, were direct attacks on the white aesthetic values that had penetrated and that were stifling the attainment of a valid self-image in the black community. Such plays therefore also projected their authors' "rejection of white aesthetics and ethics."

The Black Revolutionary Theater's rejection of the white commercial stage undoubtedly contributed greatly to its success, in a receptive era, in fostering black consciousness and demands for black autonomy. This rejection was doctrinal, not financial, for the Black Arts Movement did accept financial assistance and some of the revolutionary plays, such as *Slave Ship*, were supported by grants from the Rockefeller Foundation. Certainly such rejection by the black dramatists of the Federal Theatre era was neither possible, nor desirable; it could not even have achieved the same results in the thirties, for black drama of the thirties *was* produced largely under the direction and funding of The Man, and rejection at that time would have brought production to a complete halt. But even if financial autonomy and a large enough black audience to permit rejection of the white stage had existed, the majority of the black community would have opted for a more moderate approach, for neither legal desegregation nor reactionary black anger at continued white rejection had yet become a reality. Nevertheless, the brilliant and heroic circumvention practiced by these black playwrights to reach a larger black audience did sow the seed of many revolutionary ideas, and although most black drama of the thirties could not be projected exclusively for black audiences, many of the plays were "authenticated" by the black community as Black Revolutionary Theater doctrine demands. *Run Little Chillun'* is an outstanding example of such authentication, but even those occasions on which the black community expressed its distaste for dramatizations of its shortcomings were acknowledgments of the authenticity of those dramatizations.

It now becomes clear that the tenets that are central to the Black Revolutionary Theater started right back there in the thirties, and that the achievements of the contemporary black stage rest squarely on the shoulders of the giants of the black dramatic past, although the political criteria established by the Black Revolutionary Theater cannot be literally applied to the black playwrights of the Federal Theatre era.[10] Indeed, it was this era that laid the foundation for the future independence of the black stage by challenging the existing sociopolitical and stage practices in its drama, often beyond all the bounds of caution.

Also, in spite of—sometimes because of—the exacting dual demands made on them, the black dramatists brilliantly communicated with both black and white audiences. On pain of drastic oversimplification, one might say that the higher the hurdle, the greater their effort to clear it and the greater their achievement in doing so.

Yet although the black dramatists of the Federal Theatre era escaped the negative effects of the self-limiting factors in the Black Revolutionary Theater's doctrine, the fruit of its positive factors, many of which they introduced, also eluded them. This is not the uncommon fate of intellectual pioneers, for the dissemination of new or revolutionary ideas and their digestion and acceptance by a community— the process of historical becoming—take time.

Even within its own dramatic era, the Black Revolutionary Theater's ideologies contain flaws that contradict, sometimes nullify, some of its own criteria, which not only tends to validate the broader view of the earlier dramatists but renders some of the distinctions between past and present dramatic practices more academic than real. The pre-structuring of plays, which necessitates that their creators' ideas must be projected by actors, is a Western dramatic convention, and in spite of the Black Revolutionary Theater's professed rejection of the white stage, this and similar Western conventions still prevail in contemporary black theater. The repudiation of biracially oriented drama by the Black Revolutionary Theater, on the premise that explanations that are necessary for the understanding of white audiences are tedious to blacks,[11] is still an unrealized ambition, for black audiences, although considerably larger than in the thirties, have not yet become large enough to support black drama exclusively. This criterion is also an unwarranted assumption of a loss of expertise on the part of black literary artists, for in the historical African past the stories of the African raconteur were always well known to his audience, a fact that did not lessen its appreciation of them provided the expertise of the raconteur was such that he made old ideas seem new and exciting, and the Afro-American dramatist, even when writing for an all Afro-American audience, will for the foreseeable future continue to be challenged by differing intellectual, economic, and social strata, which will still necessitate explanations.

Consider, also, the Black Revolutionary Theater's rejection of protest drama on the grounds that it is demeaning.[12] Certainly it is no more demeaning than their revolutionary plays of white flagellation, which, instead of representing action, are emotional outlets for reaction. Actually, every one of these plays, in fact every black play that still dramatizes the violent effects of white oppression on the black community, is inherently a legitimate cry of protest. Thus the revolutionary dramatists—like the practitioners of so many other theoretical movements—have found it virtually impossible to conform to their own limitations, and their actual practice is nearer to that of the black dramatists of the Federal Theatre era than their doctrine dictates.

Yet, paradoxically, the work of the black dramatists of the Federal Theatre era did further the aims intended by the political factors of the Black Revolutionary Theater's doctrine. Historically, the aim of all revolutionary politics has been change, by whatever means it is accomplished. Change is its sole purpose for being. But while violence and bloodshed can be effective in producing political and economic change, they can also result in increased polarization and they are wholly ineffective in changing the root cause of America's racial problems, prejudice. Only understanding, achieved through exposure and education, can hope to eliminate prejudice, and the black playwrights of the thirties recognized the dramatic potential for promoting this type of change, and they accepted the additional responsibility this imposed on them as educators. Protest plays such as *Turpentine*, which projected both inward to the black community and outward to the white community, cannot be discounted as one of the influences that furthered change in their era, and thereby the primary aim of revolutionary politics.

In the thirties there was probably no more effective method of communicating with or of influencing the public than through drama (unless it was through radio, and the Federal Theatre was also active in broadcasting black radio drama, which has not been included in this study). Frank Wilson's *Walk Together Children*, which Sterling Brown described as a "not distinguished play" and which ran for only a month in New York, was seen by 10,530 people. *Turpentine*, than which he considered there was "no plainer spoken drama," ran for two and a half months and attracted an audience of 23,000.[13] Consider, also, the enormous impact that Hall Johnson's *Run Little Chillun'* had at a time when black intellectual capabilities were hardly even recognized to exist by the white public. Following its New York premier, Arthur Ruhl stated in the *New York Herald Tribune*, 2 March 1933,

. . . The singing was so good and its immediate background so interesting, that once in the last act the first nighters seemed quite to forget that they were watching a play at all, and nearly stopped the show with their demands for an encore.

When this play was later produced by the Federal Theatre, it ran at the Mayan Theater in Los Angeles from 22 July 1938 to 10 June 1939 and was later produced in San Francisco for the Golden Gate Exposition.[14] The production notebooks for the Los Angeles presentation also contain newspaper reviews which tell an impressive story. The play was unanimously declared a smash hit:

> If seats . . . retailed at $3.30 or $4.00 you'd have to beg ducats from the scalpers. *Daily News*, 27 August

and by October 29, the *Examiner* reported that in its fifteenth week it would probably pass the one hundred thousand attendance mark. This is a great many people to influence in fifteen weeks, and a glance through the reviews also shows the extent of that influence:

> . . . the extraordinary demonstration of what colored people can do in a complete theatrical unit . . . conceived, written, directed, and managed by colored people. . . . *Evening News*, 23 July

> One of the outstanding plays brought to the American Theater . . . greater in every respect than 'Green Pastures.' . . . If it had been done by the Moscow Art Theater or any group of foreign actors and actresses it would be hailed nationally for its dramatic intensity and its brilliant direction and simple staging. *Hollywood Citizen News*, 16 August

> . . . makes recent commercial efforts appear pretty labored. *Evening News*, 3 September

> . . . motivated by a desire to enlighten the world. *California Eagle*, 28 July

> . . . entirely uninhibited by the structures of the so-called technique of acting. *Saturday Night*, 13 August

> . . . deeply rooted in the occurrence of everyday life. We have read of such happenings in newspapers and books. *Jewish Community Press*, 35

> Your interest . . . will not be strictly mental for such is the power . . . one more minute of it and the audience too would have been jumping up and down in the aisles. *Examiner*, 23 July

. . . always believed that when a truly great negro show would
ever be produced it would be done by negroes. Hall Johnson
proves that decisively . . . the most vivid portrait. . . . *California
Eagle*, 28 July

This was the accomplishment of one dramatist of the Federal
Theatre era, and there are many more reviews in the same vein; furthermore, this recognition of Johnson's achievement as an educator
and cultural ambassador shows only one side of the coin, for the play's
functionality and authenticity were also proclaimed by the black
community:

No one from the South could help appreciating the authentic
reproduction of a Negro community. The actions in Church were
not exaggerated. I have witnessed just such a scene in a Negro
Church. Comment of a Negro Spectator

The production held its mixed audience enthralled throughout.
Hollywood Variety, 23 July

Today has been announced as *Run Little Chillun'* day in five of the
largest Negro Churches in Los Angeles. Members of the cast . . .
will be guest speakers and soloists. *Sunday Examiner*, 28 August

In addition, a letter to the Federal Theatre Project from John Anson
Ford announces that it is ". . . already indelibly written in the minds
and hearts of more than 100,000 patrons . . . hundreds of thousands of
others have heard of its popular power and pathos, and are standing
in line to see it."[15]
These extracts from the reviews of *Run Little Chillun'* are not intended to suggest a blossoming love affair between the drama critics
of that era and the black dramatists, but rather to demonstrate the
play's enormous effectiveness in influencing public opinion. In all but
its most self-limiting aspects, and in addition to his ambassadorial
function, in 1938 Hall Johnson more than satisfied the criteria for good
black drama proclaimed in the late sixties by spokesmen of the Black
Revolutionary Theater. As one of his reviewers even observed, he was
not committed to commercial standards. He experimented with his
own music, mode, and materials; he played Western ethics, aesthetics, and religion off against African ethics and aesthetics to conclude
with his own brilliant synthesis that was in every respect "functional"
to black traditions, history, customs, arts, and attitudes; and the play
"lured Hollywood down town without benefit of big names,"[16] so

that his achievement could not be attributed to the cult of stars. *Run Little Chillun'* was overwhelmingly "authenticated" by the black community, and the play contributed enormously to black consciousness, dignity, and pride.

And this was all achieved without the protective cloak of unified critical and creative functions!

Paradoxically, while proclaiming no commitment to contemporary revolutionary politics—which, of course, he predated by almost half a century—Hall Johnson did further their paramount aim, change, for he contributed positively to the dawn of white understanding and greatly enhanced white respect for black capabilities, both of which are clearly reflected in the newspaper reviews of his play. In the crucial decades preceding the Supreme Court's historic decision on desegregation, such positive influences on white public opinion cannot be discounted. Radical changes *did* occur.

The need to inform and influence white public opinion has not, in fact, diminished in contemporary America. At the 1977 national convention of the American Theater Association in Chicago, Oscar G. Brockett, Distinguished Professor of Theater and Drama at Indiana University and leading American drama historian, was invited to evaluate the Black Theater Program's presentation on recovery of its lost past. Brockett stated that until the white public that had lived outside the black dramatic experience was made aware of it, it would continue to remain "invisible," and that black drama history, which has enriched the American stage, also belongs to the history of American drama. It would appear, therefore, that the views of the visionary Alain Locke, who looked over the formal horizons as far back as the 1920s to an enrichment of the entire American stage by Black drama, and of the black dramatists of the Federal Theatre era, who were dedicated to making black drama "visible," are by no means outdated.

On 23 July, *Hollywood Variety* reported of *Run Little Chillun'* that "it is the sort of show which makes a spectator want to shake hands with perfect strangers." That is undoubtedly a remarkable achievement of both communality and visibility for the year 1938, and one can only conclude that this play not only satisfies the criteria stated by Miller and the Black Revolutionary Theater, but that it also justifies Alain Locke's faith in the enormous potential of black drama and suggests the way for future black dramatists to make black drama the visible force which has been advocated both by Locke in the past and Brockett in the present.

One thing is certain: while rejecting none of their multiple heritage, all of these dramatists of the Federal Theatre era were highly black identity-conscious thirty-five years before it became fashionable. They were the advance forces of black "consciousness" and "commitment," and perhaps their greatest asset in projecting this was that economic support by the Federal Theatre Project made it possible for them to write as they chose, even if some of their plays were not produced. Hallie Flanagan, one of the white liberals who was also ahead of her time, set the revolutionary policy for this new degree of freedom and defied white public opinion to preserve the artistic integrity of some of the black plays.

In pointing out that some of the problems that beset the contemporary black stage stem from the self-imposed limitations of white rejection and partial self-rejection, in which the black dramatists of the thirties could not indulge and which most black dramatists today still cannot practice, I would like to emphasize that this author is neither advocating "assimilated" theater nor the wholesale adoption of white standards by black dramatists. For the same reason that the black dramatists of the thirties fought the distorted black images projected by the white stage, assimilation of black drama by the contemporary white stage, even if commercially profitable to contemporary black dramatists, would be highly undesirable. As Locke, Adam David Miller, and Black Revolutionary Theater theorists have all essentially stated, the Afro-American playwright must be free to create black drama with his own heritage and experience in his own image—in short, to reflect his own soul.

For what shall it profit a man if he gain the whole world and lose his own soul?

An example, cited by Frank Kofsky, of the sterility that can result when art is severed from its roots was "an attempt by white musicians to divest jazz of its historical black mooring and transform it into a music to which . . . whites might more easily relate."[17] This "bleaching effort," called "cool jazz," was centered in California, and Kofsky states that what most of the cool jazz musicians had in common was exposure to European classical music and the urge to "dignify" jazz, and "there was never such a plethora of fugues, concerti, divertimentos, rondos and the like at any time in the history of jazz."[18] But on that note the cool innovation settled, and it ceased when challenged by the black innovators of hard bop—which later became soul. The black innovators, once more tapping their historical roots, stressed blues and gospel, and the white attempt to take the creative lead in an artistic mode with which it had no quintessential philosophical or cultural affinity foundered for lack of sustaining roots.[19]

This is a disaster which the black dramatists dare not court. The efforts of white dramatists of the thirties to project the black soul were a complete failure insofar as the black community was concerned, and any attempt by black dramatists to bleach their drama would not only similarly divest it of its sustaining spirituality and spontaneous vitality but would result in the dramatists' alienation from their black community, for drama is an immediate and intensified reflection of the philosophy-in-action, the culture, the soul of a community, and black drama is the most communal of dramatic modes.

But while assimilation, or even domination of the black stage by the white, would be disastrous, rejection of what the white stage has to offer is shortsighted. The politico-dramatic climate created by the Black Revolutionary Theater's doctrine has discouraged most white attempts to participate in black drama and condemned most white critiques of black drama as meaningless or presumptuous, yet leaders in the black performing arts also complain of white indifference to black drama and its achievements. Although there have recently been some encouraging departures from this trend toward white exclusion, such as a "mixed blood" theater group in California which has had considerable success with its efforts at integrated theater, Brockett also noted at the American Theater Association Convention that a conviction had developed that black drama was intended exclusively for blacks, and that this view needs to be dispelled if black drama is to become a visible force in American drama.

In actual fact, the white American stage has borrowed liberally from the black arts, and at a time when the black stage was greatly in need of trained technicians, directors, dramatists, and an audience, the Federal Theatre was of immeasurable value in training them and in bringing black drama to the black community.[20] Sterling Brown noted that until the advent of the Federal Theatre no black theater company had been so well organized.[21] Contemporarily, white drama historians have been very active in helping to recover the black dramatic past by interviewing and taping the recollections of those who took an active part in its creation,[22] and W. E. B. Du Bois' words are still valid: "We cannot refuse to cooperate with white Americans and simultaneously demand the right to cooperate."[23] As we have also seen, there are elements of Afro-American drama that have no counterpart in the African tradition, and it is obvious that cross-fertilization, rather than rejection, would be beneficial to both stages.

The history of men has been essentially a record of expanding or contracting human consciousness, a record of men's growth through the inclusion, synthesis, harmonization of new or conflicting ideas, or of men's diminution through their exclusion and rejection. Philosophies, religions, nations, even races have risen or fallen depending on their capacity to promote and achieve an expanding human consciousness. But history has also recorded that more crusades have been fought to impose limitations—such as the myths of white superiority or the total rejection of white values—than to promote an expanded consciousness, and the vision, beyond the formal horizons, of the black pioneer theorists and dramatists of the thirties should not be discarded lightly by the black stage, not because of any benefit which might indirectly accrue to the white stage, although that result is entirely possible, but for the expansion and full flowering of the Afro-American potential in a truly representative Afro-American idiom. The heritage of the Afro-American dramatist includes the highest cultural achievements of two worlds. It challenges the black dramatist to synthesize and reflect his multiracial heritage, for by exploiting their fullest potential it is within his horizon to create the richest drama ever known.

The white superiority myths and black revolutionary politics have been engaged in a life-and-death struggle, and perhaps the limitations imposed by the Black Revolutionary Theater have represented an imperative, if temporary, phase in the development of black drama and the creation of a black audience. On the other hand, they have not permitted the achievement of the potential of which black drama is capable, and their exclusion of all those whose work cannot be shown to have positively underwritten black revolutionary politics has led to an emasculation of the black dramatic past that neither the history nor the future of black drama can afford. When audience objectivity is eventually achieved—and this may have to await the achievement of black socioeconomic equality which will in turn remove any need to force art under the domination of politics—then black dramatists will inevitably have to shed their limitations, harmonize their international and interracial heritage, and recapture the expanded vision of the theoreticians and dramatists of the thirties, or wither from the type of rigidity of which they have often accused the white stage.

What, then, is the value to black drama of the talented black playwrights who emerged from the watershed of the Federal Theatre era?

Certainly, they are of great historical significance, not only as gifted writers but as experimenters, innovators, creators, and the pioneers who first bent the spine of the white distortion of the black dramatic images. They also first dramatized many of the ideas popularized by the Black Revolutionary Theater, and recorded an important phase in the development of the contemporary Afro-American identity by dramatizing the various international and interracial influences that produced it.

But their value to black drama exceeds even these multiple achievements, for they transcended both white and black prejudice, rejected self-limitations, and took positive steps toward fulfilling the prophetic vision of Alain Locke, that Afro-American theater, exploiting the entire range of its possibilities, would ultimately create masterpieces in its own idiom. And when the white superiority myths and the restrictive black reactions to them have become history, and the pendulum has stabilized, future generations of black dramatists will undoubtedly return to the scope of that vision and realize its utmost potential. Thus the black dramatists of the Federal Theatre era not only represent the past but point the way to the dramatic future of an international and interracial people.

NOTES

1. William F. McDonald, *Federal Relief Administration and the Arts* (Columbus: Ohio State University Press, 1969), pp. 184–7.
2. *Ibid.*, p. 496.
3. *Ibid.*, pp. 484–7.
4. *Ibid.*, pp. 500, 507.
5. *Ibid.*, p. 506.
6. *Ibid.*, p. 502. Harry Hopkins's words also provided the title for the first book to be published on the Federal Theatre Project since the recovery of its material. Written by John O'Connor and Lorraine Brown, who were instrumental in the recovery, *Free, Adult, Uncensored: The Living History of the Federal Theatre Project* (Washington, D.C.: New Republic, 1978) includes extensive pictorial coverage of Federal Theatre productions.
7. Elmer Rice, memorandum, 28 November 1935, New York City WPA Administration, Federal Theatre Project files.
8. Hallie Flanagan, *Arena* (New York: Benjamin Blom, 1940). This is a fine narrative account of her Federal Theatre activities. Appendix, pp. 378–436, lists all Federal Theatre productions. See also McDonald, which provides a detailed history of the conception, organization, and achievements of the Federal Theatre.
9. McDonald, pp. 513–4.
10. U. S. Congress, House Committee on Appropriations, 76th Congress, 1st Session (1939), *Hearings of a Subcommittee . . . Additional Relief Appropriations*, pp. 107–11.
11. *Writing the Living Newspaper*, instructions, Federal Theatre Project Collection, George Mason University. See also Diane Bowers, "Ethiopia: The First Living Newspaper," *Phoebe* 5, 2 (Spring 1976).
12. The Communist witch-hunt, which continued into the post–World War II period, has also been discussed by W. E. B. Du Bois in several speeches. See *W. E. B. Du Bois Speaks*, ed. Philip S. Foner (New York: Pathfinder Press, 1970), pp. 228–31.
13. Flanagan. Hallie Flanagan describes her appearances before the Dies Committee and records many of its criticisms, and questions such as the one cited.
14. Mae Mallory Krulak and John O'Connor, taped interview with Emmet Lavery, 5 January 1976 at Encino, California, the Research Center for the Federal Theatre Project, George Mason University.
15. Conversations with Lorraine Brown, George Mason University.

CHAPTER TWO

1. James V. Hatch, ed., *Black Theater USA: Forty-five Plays by Black Americans, 1847–1974* (New York: The Free Press, 1974), pp. 1–2.
2. Sterling A. Brown, "The Federal Theater," in *The Anthology of the American Negro in the Theater*, ed. Lindsay Patterson, Myrdal Carnegie Study 1940 (New York: The Publishers Co., 1967), p. 107.

3. Loften Mitchell, *Black Drama* (New York: Hawthorn Books, 1967), p. 103.
4. Brown, "The Federal Theater," p. 101.
5. Edith J. R. Isaacs, *The Negro in the American Theater* (New York: Theater Arts, 1947), p. 108.
6. Doris E. Abramson, *Negro Playwrights in the American Theater 1925–59* (New York: Columbia University Press, 1969), p. 42.
7. Mitchell, *Black Drama*, pp. 24–5; also Loften Mitchell, "The Negro Theater and the Harlem Community," in *Black Expression*, ed. Addison Gayle, Jr. (New York: Weybright and Talley, 1969), p. 150.
8. Hallie Flanagan, *Arena* (New York: Benjamin Blom, 1940) and William F. McDonald, *Federal Relief Administration and the Arts* (Columbus: Ohio State University Press, 1969) for organization of the Federal Theatre.
9. Flanagan, p. 63.
10. James V. Hatch, *Black Image on the American Stage* (New York: DBS Publications, 1970) is a comprehensive listing of plays on black life by both black and white authors. See also index to Fannin S. Belcher, Jr., *The Place of the Negro in the Evolution of the American Theater 1767–1943* (PH.D. dissertation, Yale University, 1945; Ann Arbor, Mich.: University Microfilms, #69-17, 658 1975).
11. McDonald, p. 557.
12. In 1920 the editors of *The Messenger* acknowledged: "statistics show that there are nearly four million mulattoes in America as a result of miscegenation." "The New Negro—What is He?" in *Voices from the Harlem Renaissance*, ed. Nathan Irvin Huggins (New York: Oxford University Press, 1976), p. 24.
13. Sterling A. Brown, *Negro Poetry and Drama* (1937; reprint ed., New York: Atheneum, 1969) discusses the classical Negro stereotypes of the white stage.
14. Brown, "The Federal Theater," p. 103.
15. Doris E. Abramson, "The Great White Way: Critics and the First Black Playwrights on Broadway," *Educational Theater Journal* 28, 1 (March 1976), pp. 45–55.
16. *Ibid.*
17. Belcher, *The Place of the Negro*, p. 285.
18. *Ibid.*, p. 286.
19. Mitchell, *Black Drama*, p. 94.
20. Fannin S. Belcher, Jr., "Negro Drama, Stage Center," The Federal Theatre Project Collection, George Mason University, repeats this view.
21. Belcher, *The Place of the Negro*, p. 413.
22. *Ibid.*, p. 410.
23. Ralph Ellison, *Invisible Man* (1947; reprint ed., New York: Random House, 1952).
24. August Meier and Elliott Rudwick, *From Plantation to Ghetto* (1966; revised ed., New York: Hill and Wang, 1970), pp. 1–136, discuss the historical background of this attitude. See also Richard S. Dunn, *Sugar and Slaves: The Rise of the Planter Class in the English West Indies, 1624–1713* (New York: W. W. Norton, 1972). Possibly the best discussion is Leonard E. Barrett, *Soul Force: African Heritage in Afro-American Religion* (New York: Anchor, 1974), pp. 1–56.
25. Studies on this subject are numerous. In addition to the sources cited in the previous note, Thomas Kochman, ed., *Rappin' and Stylin' Out* (Urbana: University of Illinois Press, 1972) contains a collection of articles by prominent researchers in these fields.
26. Mitchell, *Black Drama*, p. 2, acknowledges the West Indian influence on black culture and black drama. W. A. Domingo, "Gifts of the Black Tropics," in *The New*

Negro, ed. Alain Locke (1925; reprint ed., New York: Atheneum, 1975), pp. 341–9, discusses West Indian migrations to Harlem and the influences of black West Indians. Sir Alan Burns, *History of the British West Indies* (London: George Allen and Unwin, 1954) and German Arciniegas, *Caribbean: Sea of the New World*, trans. Harriet de Ones (New York: Alfred A. Knopf, 1946) show the varying conditions of slavery in the islands. Herbert Asbury, *The French Quarter* (New York: Garden City Publishing Co., 1938) records the reinvigoration of the African heritage among New Orleans blacks, both free and enslaved, through migrations of sugar planters with their slaves from the West Indies. W. E. B. Du Bois, *The Gift of Black Folk: The Negroes in the Making of America* (1924; reprint ed., New York: AMS Press, 1971), p. 160, also acknowledges this debt.

27. The Federal Theatre Project Collection includes several such plays by black playwrights.

28. Harry A. Plotski and Ernest Kaiser, eds., *Afro-USA: A Reference Work on the Black Experience* (New York: Bellweather, 1971), p. 686.

29. Alain Locke, "Negro Youth Speaks," in *The New Negro*, pp. 47–53.

30. Alain Locke, "The Legacy of the Ancestral Arts," in *The New Negro*, p. 256.

31. Alaine Locke, "The Negro and the American Theater," in *Theater: Essays on the Arts of the Theater*, ed. Edith J. R. Isaacs (1927; reprint ed., New York: Books for Libraries Press, 1968), p. 303.

32. *Ibid.*, p. 294. W. E. B. Du Bois also stated: ". . . in brief, there is nothing so indigenous, so completely 'made in America' as we." Henry Lee Moon, *The Emerging Thought of W. E. B. Du Bois* (New York: Simon and Schuster, 1972), p. 219.

33. Locke, "The Negro and the American Theater," p. 300.

34. *Ibid.*, p. 292.

35. Reflected by Abiodun Jeyifous, "Black Critics on Black Theater in America," *The Drama Review* 18 (September 1974): 34–45.

36. John O'Brien, ed., *Interviews with Black Writers* (New York: Liveright, 1973), p. 56.

CHAPTER THREE

1. Thomas Kochman, "Preface," *Rappin' and Stylin' Out* (Urbana: University of Illinois Press, 1972), p. xii.

2. W. E. B. Du Bois, *The Gift of Black Folk: The Negroes in the Making of America* (1924; reprint ed., New York: AMS Press, 1971), pp. 146–61 and 169; also V. S. Naipaul, *The Loss of El Dorado* (New York: Alfred A. Knopf, 1970), pp. 110–1.

3. Leonard E. Barrett, *Soul Force: African Heritage in Afro-American Religion* (New York: Anchor, 1974), pp. 42 and 55–8.

4. Henry H. Mitchell, *Black Preaching* (Philadelphia: J. B. Lippincott, 1970), p. 67, also Du Bois, *The Gift of Black Folk*, pp. 324–5.

5. Barrett, *Soul Force*, p. 46.

6. *Ibid.*, p. 47.

7. Grace Sims Holt, "Stylin' Outta the Black Pulpit," in *Rappin' and Stylin' Out*, pp. 189–90.

8. *Ibid.*, p. 193.

9. Mitchell, *Black Preaching*, pp. 29, 116, 124, and 138.

10. *Ibid.*, p. 30. Also W. E. B. Du Bois, "Of the Sorrow Songs," in *The Black Aesthetic*, ed. Allison Gayle, Jr. (New York: Anchor, 1971).

11. Grace Sims Holt, "'Inversion' in Black Communication," in *Rappin' and Stylin' Out*, p. 152.
12. Clarence Major, *Dictionary of Afro-American Slang* (New York: International Publishers, 1970), p. 9. William H. Wiggins, Jr., also discusses the "bad nigger" in "Jack Johnson as Bad Nigger: The Folklore of His Life," in *Contemporary Black Thought: The Best from the Black Scholar*, eds. Robert Chrisman and Nathan Hare (New York: Bobbs-Merrill, 1973), p. 54.
13. Holt, "'Inversion' in Black Communication," p. 157.
14. Thomas Kochman, "Toward an Ethnology of Black American Speech Behavior," in *Rappin' and Stylin' Out*, pp. 241–64.
15. Benjamin G. Cooke, "Nonverbal Communication Among Afro-Americans: An Initial Classification," in *Rappin' and Stylin' Out*, pp. 32–64.
16. Elkin T. Sithole, "Black Folk Music," in *Rappin' and Stylin' Out*, p. 74.
17. Holt, "Stylin' Outta the Black Pulpit," pp. 194–5.
18. Telephone conversation with Mrs. Hughes Allison, 16 June 1979.
19. Hallie Flanagan, *Arena* (New York: Benjamin Blom, 1940), p. 393.
20. Fannin S. Belcher, Jr., *The Place of the Negro in the Evolution of the American Theater 1767–1943* (PH.D. dissertation, Yale University, 1945; Ann Arbor, Mich.: University Microfilms, 1975), p. 423.
21. In this text, references to playscripts are as follows: large Roman numerals denote act numbers, small Roman numerals denote scene numbers, and Arabic numbers denote page numbers. Where small Roman numerals are absent, no scene numbers were indicated in the playscripts. References to plays published in anthologies are by page numbers only.

CHAPTER FOUR

1. Hughes Allison, *Foreword to Panyared*, Federal Theatre Project Collection, George Mason University, p. 29.
2. Unspaced ellipses are Allison's punctuation and they have been retained in all quotations from this play. They do not denote an omission.
3. Philip S. Foner, ed., *W. E. B. Du Bois Speaks* (New York: Pathfinder Press, 1970), p. 205.

CHAPTER FIVE

1. Hallie Flanagan, *Arena* (New York: Benjamin Blom, 1940), p. 428.
2. Abiodun Jeyifous, "Black Critics on Black Theater in America," *The Drama Review* 18 (September 1974), p. 42.
3. Fannin S. Belcher, Jr., *The Place of the Negro in the Evolution of the American Theater 1767–1943* (PH.D dissertation, Yale University, 1945; Ann Arbor, Mich.: University Microfilms, 1975), p. 424. This playscript is in the Federal Theatre Collection, but Flanagan does not record in *Arena* that it was ever produced by the Federal Theatre.
4. James V. Hatch, ed., *Black Theater USA: Forty-five Plays by Black Americans, 1847–1974* (New York: The Free Press, 1974), p. 241.
5. Randolph Edmonds, *Bad Man*, in *Black Theater USA*, p. 251.
6. Flanagan, p. 393.
7. Hatch, *Black Theater USA*, p. 360. All references to *Natural Man* are to the revised version in Hatch's anthology.

8. See W. E. Abraham, *The Mind of Africa* (Chicago: University of Chicago Press, 1962), p. 51–2.
9. Hatch, *Black Theater USA*, p. 360.
10. John S. Mbiti, *African Religions and Philosophies* (Garden City, N.Y.: Anchor, 1970), pp. 31, 62, and 95.
11. John C. Gibbs, memo to Mrs. Hallie Flanagan (Script Department, Federal Project No. 1, New York City), 14 December 1938, Federal Theatre Project Collection, George Mason University.
12. The dozens. A verbal contest between young males of the same peer group. Consists of ritual insults, usually directed at the recipient's mother. The purpose is to test the verbal ability and nerves. For complete description of the various forms of verbal combat see Thomas Kochman, "Toward an Ethnology of Black American Speech Behavior," pp. 241–64, and Roger D. Abrahams, "Joking: The Training of the Man of Words in Talking Broad," pp. 215–39, both in *Rappin' and Stylin' Out*, ed. Thomas Kochman (Urbana: University of Illinois Press, 1972).
13. Hatch, *Black Theater USA*, p. 262.
14. Langston Hughes, *Don't You Want to be Free?* in *Black Theater USA*, pp. 263–4.

CHAPTER SIX

1. Brooks Atkinson, "No Time for American Drama," *The Critic* 25 (December 1966–January 1967), p. 17.
2. Doris E. Abramson, *Negro Playwrights in the American Theater 1925–59* (New York: Columbia University Press, 1969), p. 269.
3. *Ibid.*, pp. 66–7.
4. Hallie Flanagan, *Arena* (New York: Benjamin Blom, 1940), p. 3.
5. Martin Esslin, *Brecht: The Man and His Work*, revised ed. (Garden City, N.Y.: Anchor, 1959), pp. 73–9.
6. Abramson, *Negro Playwrights in the American Theater*, p. 42.
7. Produced 19 March 1923 by the Theater Guild at the Garrick Theater, New York City. See John Gassner, ed., *Best American Plays: Supplementary Volume 1918–1958* (New York: Crown, 1961), p. 95.
8. Produced at the Provincetown Playhouse in Greenwich Village, 1920, with Charles Gilpin playing the lead. The Provincetown Players staged O'Neill's plays in both Provincetown and New York; they represented the Little Theater Movement.
9. James V. Hatch, ed., *Black Theater USA: Forty-five Plays by Black Americans, 1847–1974* (New York: The Free Press, 1974), p. 101.
10. *Ibid.*
11. Marita Bonner, *The Purple Flower*, in *Black Theater USA*, p. 206.
12. For a full discussion of constructivism and other European dramatic modes, see Albert and Bertha Johnson, *Directing Methods* (New York: A. S. Barnes, 1970), Stephen Bann, ed., *The Tradition of Constructivism* (New York: Viking, 1974), and Dieter Dube Wolf, *Expressionism*, trans. Mary Whittall (New York: Praeger, 1973).
13. Bertolt Brecht, *Baal*, in *Bertolt Brecht: Collected Plays*, ed. Ralph Manheim and John Willett (New York: Random House, 1971), pp. i–xxi and 3–58.
14. Abramson, *Negro Playwrights in the American Theater*, p. 16.
15. Fannin S. Belcher, Jr., *The Place of the Negro in the Evolution of the American Theater 1767–1943* (PH.D. dissertation, Yale University, 1945; Ann Arbor, Mich.; University Microfilms, 1975), p. 328, footnote 2.

16. Hatch, *Black Theater USA*, p. 61.
17. William F. McDonald, *Federal Relief Administration and the Arts* (Columbus: Ohio State University Press, 1969), p. 554.
18. Edith J. R. Isaacs, *The Negro in the American Theater* (New York: Theater Arts, 1947), p. 108.
19. Negro Arts Committee, U. S. Federal Arts Council, *Brief*, New York City Project No. 1, National Archives, Federal Theatre Project Record Group 69.
20. See production notebook for *Big White Fog*, Federal Theatre Project Collection, George Mason University.
21. Abramson, *Negro Playwrights in the American Theater*, p. 286. See also Hoyt W. Fuller, "Toward a Black Aesthetic," in *The Black Aesthetic*, ed. Addison Gayle, Jr. (1971; reprint ed., Garden City, N.Y.: Anchor, 1972), pp. 3–11.
22. Flanagan, p. 393.
23. McDonald, p. 553.
24. *Writing the Living Newspaper*, instructions, Federal Theatre Project Collection, George Mason University. See also Flanagan, and McDonald.
25. See Flanagan, and McDonald, p. 553.
26. W. E. B. Du Bois, "One Hundred Years of Negro Freedom," in *W. E. B. Du Bois Speaks*, ed. Philip S. Foner (New York: Pathfinder Press, 1970), p. 260.
27. Lorraine Brown, taped interview with Abram Hill, 27 February 1977 at New York City, The Research Center for the Federal Theatre Project, George Mason University.
28. Emmet Lavery, *Brief*, memorandum to Negro Arts Committee, Federal Arts Council, 31 March 1939, New York City Project 1, National Service Bureau, National Archives, Federal Theatre Project Record Group 69.
29. Brown, interview with Abram Hill.
30. Mae Mallory Krulak and John O'Connor, taped interview with Emmet Lavery, 5 January 1976 at Encino, California, the Research Center for the Federal Theatre Project, George Mason University.
31. John O'Connor, taped interview with Emmet Lavery, 17 October 1977 at Encino, California, The Research Center for the Federal Theatre Project, George Mason University.
32. Memorandum, suggestions for improvement of *Liberty Deferred*, Federal Theatre Project Collection, George Mason University.
33. Flanagan, p. 406.
34. Henry Lee Moon, *The Emerging Thought of W. E. B. Du Bois* (New York: Simon and Schuster, 1972), pp. 305–6.
35. Abram Hill and John Silvera, *Liberty Deferred*, Federal Theatre Project Collection, George Mason University. Page number undeterminable due to rough copy.
36. Conversation with John Silvera, 11 July 1977. This author asked if this scene was intended to be "pro-integration." He replied that in the Federal Theatre era nobody thought of it in those terms; it was basically a demand for equal justice.
37. Addison Gayle, Jr., "Cultural Strangulation: Black Literature and the White Aesthetic," in *The Black Aesthetic*, pp. 38–45.
38. John Illo, "The Rhetoric of Malcolm X," in *Language Communication and Rhetoric in Black America*, ed. Arthur L. Smith (Los Angeles: University of California, 1972), p. 178.

CHAPTER SEVEN

1. This play was first produced in 1925 by the Theater Guild, and ran for ninety-six performances. See E. B. Watson and Benfield Pressey, *Contemporary Drama: European* (1931; reprint ed., New York: Charles Scribner's Sons, 1966), p. 849. It was revived by the Federal Theatre in New York, October 1937, and ran for eighty-one performances. See Hallie Flanagan, *Arena* (New York: Benjamin Blom, 1940), p. 415.
2. Sam Smiley, *The Drama of Attack: Didactic Plays of the American Depression* (Columbia: University of Missouri Press, 1972), p. 217.
3. John Howard Lawson, *Theory and Technique of Playwriting* (New York: G. P. Putnam's Sons, 1936), pp. 87–8, and Smiley, pp. 58–9.
4. Smiley, pp. 199–217.
5. Flanagan, p. 45.
6. Martin E. Dann, "Introduction," in *The Black Press 1827–1880: The Quest for National Identity* (New York: G. P. Putnam's Sons, 1971), and William H. Grier and Price M. Cobbs, *Black Rage* (New York: Basic Books, 1968), p. 30.
7. Flanagan, p. 393.
8. Elizabeth Walsh and Diane Bowers, "WPA Federal Theatre Project," *Theater News* 8, 7 (April 1976), p. 3.

CHAPTER EIGHT

1. Ancient, traditional, and highly stylized. Still being produced.
2. Chinese street theater performed on ceremonial or festive occasions by professional companies without charge to spectators. The characters, usually from history or legend, comprise four groups, male, female, comics, and painted faces, and plots may date back as much as two thousand years, and are familiar to the audiences.
3. The traditional folk theater.
4. The Sanskrit theater of Kerala, the oldest of India's theater forms, but one that is still practiced.
5. Alain Locke, "Negro Youth Speaks," in *The New Negro*, ed. Alain Locke (1925; reprint ed., New York: Atheneum, 1975), p. 52.
6. Alain Locke, "The Negro and the American Stage," *Theater Arts Monthly* 10, 2 (February 1926), p. 119.
7. *Ibid.*
8. Luigi Pirandello, "On Humor," *Tulane Drama Review* 10 (Spring 1966), pp. 46–59.
9. Production notebook for Los Angeles production of *Run Little Chillun'*, Federal Theatre Project Collection, George Mason University, pp. 33–5.
10. *Ibid.*, p. 34.
11. Ortiz M. Walton, "A Comparative Analysis of the African and the Western Aesthetics," in *The Black Aesthetic*, ed. Addison Gayle, Jr. (1971; reprint ed., Garden City, N.Y.: Anchor, 1972), pp. 154–5. See also Ralph J. Metcalfe, "The West African Roots of Afro-American Music," in *Contemporary Black Thought: The Best from the Black Scholar*, eds. Robert Chrisman and Nathan Hare (New York: Bobbs-Merrill, 1973), pp. 26–40, and LeRoi Jones, *Black Music* (New York: William Morrow, 1967).
12. Elkin T. Sithole, "Black Folk Music," in *Rappin' and Stylin' Out*, ed. Thomas Kochman (Urbana: University of Illinois Press, 1972), pp. 75–6.

13. Walton, p. 161. See also Frank Kofsky, *Black Nationalism and the Revolution in Music* (New York: Pathfinder Press, 1970).

14. Walton, p. 161.

15. *Ibid.*, p. 162.

16. W. E. B. Du Bois, *The Gift of Black Folk: The Negroes in the Making of America* (1924; reprint ed., New York: AMS Press, 1971), p. 283.

17. Rudolph Fischer, "The Caucasian Storms Harlem," in *Voices from the Harlem Renaissance*, ed. Nathan Irvin Huggins (New York: Oxford University Press, 1976), p. 81.

18. Hallie Flanagan, *Arena* (New York: Benjamin Blom, 1940), p. 428. Previously produced at the Lyric Theater, New York, 1933, and ran for 126 performances. Production notebook for Los Angeles production, Federal Theatre Project Collection, George Mason University, p. 51.

19. Production notebook, Los Angeles production of *Run Little Chillun'*, press notices, pp. 31–54 and 57–8.

20. *Ibid.*, p. 33.

21. *Ibid.*, p. 6 is Clarence Muse's report. Copyright D (unpublished) 23034, 6 June 1933, in the Copyright Office, Library of Congress, is Hall Johnson's original script. He also indicates in it that some details of the play will be developed in the process of its production, particularly the "moon worship" scene.

22. Metcalfe, p. 28. "Griots," the strolling minstrels or songsters of Africa who played stringed instruments as vocal extensions.

23. Comprehensive discussions of these and other elements of the African cosmological, religious, and cultural background can be found in John S. Mbiti, *African Religions and Philosophies* (Garden City, N.Y.: Anchor, 1970), Leonard E. Barrett, *Soul Force: African Heritage in Afro-American Religion* (New York: Anchor, 1974), W. E. Abraham, *The Mind of Africa* (Chicago: University of Chicago Press, 1962), and Paul Carter Harrison, *The Drama of Nommo* (New York: Grove, 1972). Voodoo elements have also been discussed in John W. Fagg, *Cuba, Haiti and the Dominican Republic* (Englewood Cliffs, N.J.: Prentice-Hall, 1965). Only those elements that are of major concern to black drama have been included in this chapter.

    Living Drama: the drama of life itself which is enacted or manifested with total involvement and spontaneity. The dramatic element inherent in the process of living. Alain Locke, stating that when life itself moves dramatically drama, by comparison, suffers, indirectly indicated the superiority of living drama. A "sense of something dramatic to the core" Locke also posited as a racial attribute, a unique part of the African mystique, in "The Negro and the American Theater," in *Theater: Essays on the Arts of the Theater*, ed. Edith J. R. Isaacs (1927: reprint ed., New York: Books for Libraries Press, 1968), pp. 295–6. Contemporary literary critics and commentators have also noted a trend away from fiction writing toward journalism since such contemporary events as Watergate have made the drama of American life more dramatic than fiction.

24. These purposes included preservation of histories of migrations, wars, genealogies, royal and clan succession, heroic exploits, ritual, and the like.

25. Abraham, p. 97.

26. Elements of the African oral tradition can be found in Melville J. Herskovitz, "The Study of African Oral Literature," in *Cultural and Social Anthropology: Selected Readings*, ed. Peter B. Hammond (New York: Macmillan, 1964), pp. 361–7, Abraham, pp. 88–103, and Eugene B. Redmond, "The Black American Epic: Its Roots, Its Writers," in *Contemporary Black Thought*, pp. 41–52.

27. Thomas Kochman, "The Kinetic Element in Black Idiom," in *Rappin' and Stylin' Out*, pp. 160–9; and Mbiti.
28. Alain Locke, "The Legacy of the Ancestral Arts," in *The New Negro*, pp. 254–67.
29. *Ibid.*, p. 256.
30. *Ibid.*, pp. 260–1.
31. Condensed from Aristotle, "De Poetica," trans. Ingram Bywater, in *Great Books of the Western World*, ed. Robert Maynard Hutchins, vol. 9 (Chicago: Encyclopedia Britannica, 1952), pp. 681–99. See also Laila Gross, ed., *An Introduction to Literary Criticism* (New York: Capricorn, 1971), pp. 1–52.

CHAPTER NINE

1. Production notebook for Los Angeles production of *Run Little Chillun'*, Federal Theatre Project Collection, George Mason University, p. 45.
2. Hall Johnson, *Run Little Chillun'*, Federal Theatre Project Collection, George Mason University, 1.i.28. Two scripts have been worked with. Script A contains more detailed instructions, particularly for the scene in Hope Baptist Church. Wherever Script A has been used, this has been specified in the text.
3. See Langston Hughes, *Don't You Want to Be Free?* in *Black Theater USA: Forty-five Plays by Black Americans, 1847–1974*, ed. James V. Hatch (New York: The Free Press, 1974), pp. 263–4.
4. Arthur L. Smith, "Socio-Historical Perspectives of Black Oratory," in *Language Communication and Rhetoric in Black America*, ed. Arthur L. Smith (Los Angeles: University of California, 1972), pp. 295–305.
5. Elkin T. Sithole, "Black Folk Music," in *Rappin' and Stylin' Out*, ed. Thomas Kochman (Urbana: University of Illinois Press, 1972), p. 74.
6. Program for *Run Little Chillun'* at the Mayan Theater, Los Angeles, lists the drummer as a Nigerian, Prince Modupe. Production notebook, p. 55.
7. Arthur L. Smith, "Markings of an African Concept of Rhetoric," in *Language Communication and Rhetoric in Black America*, p. 372.
8. *The Divine Comedy* was written to fulfill a requirement for a fine arts degree at Yale University, and was presented by their drama department in 1938. Hatch, *Black Theater USA*, p. 320.
9. Kenneth Burke, "The Negro Pattern of Life," *Saturday Review of Literature* 10 (27 July 1933), p. 1.
10. Production notebook for Los Angeles production of *Run Little Chillun'*, press notices, pp. 31–54 and 57–8.
11. Hallie Flanagan, *Arena* (New York: Benjamin Blom, 1940), pp. 75–6.
12. See Vadim Uraneff, "Commedia dell'Arte and American Vaudeville," in *Theater: Essays on the Arts of the Theater*, ed. Edith J. R. Isaacs (Boston: Little, Brown, 1927), pp. 322–31.
13. Flanagan, pp. 75–6.

CHAPTER TEN

1. Production notebook for Chicago production of *Big White Fog*, press notices, p. 17.
2. *Ibid.*, p. 13.
3. Sterling A. Brown, "The Federal Theater," in *The Anthology of the American Negro in the Theater*, ed. Lindsay Patterson, Myrdal Carnegie Study 1940 (New York: The Publishers Co., 1967), p. 106.

4. Doris E. Abramson, "The Great White Way: Critics and the First Black Playwrights on Broadway," *Educational Theater Journal* 28, 1 (March 1976), pp. 45–55.

5. W. E. B. Du Bois, *The Gift of Black Folk: The Negroes in the Making of America* (1924; reprint ed., New York: AMS Press, 1971), and paraphrased in W. E. B. Du Bois, *The Souls of Black Folk* (1953; reprint ed., New York: Fawcett, 1961), p. 17.

6. *Loc. cit.*.

7. Larry Neal, "The Black Arts Movement," *The Drama Review* 12, 4 (Summer 1968), p. 34.

8. Hughes Allison, *Foreword to Panyared*, Federal Theatre Project Collection, George Mason University, pp. 2–3 and 27–8.

9. Walt Wolfram, "Sociolinguistic Premises and the Nature of Non-Standard Dialects," p. 28–40, and Henry H. Mitchell, "Black English," pp. 87–97, both in *Language Communication and Rhetoric in Black America*, ed. Arthur L. Smith (Los Angeles: University of California, 1972). See also Joan and Stephen Baratz, "Black Culture on Black Terms: A Rejection of the Social Pathology Model," in *Rappin' and Stylin' Out*, ed. Thomas Kochman (Urbana: University of Illinois Press, 1972), p. 11.

10. Thomas Kochman, "The Kinetic Elements in Black Idiom," in *Rappin' and Stylin' Out*, pp. 160–9. Zora Neale Hurston, "Characteristics of Negro Expression," in *Voices from the Harlem Renaissance*, ed. Nathan Irvin Huggins (New York: Oxford University Press, 1976), p. 225, points out the addition of action words in such phrases as "cook-pot" and "chop-axe."

11. Hurston, pp. 226–7.

12. David Dalby, "The African Element in American English," in *Rappin' and Stylin' Out*, pp. 170–86.

13. Grace Sims Holt, " 'Inversion' in Black Communication," in *Rappin' and Stylin' Out*, pp. 152–9, and Ossie Davis, "The English Language is My Enemy," in *Language Communication and Rhetoric in Black America*, pp. 49–57.

14. Elkin T. Sithole, "Black Folk Music," p. 74, and Charles Keil, "Motion and Feeling Through Music," pp. 83–100, both in *Rappin' and Stylin' Out*.

15. John S. Mbiti, *African Religions and Philosophies* (Garden City, N.J.: Anchor, 1970), pp. 285–98. Julius K. Nyerere, president of Tanzania, discusses the importance of the land and traditional values in "African Socialism: Ujamaa in Practice," in *Contemporary Black Thought: The Best from the Black Scholar*, ed. Robert Chrisman and Nathan Hare (New York: Bobbs-Merrill, 1973), pp. 211–8.

16. Paul Bohannan, "The Impact of Money on an African Subsistence Economy," in *Cultural and Social Anthropology*, ed. Peter B. Hammond (New York: Macmillan, 1964), p. 139.

17. Mbiti, p. 35.

18. In black English, the standard abbreviation for "colored people's time," described as living outside the sound and control of the white man's clock.

19. Julius Hudson, "The Hustling Ethic," p. 415, and John Horton, "Time and Cool People," pp. 19–31, both in *Rappin' and Stylin' Out*.

20. Imamu Amiri Baraka (LeRoi Jones), "A Black Value System," in *Contemporary Black Thought*, pp. 71–9.

21. Neal, p. 31.

22. August Meier and Elliott Rudwick, *From Plantation to Ghetto* (1966; revised ed., New York: Hill and Wang, 1970), pp. 74–5, and W. E. Abraham, *The Mind of Africa* (Chicago: University of Chicago Press, 1962), pp. 74–5.

23. Abraham, pp. 74–5.

24. Meier and Rudwick, p. 27.

25. *Ibid.* See also p. 56 for slave breeding.

26. Brown, "The Federal Theater," p. 104.

27. Du Bois, *The Souls of Black Folk*, p. 108.

28. *Ibid.*, p. 115. See also W. E. B. Du Bois, *The Negro American Family* (1909; reprint ed., Cambridge, Mass.: M.I.T. Press, 1970).

29. The extent of black anger is reflected in Max Stanford, "Black Guerilla Warfare: Strategy and Tactics," pp. 198–210, and Joseph White, "Guidelines for Black Psychologists," pp. 107–15, both in *Contemporary Black Thought*.

30. W. E. B. Du Bois, "Race Pride," in *Voices from the Harlem Renaissance*, p. 42.

31. Meier and Rudwick, pp. 215–50. William H. Grier and Price M. Cobbs, *Black Rage* (New York: Basic Books, 1968) is also an excellent reflection of the effects of oppression, written by psychologists.

32. Du Bois, *The Souls of Black Folk*, p. 150. See also W. E. B. Du Bois, "The Negro and Socialism," in *W. E. B. Du Bois Speaks*, ed. Philip S. Foner (New York: Pathfinder Press, 1970), pp. 297–311.

33. Allison, *Foreword to Panyared*, p. 24.

34. Sterling A. Brown, *Negro Poetry and Drama* (1937; reprint ed., New York: Atheneum, 1969), pp. 115–6. Torrence's three one-act plays on black life were *Simon the Cyrenian*, *Granny Maumee*, and *The Rider of Dreams*.

35. Brown, "The Federal Theater," p. 104.

36. Brown, *Negro Poetry and Drama*, p. 139.

37. Hallie Flanagan, *Arena* (New York: Benjamin Blom, 1940), p. 393.

38. *Ibid.*, p. 392.

CHAPTER ELEVEN

1. Hallie Flanagan, *Arena* (New York: Benjamin Blom, 1940), p. 393.

2. Alain Locke, "The Legacy of the Ancestral Arts," in *Voices from the Harlem Renaissance*, ed. Nathan Irvin Huggins (New York: Oxford University Press, 1976), p. 140.

3. Flanagan, p. 392.

4. Production notebook for Chicago production of *Big White Fog*, p. 15.

5. *Ibid.*, p. 16.

6. *Ibid.*, p. 14.

7. At the 1977 convention of the American Theater Association in Chicago, Ward acknowledged to this author that the play was an attempt, in drama, to make democracy work for all Americans.

8. W. E. B. Du Bois reported in *Crisis*, in 1929, that of 130 juniors and seniors at Lincoln University who were sent questionnaires by Langston Hughes, 81 were opposed to having colored professors. See Henry Lee Moon, *The Emerging Thought of W. E. B. Du Bois* (New York: Simon and Schuster, 1972), p. 139.

9. W. E. B. Du Bois, "One Hundred Years of Negro Freedom," in *W. E. B. Du Bois Speaks*, ed. Philip S. Foner (New York: Pathfinder Press, 1970), p. 263, states: ". . . we must understand that the exploiting class is beginning to appear among Negroes."

10. Sterling A. Brown, "The Federal Theater," in *The Anthology of the American Negro in the Theater*, ed. Lindsay Patterson, Myrdal Carnegie Study 1940 (New York: The Publishers Co., 1967), p. 106.

CHAPTER TWELVE

1. Roger D. Abrahams, "Joking: The Training of the Man of Words in Talking Broad," in *Rappin' and Stylin' Out*, ed. Thomas Kochman (Urbana: University of Illinois Press, 1972), pp. 215–40.
2. The "broad talker," using license, stylizes the creole form of language in contrast to the "sweet talker," who, using formal standard English, emphasizes eloquence and manners. *Ibid.*, p. 219.
3. Mother rhyming, a form of ritual insult among peers in which participants successively try to top previous rhymes. Also called the "dozens." See chapter five, note 12.
4. Nonverbal communication comprises an entire language of stance and gesture. For illustrations of the American equivalent, see Benjamin Cooke, "Non-verbal Communication Among Afro-Americans," in *Rappin' and Stylin' Out*, pp. 32–64.
5. Daybreak, when the air is fresh, cleaned by night breezes from the ocean.
6. See John Edwin Fagg, *Cuba, Haiti and the Dominican Republic* (Englewood Cliffs, N.J.: Prentice-Hall, 1965) for continuous attempts at Catholic conversion.
7. For further information on the fusion of these African religious customs, see Leonard E. Barrett, *Soul Force: African Heritage in Afro-American Religion* (Garden City, N.Y.: Anchor, 1974), pp. 64–104.
8. See Sir Alan Burns, *History of the British West Indies* (London: George Allen and Unwin, 1954) for Spanish administration in West Indian colonies, also Lambros Comitas and David Lowenthal, eds., *Slaves, Free Men, Citizens: West Indian Perspectives* (New York: Anchor, 1973) for West Indian development.
9. For accounts of successful Cimaroone battles and continuous resistance, see W. E. B. Du Bois, *The World of Africa* (1946; reprint ed., New York: International Publishers, 1972), pp. 60–3, also Burns, and Eric Williams, *From Columbus to Castro: A History of the Caribbean 1492–1969* (New York: Harper and Row, 1970).
10. Patrick Hylton, "The Politics of Caribbean Music," *The Black Scholar* (September 1975), pp. 23–9.
11. Abrahams, p. 226.
12. Roy Boyke, ed., *Trinidad Carnival* (Laventile, Trinidad: Key Caribbean Publications, 1974) contains photographic coverage of many of the spectacular elements of carnival, 1974.
13. This author has been a regular participant in the carnival festivities described.
14. Patrick Hylton, "The Politics of Caribbean Music," *Black Scholar* (September 1975), p. 24.
15. During this decade, Trinidad, while owned by the Spanish, who were few in number in the island, experienced two heavy French colonizations: the first by royalists and their slaves fleeing the French islands at the time of the French Revolution, the second by revolutionaries, mostly free creoles, when Britain captured the French islands. These two French factions kept the island in a virtual state of insurrection. Simultaneously, since Britain and Spain were temporarily at peace, Trinidad was being governed by a British military administrator—in accordance with Spanish Law. For details of this unusual situation see V. S. Naipaul, *The Loss of El Dorado* (New York: Alfred A. Knopf, 1970) and Burns. By the Treaty of Amiens in 1803 Britain returned all Spanish territory to Spain except Trinidad, gateway to the mainland, which became a British colony. For earlier colonization, see Philip Means, *The Spanish Main, Focus of Envy 1492–1700* (1931; reprint ed., New York: Gordian Press, 1965).

16. Herbert Asbury, *The French Quarter* (New York: Garden City Publishing Co., 1938) deals extensively with the French West Indian migrations, see pp. 254–5.

17. *Ibid.*, p. 243.

18. Romeo B. Garrett, "African Survivals in American Culture," in *Language Communication and Rhetoric in Black America*, ed. Arthur L. Smith (Los Angeles: University of California, 1972), p. 359.

19. *Ibid.*

20. John Blassingame, *Black New Orleans, 1860–1880* (Chicago: University of Chicago Press, 1973), p. 140.

21. *Ibid.*

22. W. E. B. Du Bois, *The Gift of Black Folk: The Negroes in the Making of America* (1924; reprint ed., New York: AMS Press, 1971), p. 154. Du Bois also states: "seven hundred Haitian soldiers saved the American Army at the siege of Savannah in 1779." In *W. E. B. Du Bois Speaks*, ed. Philip S. Foner (New York: Pathfinder Press, 1970), p. 95.

23. Loften Mitchell, *Black Drama* (New York: Hawthorn Books, 1967), p. 24.

24. Martin E. Dann, ed., *The Black Press: 1827–1880, The Quest for National Identity* (New York: G. P. Putnam's Sons, 1971), pp. 16 and 37.

25. W. A. Domingo, "Gifts of the Black Tropics," in *The New Negro*, ed. Alain Locke (1925; reprint ed., New York: Atheneum, 1975), p. 344.

26. *Ibid.*

27. *Ibid.*

28. *Ibid.*, p. 349.

29. Harry A. Plotski and Ernest Kaiser, eds., *Afro-USA: A Reference Work on the Black Experience* (New York: Bellweather Publishing, 1971), pp. 790–1. Fannin S. Belcher, Jr., "Negro Drama, Stage Center," Federal Theatre Project Collection, George Mason University, p. 6, also states: "If, however I were to choose the Negro actor who has possibly made the most notable contribution to the development of Negro drama I would select Bert Williams."

30. Plotski and Kaiser, p. 687.

31. James V. Hatch, *Black Theater USA: Forty-five Plays by Black Americans, 1847–1974* (New York: The Free Press, 1974), p. 192.

32. Plotski and Kaiser, p. 691.

33. Mitchell, *Black Drama*, p. 24.

34. Plotski and Kaiser, p. 691.

35. Mitchell, *Black Drama*, p. 2.

36. For details of Marcus Garvey's career and influence, see also Leonard E. Barrett, *Soul Force: African Heritage in Afro-American Religion* (Garden City, N.Y.: Anchor, 1974), pp. 129–52, and Plotski and Kaiser, pp. 232–3.

37. The first Pan African Congress which W. E. B. Du Bois attended in 1900, however, was called by a young West Indian barrister, H. Sylvester-Williams, in London. See Henry Lee Moon, *The Emerging Thought of W. E. B. Du Bois* (New York: Simon and Schuster, 1972), p. 41.

38. Production notebook for the Chicago production of *Big White Fog*, Federal Theatre Project Collection, George Mason University, pp. 13–9.

39. I.i.3. This movement was international and had other paid-up members besides those in America.

40. This exclusion has been noted by many black intellectuals, including Eric Williams, Prime Minister of Trinidad, in *British Historians and the West Indies* (New York: Charles Scribner's Sons, 1966).

41. A contemporary view of Garvey's importance is also expressed by Robert Allen, "Black Liberation and World Revolution," in *Contemporary Black Thought: The Best from the Black Scholar*, ed. Robert Chrisman and Nathan Hare (New York: Bobbs-Merrill, 1973), p. 269.

CHAPTER THIRTEEN

1. Some of the earliest of these were Thomas Dunn's *The Empire of Haiti*, 1849, J. W. Burson's *Dessalines* and William Edgar Easton's *Dessalines*, both in 1893, and Easton's *Christophe*, 1911, which was a continuation of his *Dessalines*. For a more complete listing of plays on this subject, see Fannin S. Belcher, Jr., *The Place of the Negro in the Evolution of the American Theater 1867–1943* (PH.D. dissertation, Yale University, 1945; Ann Arbor, Mich.: University Microfilms, 1975), pp. 277, 328, and 373–4. There are also several plays on this subject in the Federal Theatre Collection in addition to those analyzed here, among them Allen C. Miller's *Opener of Doors* (1923), Lester Fuller's *Babouk* (undated), and William Du Bois's *Haiti*, which was a successful production of the Federal Theatre in 1938.

2. Hallie Flanagan, *Arena* (New York: Benjamin Blom, 1940), p. 392, lists this co-authorship. However, *Black Empire* was copyrighted by Christine Ames and Clarke Painter, Copyright No. D 16548, 31 May 1932, and the program for its Los Angeles production by the Federal Theatre in 1936 reflects this co-authorship. On 22 April 1937, *Black Empire* was re-copyrighted by Christine Ames, Copyright No. D 49274, and the program for its Seattle production by the Federal Theatre in 1938 lists only Christine Ames as its author. The same script appears to have been used in both productions, however, with the name of Clarke Painter scratched off the fly leaf, for all the scripts in the Federal Theatre Collection are identical to the script re-copyrighted by Christine Ames in 1937. Ames and Painter, who both lived in Los Angeles, also collaborated on *Forever More* (1933), and Painter wrote *She Played Her King* in 1936. Christine Ames was a pseudonym for Margaret Morrison Smith, and she also wrote *Human Side* (1933), *King's Lady* (1935), and *Girl's Best Friend* (1937), using the same pseudonym.

3. Flanagan, p. 392.

4. Human sacrifice.

5. Hughes Allison, *Foreword to Panyared*, Federal Theatre Project Collection, George Mason University, p. 24.

6. See production notebook for Los Angeles production of *Black Empire*, press notices.

7. Belcher, *The Place of the Negro*, p. 287.

8. Sterling A. Brown, "The Federal Theater," in *The Anthology of the American Negro in the Theater*, ed. Lindsay Patterson, Myrdal Carnegie Study 1940 (New York: The Publishers Co., 1967), pp. 103–4.

9. Brooks Atkinson, The *New York Times*, 3 March 1938.

10. William F. McDonald, *Federal Relief Administration and the Arts* (Columbus: Ohio State University Press, 1969), p. 558.

11. Belcher, *The Place of the Negro*, p. 415.

12. *Emperor of Haiti*, copyright No. D unpub. 45056, 2 October 1936, renewed No. R 323000, 2 October 1963.

13. The original piano and libretto score of the first three acts of the opera are Library of Congress No. ML 96-S915; the fourth act is a holograph, No. ML 96.5-S82. It was copyrighted 13 December 1941, No. E unpub. 278708, and renewed.

14. While the play, *Troubled Island*, is in the Federal Theatre Project Collection, there is no record in the Copyright Office, Washington, D.C., that it has ever been copyrighted as a play under this title, or as *Drums of Haiti*. The Federal Theatre script of the play, *Troubled Island*, was compared with the original copyrighted script of *Emperor of Haiti* at the Copyright Office and with the original opera libretto at the Library of Congress.

15. Sir Alan Burns, *History of the British West Indies* (London: George Allen and Unwin, 1954).

16. See Harry A. Plotski and Ernest Kaiser, eds., *Afro-USA: A Reference Work on the Black Experience* (New York: Bellweather Publishing, 1971), pp. 229–30.

17. Alain Locke, "Negro Youth Speaks," in *The New Negro*, ed. Alain Locke (1925; reprint ed., New York: Atheneum, 1975), p. 48.

18. *Ibid.*, p. 47.

CHAPTER FOURTEEN

1. Abiodun Jeyifous, "Black Critics on Black Theater in America," *The Drama Review* 18 (September 1974), pp. 34–45, states that the issue of *The Drama Review* which was entirely devoted to Black Revolutionary drama (Summer 1968) became "the unofficial collective manifesto of the Movement." Edward Margolies, "Prospects: LeRoi Jones?" in *Native Sons* (New York: J. P. Lippincott, 1968), pp. 190–9, also discusses the development of Black Revolutionary drama's originator and chief theoretician, Jones; and *The Black Aesthetic*, ed. Addison Gayle, Jr. (1971; reprint ed., Garden City, N.Y.: Anchor, 1972) also records in 1971 the aesthetic base of this manifesto.

2. *Ibid.*

3. See *The Drama Review* 12, 4 (Summer 1968), *The Black Aesthetic*, and *Contemporary Black Thought: The Best from the Black Scholar*, ed. Robert Chrisman and Nathan Hare (New York: Bobbs-Merrill, 1973). See also Ed. Bullins, ed., *New Plays from the Black Theater* (New York: Bantam, 1969).

4. John O'Neal, "Motion in the Ocean," *The Drama Review* 12, 4 (Summer 1968), p. 72. See also Ron Karenga, "Black Cultural Nationalism," in *The Black Aesthetic*, pp. 31–7, for this commitment.

5. Adam David Miller, "It's a Long Way to St. Louis: Notes on the Audience for Black Drama," *The Drama Review* 12, 4 (Summer 1968), p. 148.

6. Jeyifous, p. 43, quotes Baraka's acknowledgment of racist charges at a Black Theater forum at the Gate Theater, Lower East Side, New York, in 1969.

7. Larry Neal, "The Black Arts Movement," *The Drama Review* 12, 4 (Summer 1968), p. 33.

8. *Ibid.*, pp. 29–39.

9. Jeyifous, pp. 34–45.

10. *Ibid.*, p. 37.

11. Alain Locke, "Art or Propaganda," in *Voices from the Harlem Renaissance*, ed. Nathan Irvin Huggins (New York: Oxford University Press, 1976), p. 312.

12. Henry Lee Moon, *The Emerging Thought of W. E. B. Du Bois* (New York: Simon and Schuster, 1972), p. 354.

13. Harry A. Plotski and Ernest Kaiser, *Afro-USA: A Reference Work on the Black Experience* (New York: Bellweather Publishing, 1971), p. 686.

14. Alain Locke, "Negro Youth Speaks," in *The New Negro*, ed. Alain Locke (1925; reprint ed., New York: Atheneum, 1975), p. 48.

15. Alain Locke, "The Negro and the American Theater," in *Theater: Essays on the Arts of the Theater*, ed. Edith J. R. Isaacs (1927; reprint ed., New York: Books for Libraries Press, 1968), pp. 296–7.
16. *Ibid.*
17. Jeyifous, p. 37.
18. *Ibid.*, p. 39.
19. *Ibid.*, pp. 39–40.
20. Grace Sims Holt, "Stylin' Outta the Black Pulpit," in *Rappin' and Stylin' Out*, ed. Thomas Kochman (Urbana: University of Illinois Press, 1972), pp. 189–204.
21. For a brief description of this myth-making play, see Neal, p. 36.
22. O'Neal, p. 73.
23. Jeyifous; or Locke, "The Negro and the American Stage," in *Theater Arts Monthly* 10, 2 (February 1926), pp. 112–20.
24. Locke, "The Negro and the American Theater," in *The Black Aesthetic*, p. 254.
25. Owen Dodson, "Playwrights in Dark Glasses," *Negro Digest* 17 (April 1968): 30–36, and Jeyifous, p. 36.
26. Jeyifous, p. 36.
27. John O'Brien, ed., *Interviews with Black Writers* (New York: Liveright, 1973), p. 227.
28. *Ibid.*, p. 57.
29. O'Neal, p. 74.
30. Miller, "It's a Long Way to St. Louis," p. 160.
31. Thomas Sowell, "Why a School Can Produce Black Achievers," The *Washington Star*, 17 June 1976.
32. *Ibid.*

CHAPTER FIFTEEN

1. Lindsay Patterson, comp., *Black Theater* (New York: Dodd Mead, 1971), p. i.
2. James Weldon Johnson, "The Dilemma of the Negro Author," *American Mercury* (December 1928), p. 477.
3. John O'Brien, ed., *Interviews with Black Writers* (New York: Liveright, 1973), p. ix.
4. Adam David Miller, "It's a Long Way to St. Louis: Notes on the Audience for Black Drama," *The Drama Review* 12, 4 (Summer 1968), p. 148.
5. Alain Locke, "Art or Propaganda," in *Voices from the Harlem Renaissance*, ed. Nathan Irvin Huggins (New York: Oxford University Press, 1976), pp. 312–3.
6. Loften Mitchell, *Black Drama* (New York: Hawthorn, 1967), p. 140.
7. Miller, "It's a Long Way to St. Louis," p. 160.
8. *Ibid.*, pp. 147–8. Miller states: "To Broadway the negro audience wanted only a nice negro to be shown."
9. *The Drama Review* 12, 4 (Summer 1968). Abiodun Jeyifous, "Black Critics on Black Theater in America," *The Drama Review* 18 (September 1974), p. 41, also quotes Baraka's canons, stated in a 1969 symposium.
10. In 1976, when Margaret Wilkerson was browsing through the newly recovered black drama of the Federal Theatre at George Mason University, she kept exclaiming, "It's here! It's all right here!"
11. See articles in *The Drama Review* 12, 4 (Summer 1968), *The Black Aesthetic*, ed. Addison Gayle, Jr. (1971; reprint ed., Garden City, N.Y.: Anchor, 1972), and *Contemporary Black Thought: The Best from the Black Scholar*, ed. Robert Chrisman and Nathan Hare (New York: Bobbs-Merrill, 1973).

12. *Ibid.*
13. For dates of production, see Hallie Flanagan, *Arena* (New York: Benjamin Blom, 1940), p. 393, and for attendance figures, see William F. McDonald, *Federal Relief Administration and the Arts* (Columbus: Ohio State University Press, 1969), p. 557, and Sterling A. Brown, "The Federal Theater," in *The Anthology of the Negro in the Theater*, ed. Lindsay Patterson, Myrdal Carnegie Study 1940 (New York: The Publishers Co., 1967), p. 105. Mitchell, *Black Drama*, p. 102, mentions other attendance figures.
14. Flanagan, p. 428, and Diane Bowers, ed., *Federal One*, vol. I.3 (Fairfax, Va.: The Research Center for the Federal Theatre Project, George Mason University, August 1976), p. 6.
15. Production notebook for Los Angeles production of *Run Little Chillun'*.
16. *Ibid.* Comment of *Evening News*, 3 September 1948.
17. Frank Kofsky, *Black Nationalism and the Revolution in Music* (New York: Pathfinder Press, 1970), p. 33.
18. *Ibid.*
19. *Ibid.*, p. 34.
20. Mitchell, *Black Drama*, p. 140; also *The Manifesto of the American Negro Theater* (New York, 1940), Edith J. R. Isaacs, *The Negro in the American Theater* (New York: Theater Arts, 1947), pp. 105–10, and Doris Abramson, *Negro Playwrights in the American Theater 1926–59* (New York: Columbia University Press, 1969), pp. 45–8.
21. Brown, "The Federal Theater," p. 106
22. James V. Hatch and members of The Research Center for the Federal Theater Project are involved in oral history projects.
23. W. E. B. Du Bois, "White Co-Workers," in *The Emerging Thought of W. E. B. Du Bois*, ed. Henry Lee Moon (New York: Simon and Schuster, 1972), p. 81.

BIBLIOGRAPHY

Abraham, W. E. *The Mind of Africa*. Chicago: University of Chicago Press, 1962.

Abrahams, Roger D. "Joking: The Training of the Man of Words in Talking Broad." In *Rappin' and Stylin' Out*, edited by Thomas Kochman, pp. 215–40. Urbana: University of Illinois Press, 1972.

Abramson, Doris. "The Great White Way: Critics and the First Black Playwrights on Broadway." *Educational Theater Journal*, 28, 1 (March 1976), pp. 45–55.

——. *Negro Playwrights in the American Theater 1926–59*. New York: Columbia University Press, 1969.

Allen, Robert C. "Black Liberation and World Revolution." In *Contemporary Black Thought: The Best from the Black Scholar*, edited by Robert Chrisman and Nathan Hare, pp. 247–70. New York: Bobbs-Merrill, 1973.

Allison, Hughes. *Foreword to Panyared*. Federal Theatre Project Collection, The Research Center for the Federal Theatre Project, George Mason University.

——. *Panyared*. Federal Theatre Project Script Collection, The Research Center for the Federal Theatre Project, George Mason University.

——. *The Trial of Dr. Beck*. Federal Theatre Project Script Collection, The Research Center for the Federal Theatre Project, George Mason University.

Ames, Christine, and Painter, Clarke. *Black Empire*. Federal Theatre Project Script Collection, The Research Center for the Federal Theatre Project, George Mason University.

Arciniegas, German. *Caribbean: Sea of the New World*. Translated by Harriet de Ones. New York: Alfred A. Knopf, 1946.

Aristotle. "De Poetica." Translated by Ingram Bywater. In *Great Books of the Western World*. Edited by Robert Maynard Hutchins. Vol. 9, pp. 681–99. Chicago: Encyclopaedia Britannica, 1952.

Asbury, Herbert. *The French Quarter*. New York: Garden City Publishing Co., 1938.

Atkinson, Brooks. "No Time for American Drama." *The Crisis* 25 (December 1966–January 1967), p. 17.

Bann, Stephen, ed. *The Documents of Twentieth Century Art: The Tradition of Constructivism*. New York: Viking, 1974.

Baratz, Joan and Stephen. "Black Culture on Black Terms: a Rejection of the Social Pathology Model." In *Rappin' and Stylin' Out*. Edited by Thomas Kochman, pp. 3–16. Urbana: University of Illinois Press, 1972.

Barrett, Leonard E. *Soul Force: African Heritage in Afro-American Religion*. Garden City, N.Y.: Anchor, 1974.

Belcher, Fannin S. "Negro Drama, Stage Center." Federal Theatre Project Collection, The Research Center for the Federal Theatre Project, George Mason University.

——. *The Place of the Negro in the Evolution of the American Theater 1867–1943*. PH.D. dissertation, Yale University 1945; reprinted, Ann Arbor, Mich.: University Microfilms, 1975.

Blassingame, John W. *Black New Orleans 1860–80*. Chicago: University of Chicago Press, 1973.

Bohannan, Paul. "The Impact of Money on an African Subsistence Economy." In *Cultural and Social Anthropology*. Edited by Peter B. Hammond, pp. 136–44. New York: Macmillan, 1964.

Bonner, Marita. *The Purple Flower*. In *Black Theater USA: Forty-five Plays by Black Americans, 1847–1974*. Edited by James V. Hatch, pp. 202–7. New York: The Free Press, 1974.

Bontemps, Arna. "Introduction to the Book of Negro Folklore." In *Black Expression: Essays By and About Black Americans in the Creative Arts*. Edited by Addison Gayle, Jr., pp. 29–36. New York: Weybright and Talley, 1969.

Bontemps, Arna, and Cullen, Countee. *Saint Louis Woman*. Federal Theatre Project Collection, The Research Center for the Federal Theatre Project, George Mason University.

Bowers, Diane. "Ethiopia: The First Living Newspaper." *Phoebe* 5, 2 (Spring 1976).

——, ed. *Federal One*. Vol 1.3. Fairfax, Va.: The Research Center for the Federal Theatre Project, August 1976.

Boyke, Roy, ed. *Trinidad Carnival*. Trinidad, West Indies: Key Caribbean Publications, 1974.

Brecht, Bertolt. *Baal, Bertolt Brecht: Collected Plays*. Edited by Ralph Manheim and John Willett. New York: Random House, 1971.

Brown, Lorraine. Taped interview with Abram Hill, 27 February 1977 at New York City. The Research Center for the Federal Theatre Project, George Mason University.

Brown, Sterling A. "The Federal Theater." In *The Anthology of the American Negro in the Theater*. Edited by Lindsay Patterson. Myrdal Carnegie Study 1940. New York: The Publishers Co., 1967.

——. "Negro Folk Expression." In *Black Expression: Essays By and About Black Americans in the Creative Arts*. Edited by Addison Gayle, Jr., pp. 3–14. New York: Weybright and Talley, 1969.

——. *Negro Poetry and Drama*. 1937; reprint ed, New York: Atheneum, 1969.

Browne, Theodore. *Go Down Moses*. Federal Theatre Project Collection, The Research Center for the Federal Theatre Project, George Mason University.

——. *Natural Man*. In *Black Theater USA: Forty-five Plays by Black Americans, 1847–1974*. Edited by James V. Hatch, pp. 64–99. New York: The Free Press, 1974.

Bullins, Ed., ed. *New Plays from the Black Theater*. New York: Bantam, 1969.

Burke, Kenneth. "The Negro Pattern of Life." *Saturday Review of Literature*, 27 July 1933.

Burns, Sir Alan. *History of the British West Indies*. London: George Allen and Unwin, 1954.

Chrisman, Robert, and Hare, Nathan, eds. *Contemporary Black Thought: The Best From the Black Scholar*. New York: Bobbs-Merrill, 1973.

Comitas, Lambros, and Lowenthal, David, eds. *Slaves, Free Men, Citizens: West Indian Perspectives*. New York: Anchor, 1973.

Cooke, Benjamin. "Non-verbal Communication Among Afro-Americans: An Initial Classification." In *Rappin' and Stylin' Out*. Edited by Thomas Kochman, pp. 32–64. Urbana: University of Illinois Press, 1972.

Cotter, Joseph. *Caleb, The Degenerate*. In *Black Theater USA: Forty-five Plays by Black Americans, 1847–1974*. Edited by James V. Hatch, pp. 64–99. New York: The Free Press, 1974.

Cullen, Countee, and Bontemps, Arna. *Saint Louis Woman*. Federal Theatre Project

Script Collection, The Research Center for the Federal Theatre Project, George Mason University.

Dalby, David. "The African Element in American English." In *Rappin' and Stylin' Out.* Edited by Thomas Kochman, pp. 170–185. Urbana: University of Illinois Press, 1972.

Dann, Martin E., ed. *The Black Press: 1827–1880, The Quest for National Identity.* New York: G. P. Putnam's Sons, 1971.

Davis, Ossie. "The English Language Is My Enemy." In *Language Communication and Rhetoric in Black America.* Edited by Arthur L. Smith, pp. 49–57. Los Angeles: University of California, 1972.

Dodson, Owen. *The Divine Comedy.* In *Black Theater USA: Forty-five Plays by Black Americans, 1847–1974.* Edited by James V. Hatch, pp. 320–49. New York: The Free Press, 1974.

——. "Playwrights in Dark Glasses." *Negro Digest* 17 (April 1968): 30–6.

Domingo, W. A. "The Gift of the Black Tropics." In *The New Negro.* Edited by Alain Locke, pp. 341–49. 1925; reprint ed., New York: Atheneum, 1975.

——. "The New Negro—What is He?" Editorial from *The Messenger* 2 (August 1920). In *Voices from the Harlem Renaissance.* Edited by Nathan Irvin Huggins, pp. 23–25. New York: Oxford University Press, 1976.

The Drama Review 12, 4 (Summer 1968).

Du Bois, W. E. B. *Dusk at Dawn.* 1940; reprint ed., New York: Schocken, 1968.

——. *The Gift of Black Folk: The Negro in the Making of America.* 1924; reprint ed, New York: AMS Press, 1971.

——. ed. *The Negro American Family.* 1909; reprint ed., Cambridge, Mass.: The MIT Press, 1970.

——. "Of the Sorrow Songs." In *The Black Aesthetic.* Edited by Addison Gayle, Jr., pp. 92–103. 1971; reprint ed., Garden City, N.Y.: Anchor, 1972.

——. "Race Pride." In *Voices from the Harlem Renaissance.* Edited by Nathan Irvin Huggins. New York: Oxford University Press, 1976.

——. *The Souls of Black Folk.* 1953; reprint ed., New York: Fawcett, 1961.

——. *W. E. B. Du Bois Speaks.* Edited by Philip S. Foner. New York: Pathfinder Press, 1970.

——. "White Co-Workers." From *Crisis,* 1920. In *The Emerging Thought of W. E. B. Du Bois.* Edited by Henry Lee Moon, pp. 79–82. New York: Simon and Schuster, 1972.

——. *The World of Africa.* 1946; reprint ed., New York: International Publishers, 1972.

Dunn, Richard S. *Sugar and Slaves: The Rise of the Planter Class in the English West Indies 1624–1713.* New York: W. W. Norton, 1972.

Edmonds, Randolph. *Bad Man.* In *Black Theater USA: Forty-five Plays by Black Americans, 1847–1974.* Edited by James V. Hatch, pp. 243–51. New York: The Free Press, 1974.

Ellison, Ralph. *Invisible Man.* 1947; reprint ed., New York: Random House, 1952.

Esslin, Martin. *Brecht, The Man and His Work.* 1959; revised ed., Garden City, N.Y.: Anchor, 1971.

Fagg, John Edwin. *Cuba, Haiti and the Dominican Republic.* Englewood Cliffs, N.J.: Prentice-Hall, 1965.

Federal Theatre Project Collection, The Research Center for the Federal Theatre Project, George Mason University, Fairfax, Virginia.

Fischer, Rudolph. "The Caucasian Storms Harlem." In *Voices from the Harlem Renaissance.* Edited by Nathan Irvin Huggins. New York: Oxford University Press, 1976.

Flanagan, Hallie. *Arena*. New York: Benjamin Blom, 1940.

Fuller, Hoyt W. "Toward a Black Aesthetic." In *The Black Aesthetic*. Edited by Addison Gayle, Jr., pp. 3–11.1971; reprint ed., Garden City, N.Y.: Anchor, 1972.

Garrett, Romeo B. "African Survivals in American Culture." In *Language Communication and Rhetoric in Black America*. Edited by Arthur L. Smith, pp. 356–62. Los Angeles: University of California, 1972.

Gassner, John. *Best American Plays: Supplementary Volume 1918–58*. New York: Crown, 1961.

Gayle, Addison, Jr., ed. *The Black Aesthetic*. 1971; reprint ed., Garden City, N.Y.: Anchor, 1972.

———."Cultural Strangulation: Black Literature and the White Aesthetic." In *The Black Aesthetic*. Edited by Addison Gayle, Jr., pp. 38–45. 1971; reprint ed., Garden City, N.Y.: Anchor, 1972.

Gibbs, John C. Memo to Mrs. Hallie Flanagan. Script Department, Federal Project No. 1, New York City. Federal Theatre Collection, The Research Center for the Federal Theatre Project, George Mason University.

Green, Paul. *Hymn to the Rising Sun*. Federal Theatre Project Script Collection, The Research Center for the Federal Theatre Project, George Mason University.

Grier, William H., and Cobbs, Price M. *Black Rage*. New York: Basic Books, 1968.

Gross, Laila. *An Introduction to Literary Criticism*. New York: Capricorn, 1972.

Harrison, Paul Carter. *The Drama of Nommo*. New York: Grove, 1972.

Hatch, James V. *Black Image on the American Stage*. New York: DBS Publications, 1970.

———, ed. *Black Theater USA: Forty-five Plays by Black Americans, 1847–1974*. New York: The Free Press, 1974.

Hatcher, Harlan. *Modern American Dramas*. New York: Harcourt Brace and World, 1941.

Herskovitz, Melville. "The Study of African Oral Literature." In *Cultural and Social Anthropology: Selected Readings*. Edited by Peter B. Hammond, pp. 361–7. New York: Macmillan, 1964.

Hill, Abram, and Silvera, John. *Liberty Deferred*. Federal Theatre Project Script Collection, The Research Center for the Federal Theatre Project, George Mason University.

Holt, Grace Sims. "'Inversion' in Black Communication." In *Rappin' and Stylin' Out*. Edited by Thomas Kochman, pp. 151–9. Urbana: University of Illinois Press, 1972.

———. "Stylin' Outta the Black Pulpit."In *Rappin' and Stylin' Out*. Edited by Thomas Kochman, pp. 189–204. Urbana: University of Illinois Press, 1972.

Horton, John. "Time and Cool People." In *Rappin' and Stylin' Out*. Edited by Thomas Kochman. Urbana: University of Illinois Press, 1972.

Hudson, Julius. "The Hustling Ethic." In *Rappin' and Stylin' Out*. Edited by Thomas Kochman. Urbana: University of Illinois Press, 1972.

Hughes, Langston. *Don't You Want to Be Free?* In *Black Theater USA: Forty-five Plays by Black Americans, 1847–1974*. Edited by James V. Hatch, pp. 263–77. New York: The Free Press, 1974.

———. *Emperor of Haiti*. Library of Congress, Copyright Office, No. D 45056, R 323000. Washington, D.C.

———. "The Negro Artist and the Racial Mountain." In *The Black Aesthetic*. Edited by Addison Gayle, Jr., pp. 167–72. Garden City, N.Y.: Anchor, 1971.

———. *Troubled Island* (playscript). Federal Theatre Project Script Collection, The Research Center for the Federal Theatre Project, George Mason University.

Hughes, Langston, and Still, William Grant. *Troubled Island* (opera). Library of Congress. Nos. ML 96-S915 and ML 96.5-S82. Washington, D.C.

Hurston, Zora Neale. "Characteristics of Negro Expression." In *Voices from the Harlem Renaissance*. Edited by Nathan Irvin Huggins, pp. 224–38. New York: Oxford University Press, 1976.

Hylton, Patrick. "The Politics of Caribbean Music." *The Black Scholar* (September 1975), pp. 23–9.

Illo, John. "The Rhetoric of Malcolm X." In *Language Communication and Rhetoric in Black America*. Edited by Arthur L. Smith, pp. 158–75. Los Angeles: University of California, 1972.

Isaacs, Edith J. R. *The Negro in the American Theater*. New York: Theater Arts, 1947.

Jeyifous, Abiodun. "Black Critics on Black Theater in America." *The Drama Review* 18 (September 1974), pp. 34–45.

Johnson, Albert and Bertha. *Directing Methods*. New York: A. S. Barnes, 1970.

Johnson, Georgia Douglas. *Blue Eyed Black Boy*. Federal Theatre Project Script Collection, The Research Center for the Federal Theatre Project, George Mason University.

———. *Ellen and William Craft*. Federal Theatre Project Script Collection, The Research Center for the Federal Theatre Project, George Mason University.

———. *Frederick Douglass*. Federal Theatre Project Script Collection, The Research Center for the Federal Theatre Project, George Mason University.

———. *A Sunday Morning in the South*. Federal Theatre Project Script Collection, The Research Center for the Federal Theatre Project, George Mason University.

Johnson, Hall. *Run Little Chillun'*. Federal Theatre Project Script Collection, The Research Center for the Federal Theatre Project, George Mason University.

Johnson, James Weldon. "The Dilemma of the Negro Author." *The American Mercury* (December 1928).

Jones, LeRoi. *Black Music*. New York: William Morrow, 1967.

———. "A Black Value System," *Contemporary Black Thought: The Best from the Black Scholar*. Edited by Robert Chrisman and Nathan Hare, pp. 71–9. New York: Bobbs-Merrill, 1973.

Karenga, Ron. "Black Cultural Nationalism." In *The Black Aesthetic*. Edited by Addison Gayle, Jr., pp. 31–7. 1971; reprint ed., Garden City, N.Y.: Anchor, 1972.

Keil, Charles. "Motion and Feeling through Music." In *Rappin' and Stylin' Out*. Edited by Thomas Kochman, pp. 83–100. Urbana: University of Illinois Press, 1972.

Knaster, Ira H. Memorandum to Mr. Ben Russak, Mr. John Silvera and Mr. Abram Hill: Suggestions for improvement of *Liberty Deferred*, 3 August 1938. Federal Theatre Project Collection, The Research Center for the Federal Theatre Project, George Mason University.

Kochman, Thomas. "The Kinetic Element in Black Idiom." In *Rappin' and Stylin' Out*. Edited by Thomas Kochman, pp. 160–69. Urbana: University of Illinois Press, 1972.

———, ed. *Rappin' and Stylin' Out*. Edited by Thomas Kochman. Urbana: University of Illinois Press, 1972.

———. "Toward an Ethnology of Black American Speech Behavior." In *Rappin' and Stylin' Out*. Edited by Thomas Kochman, pp. 241–64. Urbana: University of Illinois Press, 1972.

Kofsky, Frank. *Black Nationalism and the Revolution in Music*. New York: Pathfinder Press, 1970.

Krulak, Mae Mallory, and O'Connor, John. Taped interview with Emmet Lavery, 5

January 1976 at Encino, California. The Research Center for the Federal Theatre Project, George Mason University.

Lavery, Emmet. Reply to Brief of the Negro Arts Committee of the U. S. Federal Arts Council, March 1939. U. S. National Archives. Records of the WPA Federal Theatre Project Record Group 69.

Lawson, John Howard. *Processional*. Federal Theatre Project Script Collection, The Research Center for the Federal Theatre Project, George Mason University.

——— . *Theory and Technique of Playwriting*. New York: G. P. Putnam's Sons, 1936.

Locke, Alain. "Art or Propaganda." In *Voices from the Harlem Renaissance*. Edited by Nathan Irvin Huggins, pp. 312–3. New York: Oxford University Press, 1976.

——— . "The Drama of Negro Life." In *Black Expression: Essays by and About Black Americans in the Creative Arts*. Edited by Addison Gayle, Jr., pp. 123–33. New York: Weybright and Talley, 1969.

——— . "The Legacy of the Ancestral Arts." In *The New Negro*. Edited by Alain Locke, pp. 254–67. 1925; reprint ed., New York: Atheneum, 1975.

——— . "The Negro and the American Stage." *Theater Arts Monthly* 10, 2 (February 1926), pp. 112–20.

——— . "The Negro and the American Theater." In *The Black Aesthetic*. Edited by Addison Gayle, Jr., pp. 249–56. 1971; reprint ed., Garden City, N.Y.: Anchor, 1972.

——— . "The Negro and the American Theater." In *Theater: Essays on the Arts of the Theater*. Edited by Edith J. R. Isaacs, pp. 290–303. Boston: Little, Brown, 1927.

——— . "The Negro and the American Theater." *Theater: Essays on the Arts of the Theater*. Edited by Edith J. R. Isaacs, pp. 290–303. 1927; reprint ed., New York: Books for Libraries Press, 1968.

——— . "The Negro Spirituals." In *The New Negro*. Edited by Alain Locke, pp. 199–210. 1925; reprint ed., New York: Atheneum, 1975.

——— . "Negro Youth Speaks." In *The New Negro*. Edited by Alain Locke, pp. 47–53. 1925; reprint ed., New York: Atheneum, 1975.

——— . "The New Negro." In *The New Negro*. Edited by Alain Locke, pp. 3–16. 1925; reprint ed., New York: Atheneum, 1975.

——— , ed. *The New Negro*. 1925: reprint ed., New York: Atheneum, 1975.

McDonald, William F. *Federal Relief Administration and the Arts*. Columbus: Ohio State University Press, 1969.

Major, Clarence. *Dictionary of Afro-American Slang*. New York: International Publishers, 1970.

The Manifesto of The American Negro Theater. New York, 1940.

Margolies, Edward. "Prospects: LeRoi Jones?" In *Native Sons*, pp. 190–9. New York: J. B. Lippincott, 1968.

Mbiti, John S. *African Religions and Philosophies*. Garden City, N.Y.: Anchor, 1970.

Means, Philip Ainsworth. *The Spanish Main, Focus of Envy 1492–1700*. 1931; reprint ed., New York: Gordian Press, 1965.

Meier, August and Rudwick, Elliott. *From Plantation to Ghetto*. 1966; revised ed., New York: Hill and Wang, 1970.

Memorandum. Suggestions for improvement of *Liberty Deferred*. 20 August 1938. The Research Center for the Federal Theatre Project, George Mason University.

Metcalfe, Ralph J. "The West African Roots of Afro-American Music." In *Contemporary Black Thought: The Best from the Black Scholar*. Edited by Robert Chrisman and Nathan Hare, pp. 126–40. New York: Bobbs-Merrill, 1973.

Miller, Adam David. "It's a Long Way to St. Louis: Notes on the Audience for Black Drama." *The Drama Review* 12, 4 (Summer 1968).

———. "Some Observations on a Black Aesthetic." In *The Black Aesthetic*. Edited by Addison Gayle, Jr., pp. 374–80. 1971; reprint ed., Garden City, N.Y.: Anchor, 1972.

Mitchell, Henry H. "Black English." In *Language Communication and Rhetoric in Black America*. Edited by Arthur L. Smith, pp. 87–97. Los Angeles: University of California, 1972.

———. *Black Preaching*. New York: J. B. Lippincott, 1970.

Mitchell, Loften. *Black Drama*. New York: Hawthorn Books, 1967.

———. "The Negro and the Harlem Community." In *Black Expression: Essays By and About Black Americans in the Creative Arts*. Edited by Addison Gayle, Jr., pp. 148–59. New York: Weybright and Talley, 1969.

Moon, Henry Lee. *The Emerging Thought of W. E. B. Du Bois*. New York: Simon and Schuster, 1972.

Naipaul, V. S. *The Loss of El Dorado*. New York: Alfred A. Knopf, 1970.

Neal, Larry. "The Black Arts Movement." *The Drama Review* 12, 4 (Summer 1968).

Negro Arts Committee of the U. S. Federal Arts Council. *Brief*. New York City Project No. 1, U. S. National Archives. Federal Theatre Project Record Group 69.

Nyerere, Julius K. "African Socialism: Ujamaa in Practice." In *Contemporary Black Thought: The Best from the Black Scholar*. Edited by Robert Chrisman and Nathan Hare, pp. 211–8. New York: Bobbs-Merrill, 1973.

O'Brien, John, ed. *Interviews with Black Writers*. New York: Liveright, 1973.

O'Connor, John. Taped interview with Emmet Lavery, 17 October 1977 at Encino, California. The Research Center for the Federal Theatre Project, George Mason University.

O'Neal, John. "Motion in the Ocean." *The Drama Review* 12, 4 (Summer 1969).

O'Neill, Eugene. *The Emperor Jones*. In *Modern American Dramas*. Edited by Harlan Hatcher, p. 8–26. New York: Harcourt, Brace and World, 1941.

Patterson, Lindsey, comp. *Black Theater*. New York: Dodd Mead, 1971.

Pirandello, Luigi. "On Humor." *Tulane Drama Review* 10 (Spring 1966), pp. 46–59.

———. *Six Characters in Search of an Author*. In *Sixteen Famous European Plays*. Compiled by Bennett A. Cerf, et al. New York: Modern Library, 1943.

Plotski, Harry A., and Kaiser, Ernest, eds. and comps. *Afro-USA: A Reference Work on the Black Experience*. New York: Bellweather Publishing, 1971.

Porter, P. Washington. *Return to Death*. Federal Theatre Project Script Collection, The Research Center for the Federal Theatre Project, George Mason University.

Production notebook for Chicago production of *Big White Fog*. The Research Center for the Federal Theatre Project, George Mason University.

Production notebook for Los Angeles production of *Run Little Chillun'*. The Research Center for the Federal Theatre Project, George Mason University.

Program for *Run Little Chillun'* at the Mayan Theater, Los Angeles. Production notebook, The Research Center for the Federal Theatre Project, George Mason University.

Programs for *Black Empire*, Los Angeles and Seattle productions. Production notebooks, The Research Center for the Federal Theatre Project, George Mason University.

Randall, Dudley. "The Black Aesthetic in the Thirties, Forties, and Fifties." In *The Black Aesthetic*. Edited by Addison Gayle, Jr., pp. 212–21. 1971; reprint ed., Garden City, N.Y.: Anchor, 1972.

Redmond, Eugene B. "The Black American Epic: Its Roots Its Writers." In *Contemporary*

Black Thought: The Best from the Black Scholar. Edited by Robert Chrisman and Nathan Hare, pp. 41–52. New York: Bobbs-Merrill, 1973.

Rice, Elmer. *The Adding Machine.* In *Best American Plays: Supplementary Volume 1918–58.* Edited by John Gassner, pp. 95–128. New York: Crown, 1961.

——— . Memorandum, New York City WPA Administration, Federal Theatre Project Files, 28 November, 1935.

Sanders, Leslie. *From Shadows to Selves: Developing Black Theater.* PH.D. dissertation, University of Toronto, 1978.

Silvera, John and Hill, Abram. *Liberty Deferred.* Federal Theatre Project Script Collection, The Research Center for the Federal Theatre Project, George Mason University.

Sithole, Elkin T. "Black Folk Music." In *Rappin' and Stylin' Out.* Edited by Thomas Kochman, pp. 65–81. Urbana: University of Illinois Press, 1972.

Smiley, Sam. *The Drama of Attack: Didactic Plays of the American Depression.* Columbia: University of Missouri Press, 1972.

Smith, Arthur L. "Markings of an African Concept of Rhetoric." In *Language Communication and Rhetoric in Black America.* Edited by Arthur L. Smith, pp. 363–72. Los Angeles: University of California, 1972.

——— . "Socio-Historical Perspectives of Black Oratory." In *Language Communication and Rhetoric in Black America.* Edited by Arthur L. Smith, pp. 295–304. Los Angeles: University of California, 1972.

Smith, J. Augustus and Morrell, P. *Turpentine.* Federal Theatre Project Script Collection, The Research Center for the Federal Theatre Project, George Mason University.

Sowell, Thomas. "Why A School Can Produce Black Achievers." The *Washington Star*, 17 June 1976.

Stanford, Max. "Black Guerilla Warfare: Strategy and Tactics." In *Contemporary Black Thought: The Best from the Black Scholar.* Edited by Robert Chrisman and Nathan Hare, pp. 198–210. New York: Bobbs-Merrill, 1973.

Stephenson, George M. *A History of American Immigration 1820–1924.* New York: Russell and Russell, 1964.

Titiev, Misha. "A Fresh Approach to the Problem of Magic and Religion." In *Cultural and Social Anthropology.* Edited by Peter B. Hammond, pp. 284–8. New York: Macmillan, 1964.

Turner, Darwin T., ed. *Black Drama in America: An Anthology.* New York: Fawcett, 1971.

U.S. Congress. House Committee on Appropriations, 76th Congress, 1st Session (1939). *Hearings of a Subcommittee . . . further Additional Relief Appropriation*, pp. 107–11.

Uraneff, Vadim. "Commedia dell'Arte and American Vaudeville." In *Theater: Essays on the Arts of the Theater.* Edited by Edith J. R. Isaacs, pp. 322–31. Boston: Little, Brown, 1927.

Walsh, Elizabeth and Bowers, Diane. "WPA Federal Theater Project." *Theater News* 8, 7 (April 1976).

Walton, Ortiz M., "A Comparative Analysis of the African and the Western Aesthetic." In *The Black Aesthetic.* Edited by Addison Gayle, Jr. 1971; reprint ed., Garden City, N.Y.: Anchor, 1972.

Ward, Theodore. *Big White Fog.* Federal Theatre Project Script Collection, The Research Center for the Federal Theatre Project, George Mason University.

Watson, E. B., and Pressey, Benfield. *Contemporary Drama: European.* 1931; reprint ed., New York: Charles Scribner's Sons, 1966.

Wells, Frank B. *John Henry*. Federal Theatre Project Script Collection, The Research Center for the Federal Theatre Project, George Mason University.

White, Joseph. "Guidelines for Black Psychologists." In *Contemporary Black Thought: The Best from the Black Scholar*. Edited by Robert Chrisman and Nathan Hare, pp. 107–15. New York: Bobbs-Merrill, 1973.

Wiggins, William H., Jr. "Jack Johnson as Bad Nigger." In *Contemporary Black Thought: The Best from the Black Scholar*. Edited by Robert Chrisman and Nathan Hare, pp. 53–70. New York: Bobbs-Merrill, 1973.

Williams, Eric. *British Historians and the West Indies*. New York: Charles Scribner's Sons, 1966.

———. *From Columbus to Castro: The History of the Caribbean 1492–1969*. New York: Harper and Row, 1970.

Wolf, Dieter Dube. *Expressionism*. Translated by Mary Whittall. New York: Praeger, 1973.

Wolfram, Walt. "Sociolinguistic Premises and the Nature of Non-Standard Dialects." In *Language Communication and Rhetoric in Black America*. Edited by Arthur L. Smith, pp. 28–40. Los Angeles: University of California, 1972.

Writing the Living Newspaper. Instructions. Federal Theatre Project Collection, The Research Center for the Federal Theatre Project, George Mason University.

INDEX

Library of Congress Cataloging in Publication Data

Craig, Evelyn Quita, 1917–
Black drama of the Federal theatre era.

Bibliography: p. 222
Includes index.
1. American drama—Afro-American authors—History and
criticism. 2. American drama—20th century—History and
criticism. 3. Federal Theatre Project. I. Title.
PS338.N4C7   812'.5'209   79–22924
ISBN 0–87023–294–0